ELECTION LAW
IN A NUTSHELL

By

DANIEL P. TOKAJI
Robert M. Duncan/Jones Day Designated
Professor of Law
The Ohio State University
Moritz College of Law

Mat #41078519

Nutshell Series, In a Nutshell and the Nutshell Logo are trademarks registered in the U.S. Patent and Trademark Office.

© 2013 LEG, Inc. d/b/a West Academic Publishing

      610 Opperman Drive
      St. Paul, MN 55123
      1-800-313-9378

West, West Academic Publishing, and West Academic are trademarks of West Publishing Corporation, used under license.

Printed in the United States of America

ISBN: 978–0–314–26847–1

In memory of my parents
Lynne and Ted Tokaji

PREFACE

The subject matter of this nutshell goes by multiple names. Some call it the Law of the Political Process, others the Law of Democracy. Portions are sometimes taught as a course in Voting Rights or included in Legislation. But the most commonly used name for the field, and the one adopted here, is Election Law.

Two decades ago, when I was in law school, the field scarcely existed. Interest in the law of elections and politics has grown exponentially in the intervening years—and not just among lawyers, law students, and legal academics. There has also been considerable interest in Election Law among the general public. This is due in no small part to the disputed 2000 presidential election and its controversial resolution by the Supreme Court in *Bush v. Gore*, 531 U.S. 98 (2000). These events had a major impact on the field's profile. In the years that followed, the infrastructure of American democracy received an unprecedented level of attention. We have also seen greater interest in campaign finance due to the enactment of the Bipartisan Campaign Reform Act of 2002 and, more recently, the Supreme Court's controversial decision in *Citizens United v. Federal Election Commission*, 558 U.S. 310 (2010), striking down a key portion of that statute. Minority voting rights have also commanded greater public interest, most recently with the invalidation of a core provision of the

Voting Rights Act in *Shelby County v. Holder*, 133 S.
Ct. 2612 (2013).

Today, the field of Election Law boasts four
casebooks with a fifth on the way. ELECTION LAW:
CASES AND MATERIALS, originally written by Dan
Lowenstein, later joined by Rick Hasen and still
later by me, is in its fifth edition. Sam Issacharoff,
Pam Karlan, and Rick Pildes' THE LAW OF
DEMOCRACY: LEGAL STRUCTURE OF THE POLITICAL
PROCESS is currently in its fourth edition. The first
edition of Michael Dimino, Brad Smith, and Michael
Solimine's VOTING RIGHTS AND ELECTION LAW was
published in 2010, and the first edition of Jim
Gardner and Guy Charles' ELECTION LAW IN THE
AMERICAN POLITICAL SYSTEM in 2012. A fifth
casebook, by Ned Foley, Mike Pitts, and Josh
Douglas, is due out soon. There is also a peer-
reviewed journal, *Election Law Journal*, now in its
twelfth year of publication.

No doubt, Election Law has arrived. It is long
past time for a summary of the law in the field. This
nutshell is designed as a resource for students using
any of the above casebooks. It should also be of
assistance to practitioners, election officials,
candidates, legislators, and others seeking to bone
up on particular points of election law, as well as
those seeking a starting point for legal research.

For the past decade, I've been privileged to study
Election Law—and occasionally work on voting
rights cases pro bono—in Ohio, a quadrennial
hotbed of election activity. I thank The Ohio State
University, Moritz College of Law, especially Dean

Alan Michaels, for generous research support. I owe a debt of gratitude to my colleagues at *Election Law @ Moritz*, especially Terri Enns, Ned Foley, and Steve Huefner. Special thanks to Donald Tobin, who was kind enough to help me with the details of campaign finance and tax law addressed in Chapter 10. I'm also grateful to Dan Lowenstein and Rick Hasen for allowing me to join them as co-authors on the casebook ELECTION LAW: CASES AND MATERIALS. Accepting their invitation was the best career decision I have made since coming to Ohio, and I continue to learn from their work.

Two of my former students, Owen Wolfe and Nikki Trautman Baszynski, provided outstanding research assistance on this project. I thank them, as well as the many other students whom I've had the good fortune to teach and learn from over the past ten years. Their idealism and enthusiasm are a continuing source of inspiration to me. Most important, I thank my wife Renuka and my daughter Aria for their love, support, and companionship. This volume is dedicated to the memory of my mom and dad, Lynne and Ted Tokaji, who instilled in me a love for democracy and a belief in its transformative potential.

The common ground among all of us who study or practice Election Law is our passionate belief in democracy. We want it to work, in the United States and around the world. Of course, there are fierce disagreements about how democracy *should* work, including the proper role of unelected judges in overseeing elections and politics. Without taking a position on these essential debates, this nutshell attempts to introduce them to its readers. I hope you will delve into these questions more deeply— and that you will do your part to help make democracy work better.

DAN TOKAJI

Columbus, Ohio
July 2013

OUTLINE

PREFACE V
TABLE OF CASES XV

Chapter 1. Perspectives on Law and Democracy 1
A. The Republican Form of Government 2
B. The Role of Representatives 4
C. Theories of the Political Process 6
D. Judicial Review of Election Laws 8

Chapter 2. The History of Voting Rights in the U.S. 13
A. Property Restrictions and Their Elimination 14
B. Reconstruction and Disenfranchisement 16
C. The Struggle for Women's Suffrage 22
D. The Second Reconstruction 25
E. Expansion of the Franchise and Recent Controversies 28
   1. Age Restrictions 28
   2. Durational Residency Requirements 29
   3. Noncitizens 30
   4. Prisoners and Felons 30
   5. Election Administration Reform 31

Chapter 3. The Constitutional Right to Vote 33
A. Constitutional Text and Structure 33
B. Restrictions on Who May Vote 35
   1. Literacy Tests 35
   2. Gerrymandering 37

3. Poll Taxes... 37
4. Exclusions Based on Lack of an Interest........ 39

Chapter 4. Representation and Districting ... 45
A. The Political Question Doctrine 46
B. One Person, One Vote 51
1. The Equal Population Rule............................... 51
2. Application and Extension of the Rule 58
a. The Degree of Equality Required 59
b. Measurement of Equal Population.............. 62
c. Localities and Special–Purpose Entities..... 64
d. Other Democratic Processes 67
e. "Fair and Effective Representation"........... 69
C. Districting Criteria... 69

Chapter 5. Partisan Gerrymandering 77
A. What Is Gerrymandering?.................................... 77
B. Constitutional Limits on Gerrymandering......... 81
1. Gerrymandering and Population Equality..... 81
2. Gerrymandering and Justiciability................. 83
a. *Davis v. Bandemer*..................................... 83
b. *Vieth v. Jubelirer* 86
c. *LULAC v. Perry* 90

Chapter 6. Minority Representation............... 93
A. The Voting Rights Act.. 94
1. Section 5... 94
a. The Preclearance Process 94
b. The Legal Standard for Preclearance 101
(1) Retrogressive Effect 101
(2) Discriminatory Purpose........................ 106
c. The Constitutionality of Preclearance 107
2. Section 2... 112

a. The Constitutional Standard for Vote Dilution 113
b. The 1982 Amendments to Section 2 118
c. *Thornburg v. Gingles* 122
d. Refinement of the *Gingles* Standard 126
   (1) "Sufficiently Large and Geographically Compact" 127
   (2) Racial Polarization 131
   (3) Totality of Circumstances 133
e. Extension and Limitation of *Gingles* 134
B. Racial Gerrymandering 136
1. Background 136
2. *Shaw v. Reno* 138
3. Post–*Shaw* Cases 141

Chapter 7. Election Administration and Remedies 149
A. Constitutional Requirements 151
1. The 2000 Election Litigation 151
a. The Electoral College 151
b. The Protest and Contest 152
c. *Bush v. Gore* 155
   (1) The Equal Protection Holding 156
   (2) The Remedy 158
   (3) The Article II Issue 160
   (4) The Dissents 161
   (5) The Aftermath 162
2. Burdens on Voting 163
a. Voter Identification 163
b. Other Burdens 168
3. Unequal Treatment 169
a. Voting Equipment 170
b. Absentee Voting, Early Voting, and Provisional Voting 173

B. Federal Statutes 177
   1. The Voting Rights Act 177
     a. Section 2's "Results" Test 178
     b. Section 5 Preclearance 180
     c. Language Assistance 181
   2. The National Voter Registration Act 182
   3. The Help America Vote Act 183
C. State Laws 186
   1. Institutional Arrangements 187
   2. Voter Registration 188
   3. Voter Identification 188
   4. Provisional Voting 189
   5. Early and Absentee Voting 190
   6. Voting Equipment 191
   7. Polling Place Operations 191
   8. Canvasses, Recounts, and Contests 193
D. Judicial Remedies 193
   1. Enjoining a Particular Practice 195
   2. Enjoining an Election 196
   3. Adjusting Vote Totals 197
   4. Voiding an Election 199
   5. Civil Damages 201
   6. Criminal Penalties 202

Chapter 8. Direct Democracy 205
A. Background 205
B. State Requirements and Judicial Review 210
   1. Single Subject Rules 210
   2. Amendments and Revisions 215
   3. Other Content Limitations 217
   4. Procedural Requirements 219
   5. Judicial Review 221
C. Federal Constitutional Limits 223
   1. The Republican Guarantee Clause 223

2. Speech and Petition Rights Under the
First Amendment 224
3. Political Restructuring and the Equal
Protection Clause 229
4. Term Limits and the Qualifications
Clauses 235

Chapter 9. Political Parties 241
A. Parties in the U.S. Political System 241
B. Constitutional Obligations of Parties:
The White Primary Cases 245
C. Associational Rights of Parties 252
1. Presidential Nominations 253
2. State Primaries 255
3. Party Governance 261
D. Ballot Access 262

**Chapter 10. Campaign Finance
Regulation 273**
A. Background 274
1. Modes of Regulation 274
2. Competing Values 276
3. The Constitutional Framework:
Buckley v. Valeo 280
B. Expenditure Limits 288
1. Ballot Measure Campaigns 289
2. Political Party Expenditures 291
3. Corporations and Unions 293
a. Federal Law 293
b. Nonprofit Corporations 294
c. For–Profit Corporations and Unions 295
(1) *Austin v. Michigan Chamber
of Commerce* 295
(2) *McConnell v. FEC* 296

(3) *Citizens United v. FEC* 298
4. Judicial Elections 302
C. Contribution Limits 303
1. Ballot Measure Elections 304
2. Contributions to Candidates......................... 305
3. Contributions to Political Parties................. 309
4. Outside Groups.. 311
   a. PACs.. 311
   b. 527s 313
   c. Super PACs and Nonprofits....................... 314
5. Aggregate Limits.. 316
D. Public Financing... 316
1. Presidential Elections 317
2. State Public Financing.................................... 318
3. Constitutional Limits..................................... 319
E. Disclosure... 322
INDEX.. 327

TABLE OF CASES

References are to Pages

Cases

ACORN v. Edgar -- 182
AFL–CIO v. Eu --- 219
Akizaki v. Fong --- 198, 199
Allen v. State Board of Elections ------------------------------- 97
American Tradition Partnership v. Bullock --------------- 302
Ammond v. McGahn -- 251
Anderson v. Celebrezze ------------------------------------ 165, 265
Arizona Free Enterprise Club's Freedom Club PAC v.
    Bennett --- 319
Arizona v. Inter Tribal Council of Arizona------------------ 183
Austin v. Michigan Chamber of Commerce---------------- 295
Avery v. Midland County--- 64
Baker v. Carr --- 46, 49
Ball v. James--- 66, 67
Bartlett v. Strickland--------------------------------------- 130
Beer v. United States-- 102
Bell v. Southwell --- 201
Black v. McGuffage --- 171
Board of Estimate of City of New York v. Morris---------- 65
Bradley v. Perrodin --------------------------------------- 199
Breedlove v. Suttles-- 39
Brown v. Socialist Workers '74 Campaign Committee- 324
Brunner v. Ohio Republican Party -------------------------- 186
Buckley v. American Constitutional Law
    Foundation-- 226, 325
Buckley v. Valeo ----------------------------- 225, 274, 280, 325
Bullock v. Carter-- 271
Burdick v. Takushi-- 165, 265
Burns v. Richardson --- 63
Bush v. Gore--- 149, 151, 154, 155, 157, 158, 159, 162, 163,
    170, 171, 173, 174, 176, 191, 194, 195
Bush v. Palm Beach County Canvassing
    Board --- 153, 154, 195
Bush v. Vera-- 143
California Democratic Party v. Jones ---------- 257, 260, 267
Caperton v. A.T. Massey Coal Co. --------------------------- 303

Carrington v. Rash -- 39
Chicago Bar Association v. State Board of Elections --- 218
Chisom v. Roemer -- 135, 196
Citizens Against Rent Control v. City of Berkeley ------ 304
Citizens for Tax Reform v. Deters --------------------------- 226
Citizens United v. Federal Election
    Commission--- 273, 293, 299
City of Boerne v. Flores-- 108
City of Mobile v. Bolden ----------------------------------- 113, 116
City of Rome v. United States ------------------------------- 108
Clingman v. Beaver--- 256
Coalition for Economic Equity v. Wilson ------------------- 233
Coalition for Political Honesty v. State Board of
    Elections-- 218
Coalition to Defend Affirmative Action v. Regents
    of the University of Michigan------------------------------ 233
Colegrove v. Green --- 48
Colorado Republican Federal Campaign Committee v.
    Federal Election Commission (Colorado
    Republican I)--- 291
Committee to Recall Robert Menendez from the Office
    of U.S. Senator v. Wells------------------------------------- 239
Common Cause v. Jones-- 171
Cook v. Gralike-- 238
Costa v. Superior Court-- 221
Cousins v. Wigoda -- 254
Cox v. Larios --- 61
Crawford v. Board of Education----------------------------- 233
Crawford v. Marion County Election
    Board --------------------------------- 149, 164, 189, 265
Davids v. Akers-- 251
Davis v. Bandemer -- 83
Davis v. Federal Election Commission---------------- 308, 320
Democratic Party of the United States v. Wisconsin
    ex rel. La Follette--- 255
Doe v. Reed ------------------------------- 227, 228, 229, 325
Dunn v. Blumstein --- 29, 41
Easley v. Cromartie--- 144
East Carroll Parish School Board. v. Marshall----------- 115
Eu v. San Francisco County Democratic Central
    Committee --- 261
Evans v. Romer-- 234
Fair Political Practices Commission v. Superior
    Court--- 213

Family PAC v. McKenna --------------------------------------- 309
Farrakhan v. Gregoire -------------------------------------- 179
Federal Election Commission v. Beaumont --------------- 308
Federal Election Commission v. Colorado Republican
    Federal Campaign Committee (Colorado
    Republican II)--- 291
Federal Election Commission v. Massachusetts
    Citizens for Life, Inc. --------------------------------- 294
Federal Election Commission v. National
    Conservative Political Action Committee --------------- 294
Federal Election Commission v. National Right to
    Work Committee---294, 312
Federal Election Commission v. Wisconsin Right to
    Life -- 298
Fine v. Firestone --- 212
First National Bank of Boston v. Bellotti ------------------ 289
Fladell v. Palm Beach County Canvassing Board ------- 200
Florida v. United States --------------------------------- 180
Foster v. Clark-- 219
Gaffney v. Cummings --------------------------------------- 61, 81
Garza v. County of Los Angeles -------------------------------- 63
Georgia v. Ashcroft--------------------------------- 103, 104, 105
Giles v. Harris --- 19
Gomillion v. Lightfoot ------------------------- 9, 37, 48, 78, 139
Gordon v. Lance--- 68
Gray v. Sanders --- 51, 68
Grovey v. Townsend -- 248
Growe v. Emison--- 75, 132
Guinn v. United States ------------------------------------- 20
Hamer v. Ely--- 201
Harper v. Virginia Board of Elections---------- 9, 20, 37, 157
Hayden v. Paterson -- 179
Holder v. Hall--130, 135
Hollingsworth v. Perry-------------------------------------- 235
Holt Civic Club v. City of Tuscaloosa ------------------------- 41
Houston Lawyers' Association v. Attorney General of
    Texas -- 135
Hunter v. Erickson--- 231
Hunter v. Hamilton County Board of Elections---------- 174
Hunter v. Underwood --------------------------------------- 31
In re Advisory Opinion to the Attorney General--------- 212
In re Contest of General Election Held on November 4,
    2008, for Purpose of Electing a U.S. Senator from
    State of Minnesota (Sheehan v. Franken) ------------- 173

In re Marriage Cases -- 216
In re the Matter of the Protest of Election Returns
    and Absentee Ballots --------------------------------------- 197
Independent Energy Producers Association v.
    McPherson --- 223
Initiative and Referendum Institute v. Jaeger ----------- 226
Ippolito v. Power --- 199
Jenness v. Fortson--- 264
Johnson v. De Grandy--- 134, 135
Karcher v. Daggett --- 59, 82
Katzenbach v. Morgan --- 108
Kirkpatrick v. Preisler --- 59
Kramer v. Union Free School District No. 15 -------------- 40
Lassiter v. Northampton County Board of
    Elections-- 20, 36
League of United Latin American Citizens v.
    Clements -- 133
League of United Latin American Citizens v.
    Perry------------------------------------- 90, 128, 131, 135, 146
Legislature v. Eu-- 216
Legislature v. Reinecke -- 75
Lewis v. Alamance County--------------------------------------- 133
Lopez v. Monterey County --------------------------------------- 109
Lowe v. Keisling--- 224
Lubin v. Panish --- 271
Lucas v. 44th General Assembly of Colorado -------------- 56
Luther v. Borden----------------------------- 16, 47, 49, 50, 224
Mahan v. Howell--- 60
Manduley v. Superior Court------------------------------------- 214
Marbury v. Madison -- 47
Marston v. Lewis-- 30
McConnell v. Federal Election Commission-- 296, 307, 310
McCulloch v. Maryland -- 108
McIntyre v. Ohio Elections Commission------------------- 325
McPherson v. Blacker --------------------------------------- 153, 160
Meyer v. Grant -- 224
Miller v. Johnson --- 142
Minor v. Happersett -- 23
Moore v. Ogilvie--- 68
Morris v. Gressette-- 99
Munro v. Socialist Workers Party --------------------------- 267
Nevada Department of Human Resources v. Hibbs ---- 109
New York State Board of Elections v. Lopez Torres ---- 262
Newberry v. United States --------------------------------------- 246

Nixon v. Condon-- 248
Nixon v. Herndon------------------------------------- 201, 247, 248
Nixon v. Shrink Missouri Government PAC - 283, 304, 305
Northeast Ohio Coalition for the Homeless v.
  Husted -- 168, 190, 195
Northwest Austin Municipal Utility District Number
  One v. Holder -- 110
O'Brien v. Brown--- 253
Obama for America v. Husted --------------------------------- 175
Ognibene v. Parks--- 309
Oregon v. Mitchell-- 29, 108
Pacific States Telephone & Telegraph Co. v.
  Oregon -- 47, 224
Palm Beach County Canvassing Board v. Harris ------- 154
People's Advocate v. Superior Court------------------------ 217
Perry v. Brown -- 235
Perry v. Perez--- 100
Pope v. Williams --- 29
Powell v. McCormack-- 237
Presley v. Etowah County Commission----------------------- 98
Purcell v. Gonzalez------------------------------------- 163, 195
Randall v. Sorrell--- 306
Raven v. Deukmejian-- 215
Reno v. Bossier Parish School Board ---------------------- 106
Republican Party v. White------------------------------------ 302
Reynolds v. Sims---------------------------- 9, 38, 53, 157, 196
Rice v. Cayetano --- 43
Richardson v. Ramirez--- 31
Rideout v. City of Los Angeles ------------------------------ 200
Rogers v. Lodge--- 117
Romer v. Evans-- 233
Sailors v. Board of Education of Kent County ------------- 65
Salyer Land Co. v. Tulare Lake Basin Water Storage
  District-- 66
Sandusky County Democratic Party v. Blackwell------- 185
Scheer v. City of Miami--------------------------------------- 198
Scott v. Germano-- 75
Senate of the State of California v. Jones ----------------- 213
Shaw v. Hunt (Shaw II)--------------------------------------- 143
Shaw v. Reno (Shaw I) ---------------------------- 128, 137, 138
Shelby County v. Holder----------------------- 28, 94, 110, 178
Simmons v. Galvin -- 179
Skafte v. Rorex --- 30
Slaughter-House Cases -------------------------------------- 23

Smith v. Allwright-------------------------- 22, 25, 249, 250, 251
South Carolina v. Katzenbach --------------------- 96, 108, 109
Southwest Voter Registration Education Project v.
　　Shelley --- 171, 196
Speechnow.org v. Federal Election Commission --------- 314
Stewart v. Blackwell-- 171, 179
Storer v. Brown-- 264, 285
Strauss v. Horton--- 216
Sugarman v. Dougall -- 30
Tashjian v. Republican Party of Connecticut ------------- 256
Taylor v. Howe--- 202
Tennant v. Jefferson County Commission ------------------- 60
Tennessee v. Lane --- 109
Terry v. Adams --- 22, 250, 251
Texas v. Holder--- 180
Thalheimer v. City of San Diego --------------------------- 309
Thornburg v. Gingles ------------------------------ 113, 122, 179
Tilson v. Mofford-- 222
Timmons v. Twin Cities Area New Party ------------------ 269
Town of Lockport v. Citizens for Community Action at
　　the Local Level --- 68
U.S. Term Limits v. Thornton ------------------------------- 236
United Jewish Organizations, Inc. v. Carey-------------- 137
United States v. Carolene Products---------------------------- 8
United States v. Classic ------------------------------- 202, 249
United States v. Danielczyk---------------------------------- 309
VanNatta v. Keisling --- 309
Vieth v. Jubelirer--- 86
Village of Arlington Heights v. Metropolitan Housing
　　Development Corp. --- 107
Voting Rights Coalition v. Wilson --------------------------- 182
Washington State Grange v. Washington State
　　Republican Party --- 166, 259
Washington v. Davis--- 231
Washington v. Seattle School District No. 1 ------------- 232
Wayne v. Venable--- 202
Weber v. Shelley --- 173
Weinschenk v. State of Missouri---------------------------- 189
Wesberry v. Sanders--- 52
Wexler v. Anderson --- 172
Whitcomb v. Chavis--- 113
White v. Regester-- 114, 119
Whitley v. Cranford--- 200
Williams v. Rhodes -- 264

Wyoming National Abortion Rights League v.
  Karpan --- 222
Yick Wo v. Hopkins -- 33
Zimmer v. McKeithen --- 115

ELECTION LAW

CHAPTER 1

PERSPECTIVES ON LAW AND DEMOCRACY

Democracy does not exist in a vacuum. It is instead a product of the laws that structure the political process and define the rights of participants. The distinctive characteristics of democracy in the United States—including the dominance of two major parties, the manner in which election campaigns are financed, the representation that different groups enjoy, and even the composition of the electorate—are inextricably tied to the laws regulating elections and politics. This nutshell summarizes that body of law, which includes the United States Constitution, federal statutes, and state laws, as well as judicial decisions interpreting all these laws.

To understand the law governing elections and politics in the United States, it is helpful to be familiar with some basic information regarding its system of government, including core democratic values enshrined in the U.S. Constitution and considered by leading political thinkers. Accordingly, this chapter begins with an overview of the republican or representative system of government in the U.S. It then proceeds to some themes and theories that may be used to frame the study of American election law.

A. THE REPUBLICAN FORM OF GOVERNMENT

Under the U.S. Constitution, federal statutes are enacted by the Congress and usually signed into law by the President. Both the members of Congress and the President are chosen by the people through elections. The people therefore do not make federal laws directly but indirectly, through their elected representatives. All the states likewise have legislative bodies that enact state laws, although many state constitutions also provide for "direct democracy," by which the people may enact laws directly through ballot measures (the subject of Chapter 8). Elections are the means through which citizens choose the officials who occupy certain government positions, including those who make our laws.

A system in which laws are made by elected representatives, rather than directly by the people, is commonly known as a republican system of government or representative democracy. This type of system exists in the United States at the federal, state, and local levels.

Federalist #10 (1787), written by James Madison, is perhaps the most famous articulation of the rationale for the republican form of government. Madison argued that republican government at the federal level would control the effects of "faction," which he defined as a group of citizens "united and actuated by some common impulse of passion, or of interest, adverse to the rights of other citizens, or to the permanent and aggregate interests of the community." Madison believed that factions are inevitable in a society committed to the preservation of liberty, but that they would have negative effects on governance unless their effects were cabined. He argued that a republican form of government, in which citizens delegate power to a relatively small number of representatives, would guard against the negative effects of faction. Those elected to the national legislature would have the wisdom and capacity to rise above parochial considerations and promote the "public good."

Though Madison wrote well over two centuries ago, *Federalist #10* addresses concerns about the democratic process that remain very much alive today. Prominent among those concerns is the danger of faction, roughly the equivalent of what we would today call "special interests." Another concern is the tyranny of the majority, the danger that an inflamed majority will coalesce to oppress an unpopular minority of citizens. Madison argued that one advantage of the republican system was its imposition of obstacles to the tyranny of the majority. He thought that representative democracy at the *federal* level would make it more difficult for any particular faction to control the reins of the national government. By encompassing a greater number of people with a variety of interests, Madison argued, the United States government would be more resistant to faction than state or local governments.

Madison's argument for a republican system of government rested in part on the idea of a transcendent "public good" that elected representatives would try to pursue. In modern times, political theorists are generally more skeptical that there is any universal public good, tending instead to focus on a fair process that will accommodate multiple competing interests. Still, Madison's arguments for a republican system of government retain considerable force today, especially his idea that such a system provided a safeguard against the tyranny of the majority.

At the same time, most everyone now agrees that a republican system of government is by itself inadequate to protect basic rights, including those of unpopular groups and individuals. The Bill of Rights contained in the first ten amendments to the U.S. Constitution, as well as the Fourteenth Amendment and other amendments protecting individual rights, provide additional protections against the tyranny of the majority. The application of these rights-creating provisions of the Constitution to the political process constitutes much of the field of election law.

B.   THE ROLE OF REPRESENTATIVES

One of the major questions of democratic theory underlying the republican system of government is how elected officials should conceive of their responsibilities. Should they serve as *agents* of those who elected them, giving the people who elected them what they want? Or should legislators exercise their own *independent judgment*, supporting policies that promote their own vision of the public good?

This is the question underlying the so-called "Burkean debate," named for British statesman Edmund Burke's classic *Speech to the Electors of Bristol* (1774). Burke famously argued that the legislator's job was to follow his own "mature judgment" and "enlightened counsel" rather than merely acceding to the wishes of citizens. He also argued that legislators should attend to the interests of the nation as whole, rather than just to those of his or her local constituency. The Burkean view is subject to the criticism that it is unrealistic, particularly in the modern political world where elected officials risk of losing the next election if they contravene the wishes of voters in their district. On the other hand, elected officials may sometimes have the latitude to follow their own judgment, rather than simply advancing the interests of their constituents.

Whether legislators should follow the wishes of voters in their district or pursue their own view of the public good remains a disputed question of political theory. It is important to the study of election law, because our conception of the legislators' proper role will necessarily inform the way in which we think the democratic process should be structured—including the manner in which elected officials are held accountable to the people, and the role of courts in policing the political process.

C. THEORIES OF THE POLITICAL PROCESS

A related theme in election law is the relative importance of individuals and groups in the political process. *Pluralism* sees groups as the fundamental unit of analysis, and therefore seeks to develop a system of rules that best accommodates multiple groups with competing interests. It bears a resemblance to Madison's discussion of factions in *Federalist #10,* although Madison saw interest groups as a necessary evil while pluralists tend to view them more favorably.

While pluralism focuses on inter-group dynamics, *progressivism* sees the individual as the fundamental unit of analysis. It views individuals as capable of making reasonable and informed decisions that promote the common good, and therefore advocates election rules that tend to facilitate participation by all citizens and, more broadly, social practices that cultivate civic virtue. This theory is associated with the progressive political movement of the early 1900s, though its roots can be traced at least as far back as Thomas Jefferson.

Closely related to progressivism is *civic republicanism,* which argues for a politics that promotes the public good by promoting reasoned deliberation among legislators. It draws on Burke's idea that representative democracy should serve the "general good, resulting from the general reason of the whole." The idea is that deliberation among a varied group of people tends to yield better decisionmaking—the "wisdom of the multitude," in the words of Jeremy Waldron. One question to consider in studying election law is how well our laws and institutions promote such group deliberation.

Some political thinkers view the civil republican ideal of deliberative democracy as unrealistic, arguing that citizens and legislators cannot realistically be expected to engage in such reasoned deliberation. Among the critics are those espousing economic theories of democracy like *public choice theory,* which sees voters and politicians as rational, self-interested actors. Broadly speaking, public choice theory seeks to apply the tools of economics to the political process. It views candidates for office as seeking to maximize their chances for election, and individual citizens as seeking to promote their own interests.

Strains of these theories may be seen in the various subjects that constitute the field of election law. In some cases, the focus tends to be on the accommodation of group interests—including protection against tyranny of the majority—while in other instances the focus is on protecting the rights of individuals to participate as equals in the democratic process. How one thinks politics ought to be structured, including the appropriate role of courts in reviewing election rules, will depend largely on the theory of democracy that one finds most persuasive.

D.   JUDICIAL REVIEW OF ELECTION LAWS

The political theories described above undergird a major ongoing debate in the field of election law today: whether judicial review should focus on the rights of citizens or, alternatively, on a fair political structure. The rights-versus-structure debate in election law grows out of the broader question of how to interpret open-ended provisions of the U.S. Constitution, like those protecting "freedom of speech," "equal protection," and "due process." Proponents of *process-based theory* (also known as "representation-reinforcement" theory) argue that judicial review should focus on laws and practices that tend to advantage incumbents and to harm numerical minorities.

Process-based theory has roots in footnote 4 of *United States v. Carolene Products,* 304 U.S. 144 (1938). While the Court held that legislation regulating commercial activity is subject to deferential judicial review, footnote 4 suggested that "more exacting judicial scrutiny" might be appropriate for legislation that restricts the political process or that targets "discrete and insular minorities." As John Hart Ely explained in DEMOCRACY AND DISTRUST: A THEORY OF JUDICIAL REVIEW (1980), the basic idea is that courts should be especially attentive in areas where the political process may be "malfunctioning," either because (1) those in power are "choking off the channels of political change to ensure that they will stay in and the outs will stay out," or (2) the governing majority is "systematically disadvantaging some minority . . . and thereby denying the minority the protection afforded to other groups by a representative system." Consistent with process-based theory, the U.S. Supreme Court has sometimes given heightened scrutiny to laws and practices that tend to advantage incumbent politicians, such as the malapportioned legislative districts struck down in *Reynolds v. Sims,* 377 U.S. 533 (1964), and the other "one person, one vote" cases (discussed in Chapter 4). The Court has also accorded heightened scrutiny to some laws that disadvantage a minority of citizens, such as the racial gerrymander struck down in *Gomillion v. Lightfoot,* 364 U.S. 339 (1960), and the poll tax struck down in *Harper v. Virginia Board of Elections,* 383 U.S. 663 (1966) (both discussed in Chapter 3).

In the field of election law, process-based theory has been used to argue for searching judicial review of structural rules that inhibit competition and entrench those in power. The most prominent proponents of this "structuralist" view are Samuel Issacharoff and Richard Pildes, who argue that politics should be viewed as a "marketplace" in which courts help ensure fair competition. Issacharoff and Pildes contend that judicial review should focus on structures that entrench the party in power or incumbents generally: "Where there is an appropriately robust market in partisan competition, there is less justification for judicial intervention. Where courts can discern that existing partisan forces have manipulated those background rules, courts should strike down those manipulations to ensure an appropriately competitive political environment." *Politics as*

Markets: Partisan Lockups of the Democratic Process, 50 STAN. L. REV. 643 (1998). In other words, courts engaging in judicial review of election laws should focus primarily on anti-competitive practices, rather than on the protection of individual rights.

There are factual as well as theoretical disagreements over competitiveness in elections. There is strong evidence that incumbents enjoy an advantage over challengers in elections. For example, between 1968 and 2010, U.S. House incumbents seeking reelection were successful 94% of the time, with the percentage of incumbents defeated never exceeding 15%. It is less clear *why* incumbents are reelected to office at such high rates—and, in particular, whether it is because of election laws or for some other reason. Among the possible explanations for the success of incumbents are: (1) gerrymandered legislative districts, (2) people usually voting along party lines, (3) incumbents' activities in their districts which tend to generate public support, (4) incumbents' greater ability to raise money than challengers, and (5) the fact that incumbents are usually stronger candidates than their challengers. In short, it is clear that incumbents have high rates of success when they seek reelection, but the reasons why— and specifically, the extent to which election laws are responsible for this success—are less clear.

Notwithstanding the success of incumbents generally, some scholars are skeptical of process-based theory of judicial review. One line of criticism is that the ideal of a well-functioning democratic process is the subject of vigorous contestation. There is no agreement on what the political process should look like—or even what fair competition should be understood to mean. In this vein, Richard Hasen criticizes Issacharoff and Pildes' use of the market metaphor on the ground that the meaning of political competition is not adequately defined. Hasen advocates a rights-based approach to judicial review, which would focus on places where there is broad consensus that a particular political right should be protected. Richard L. Hasen, THE SUPREME COURT AND ELECTION LAW: JUDGING EQUALITY FROM *BAKER V. CARR* TO *BUSH V. GORE* (2003).

Daniel Lowenstein is likewise critical of theories that target anti-competitive practices, believing that overly aggressive judicial review can do great harm. Lowenstein thus calls for judicial restraint in constitutional challenges to election laws. Responding to proponents of process-based theory, Lowenstein writes: "If the Court accepted this theory and were truly sophisticated . . . they would simply deconstitutionalize election law and have done with it." Daniel H. Lowenstein, *The Supreme Court Has No Theory of Politics–And Be Thankful for Small Favors,* in THE U.S. SUPREME COURT AND THE ELECTORAL PROCESS (2000). He argues that disputes over competing political values are usually best left to the political process.

Because much (though certainly not all) of election law is constitutional law, it is important to be aware of the debate over process-based theory. Still, this is just one of several theories of constitutional interpretation that might be brought to bear on election law questions. Others include originalism, rights-based theories, critical race theory, feminism, and economic theories of constitutional interpretation. Different theories will tend to yield different conclusions with respect to the various issues discussed in the remainder of this nutshell.

CHAPTER 2

THE HISTORY OF VOTING RIGHTS IN THE U.S.

It is tempting to view history as a steady forward march, with progress coming slowly but surely over time. This has not, however, been the story of voting rights in the United States. Progress has neither been constant nor inevitable; instead, it has come in fits and starts, with short bursts of progress followed by long periods of stagnation and even regression. That is especially true of African Americans' struggle for the right to vote in the states of the former Confederacy, which was won after the Civil War only to be lost in the decades that followed and not regained again for over a half-century. The story of the right to vote in the U.S. is integrally linked to African Americans' struggle for equal rights, as summarized below.

While progress has not been steady, over the course of time non-property holding white men, racial minorities, women, and young adults have all gained the right to vote. Those who are still generally not permitted to vote include noncitizens, nonresidents, minors, people deemed incompetent, and (in some states) people convicted of felonies. What follows is a very brief summary of key developments in the history of the right to vote in the U.S.*

---

* For a comprehensive history, see Alexander Keyssar, THE RIGHT TO VOTE: THE CONTESTED HISTORY OF DEMOCRACY IN THE

A. PROPERTY RESTRICTIONS AND THEIR ELIMINATION

At the time of the American Revolution, voting was generally limited to property-holding men 21 and over, a restriction inherited from British law. Every colony limited voting to people who were either "freeholders" owning a certain quantity of land or taxpayers (a more limited category than today, given the absence of an income tax). Although it is hard to say precisely what percentage of the population was excluded by property qualifications, more than half of white adult men were probably eligible to vote. Because land was relatively inexpensive, it was often possible for men to obtain the right to vote by the time they reached middle age. In addition to property requirements, a number of states had religious exclusions from voting, though these were largely eliminated by the end of the Revolution.

The original Constitution did not dictate who was allowed to vote. Instead, Article I, Section 2 of the Constitution provided that those voting for representatives in *U.S. House* must meet the qualifications for voting for the lower house of *state legislatures*. In other words, the qualifications for

UNITED STATES (revised ed. 2009). For a shorter account, linking the enfranchisement of various groups to their participation in military conflicts, see Pamela Karlan, *Ballots and Bullets: The Exceptional History of the Right to Vote,* 71 U. CIN. L. REV. 1345 (2003). The discussion that follows relies primarily on these sources, as well as Daniel Lowenstein, Richard L. Hasen & Daniel P. Tokaji, ELECTION LAW: CASES AND MATERIALS 26–38 (5th ed. 2012).

voting in U.S. House elections were tied to state qualifications, a requirement that remains to this day. Direct election for the *U.S. Senate*, by contrast, were not required until the ratification of the Seventeenth Amendment in 1913, with qualifications for voting for that office likewise tied to qualifications for voting in state legislative elections.

Questions about the disenfranchisement of non-propertyholders emerged during the Revolution, driven in part by questions about why those participating in the war effort ought not be allowed to vote. By the dawn of the Nineteenth Century, the idea of universal suffrage for white men had gained traction. By the middle of the Nineteenth Century, every state had gotten rid of its property-holding and wealth requirements for voting. Military service was, in some states, a means by which non-propertyholding white men could qualify to vote. In addition, the payment of a poll tax provided an alternative means by which to qualify. Although we think of the poll tax as a disenfranchising device today—and not without good reason, given its predominant use in the Twentieth Century—the poll tax was originally a way of expanding the vote to those who did not own land.

The last state to move to universal suffrage for adult white males was Rhode Island, which did so only after an armed insurrection known as the Dorr Rebellion. As of 1841 when the conflict began, Rhode Island was still operating under a charter granted by the Crown in 1663, under which only property-holding males could vote. With more people moving to cities, the eligible voting population in Rhode Island actually declined to less than half of white men. Many of those excluded from voting were Irish Catholic immigrants. Thomas Dorr led the movement for universal white male suffrage, organizing a "People's Convention" to draft a new constitution, while the old Charter government held its own convention. The constitution drafted by the People's Convention provided for universal white male suffrage, while the Charter government convention's constitution did not. The U.S. government (under President John Tyler) threw its support behind the Charter government. Years later, the Supreme Court held in *Luther v. Borden*, 48 U.S. 1 (1849) (Chapter 4.A) that the decision which government was the legitimate one was a "political question" not appropriate for federal judicial resolution. After a brief armed conflict in 1842, the Charter government emerged victorious with Dorr fleeing the state. A new constitution adopted in 1843 liberalized voting requirements by extending the right to vote to any free man (regardless of race) who paid a $1 poll tax.

B. RECONSTRUCTION AND DISENFRANCHISEMENT

By the second half of the Nineteenth Century, white adult males were generally eligible to vote. But large segments of the population—most notably African Americans and women—were disallowed from voting. In fact, there had actually been a regression of blacks' voting rights in the decades since the Revolution. While many state constitutions did not originally include race as a requirement for voting, only five states (all of them in New England) allowed African Americans to vote by the time the Civil War began.

Even after the Civil War, there was considerable resistance to allowing African Americans to vote— not only in the predominantly Democratic South, but also in the North. But the Republican-led national government realized that their continuing hold on power depended on the enfranchisement of African Americans. After Republicans won convincing victories in the 1866 congressional elections, Congress enacted the Reconstruction Act of 1867, which made the enfranchisement of African Americans a condition for readmission of the states of the former Confederacy. The Fourteenth Amendment, ratified in 1868, did not expressly grant the right to vote to African Americans, but it did prohibit the denial of "equal protection of the laws," as well as abridgement of the "privileges or immunities of citizens of the United States." After Ulysses S. Grant's victory in the 1868 presidential election, Republicans—worried about their future electoral prospects—rushed the Fifteenth Amendment through Congress in early 1869. The Fifteenth Amendment expressly provided that "the right of citizens of the United States to vote shall not be denied or abridged on account of race, color, or previous condition of servitude." It was ratified in early 1870. African Americans had already gained the right to vote in the South, as a condition for readmission of those states. A major reason for the enactment of the Fifteenth Amendment—in addition to reinforcing black voting rights in the South—was to shore up Republicans' electoral prospects in the *North*, where the party believed it could count on black voters' support. Nearly one million people were enfranchised as a result.

For several years, African Americans in the South not only exercised their right to vote, but also were elected to office in significant numbers. As of 1872, there were over 300 African American legislators elected from states of the former Confederacy. At the end of Reconstruction, however, white Democrats began the mass disenfranchisement of African Americans that eventually created the one-party "Solid South." Black enfranchisement was not immediate—in fact, it took about a quarter century from the end of Reconstruction in 1876 to 1900–for the process to be completed. In the early stages of black disenfranchisement (the 1870s and 1880s), white Democrats used violence and fraud to keep blacks from voting, rig election results, and thereby win control of state legislatures. In the later stages (the 1890s through 1900) southern Democrats amended their state constitutions to keep blacks— as well as many poor whites—from voting. By 1901, virtually all African Americans in the South were denied the right to vote, and there were no African Americans left serving as legislators from southern states. And that was essentially how things remained until the second half of the Twentieth Century.

For the most part, the Supreme Court declined to intervene when southern blacks were disenfranchised en masse in southern states. The most notorious example is *Giles v. Harris*, 189 U.S. 475 (1903), in which the Supreme Court declined to grant relief to a man seeking to challenge Alabama's refusal to allow him to register. Giles brought suit on behalf of himself and more than 5,000 other African Americans, challenging state and county officials' refusal to let them register and vote. Despite the clear language of the Fifteenth Amendment prohibiting racial discrimination in voting, Justice Oliver Wendell Holmes' opinion for the Court refused to grant him relief. Justice Holmes' opinion reasoned that, if plaintiff's allegations were true, then Alabama's entire registration scheme was "a fraud on the Constitution" to which the Court would be made a party by granting Giles relief. This line of reasoning effectively gave a green light to southern states, allowing them to persist in the mass disenfranchisement of African Americans. Justice Holmes went on to say that the Court lacked the practical power to enforce any order requiring that blacks be allowed to register and vote. Thus, if relief were to be had, it would have to come from the people of Alabama or the political branches of the federal government—not the federal courts. That is what eventually happened through Congress' enactment of the Voting Rights Act of 1965 (discussed in Part D below).

During the period from the late 1800s through the 1960s, the devices used to impede blacks from voting in the South included the following:

• *Literacy and Interpretation Tests.* Tests requiring voters to read or interpret texts were often administered in a discriminatory manner. To avoid disenfranchising illiterate whites, exceptions like the "grandfather clause" waived the requirement for those whose ancestors had been eligible to vote before black disenfranchisement. The grandfather clause was struck down in *Guinn v. United States*, 238 U.S. 347 (1915), but literacy tests persisted until the 1960s, with the Supreme Court holding in *Lassiter v. Northampton County Board of Elections*, 360 U.S. 45 (1959), that a fairly administered literacy test did not violate the Equal Protection Clause.

• *Poll Taxes.* By 1904, all the southern states had adopted a poll tax. Like literacy tests, these were often expressly justified as a means by which to disenfranchise blacks. Poll taxes also had the effect and sometimes the intent of keeping less affluent whites from voting as well. The Twenty–Fourth Amendment, ratified in 1964, prohibited poll taxes in federal elections. In *Harper v. Virginia Board of Elections*, 383 U.S. 663 (1966) (Chapter 3), the Supreme Court held that poll taxes in state elections violated the Equal Protection Clause.

• *Secret Ballots.* Today, we think of the secret ballot as a means by which to protect voter privacy and prevent the selling or buying of votes. While the secret ballot does serve this function, southern officials often used it as a means by which to prevent illiterate people from voting. Some states had separate boxes for each office, with only ballots placed in the correct box counted device. The boxes were moved around during the day, to prevent literate voters from informing illiterate voters which box was which. Election officials would sometimes assist white voters, while denying the same help to blacks.

- *Voter Registration.* Although voter registration is justified as a means of promoting election integrity, it has sometimes been used to keep eligible citizens from voting. Laws requiring registration in order to vote began to proliferate in the latter part of the Nineteenth Century. White Democrats' control over registration lists was a critical component of their effort to disenfranchise blacks. Southern election officials extended residency requirements, required periodic registration, and demanded voluminous information, while having considerable discretion to reject registration applications that they deemed insufficient. In the North as well, registration requirements were sometimes used to impede registration by blacks, recent immigrants, and other working-class voters.

- *The White Primary.* Democratic Party officials often excluded blacks from voting in their primaries. Because the South was solidly Democratic, the Democratic primary was the only game in town, so exclusion from that party's primary was the functional equivalent of disenfranchisement. While local party primaries were used in the South starting in the 1870s, statewide primaries did not come into being until the 1890s. The most important legal battles over white primaries emerged from the state of Texas. In a series of cases decided between the 1920s and 1950s, culminating with *Smith v. Allwright*, 321 U.S. 649 (1944), and *Terry v. Adams*, 345 U.S. 461 (1953), the Supreme Court struck down laws and practices that excluded blacks from voting in Texas primary elections. These cases, discussed at greater length in Chapter 9.B, are collectively known as the "White Primary Cases."

C. THE STRUGGLE FOR WOMEN'S SUFFRAGE

The Nineteenth Amendment to the Constitution, ratified in 1920, was the product of a struggle that went on for decades. The beginning of the women's suffrage movement is generally considered to be an 1848 meeting in Seneca Falls, New York, at which was adopted a "Declaration of Sentiments" calling for women to be granted the constitutional right to vote. Elizabeth Cady Stanton and Susan B. Anthony were among the leaders of the movement. They argued their case in various forums, including newspapers and petitions to Congress after the Civil War. They were disappointed when the Republican Party adopted measures granting blacks the right to vote, but declined to push for the enfranchisement of women. After losing the political battle, they sought the right to vote in court.

In *Minor v. Happersett*, 88 U.S. 162 (1875), the Supreme Court unanimously held that the Fourteenth Amendment did not extend the right to vote to women. Like the *Slaughter–House Cases*, 83 U.S. 36 (1873), *Minor* rests on a narrow reading of the Privileges or Immunities Clause of the Fourteenth Amendment. While acknowledging that women could be citizens if born in the U.S. or naturalized, the Court rejected the argument that voting was one of the "privileges or immunities of citizens of the United States" under Section 1 of that amendment. In support of its holding, *Minor* relied on Section 2 of the Fourteenth Amendment, which provides that the representation of a state in the U.S. House shall be reduced if the vote is denied to certain adult "male inhabitants" (the first textual reference to sex in the Constitution.) The Court thought that this language showed women and children were not meant to be given the vote by the adoption of the Fourteenth Amendment. The Court also cited the Fifteenth Amendment's express prohibition on race discrimination in voting, reasoning that this amendment would have been unnecessary if voting was one of the "privileges or immunities" of U.S. citizens. Finally, it noted that all of the states of the former Confederacy had been readmitted despite the fact that they did not confer suffrage on women, which it saw as further evidence that the Fourteenth Amendment did not enfranchise women. "Our province is to decide what the law is," the Court concluded, "not to declare what it should be."

With *Minor* holding that the Constitution did not give women the right to vote, the battle again became a political one. In fact, even before *Minor*, women gained voting rights in some western territories. In 1890, the National American Women's Suffrage Association (NAWSA) was formed through the merger of two predecessor groups. That same year, Wyoming was the first admitted state to grant full voting rights to women. Although three other new states granted women voting rights in 1896, the movement stalled after that and it was not until 1910 that another state did the same.

Women's entrance into the labor force and support for the military effort in World War I helped turn public sentiment in favor of women's suffrage. A pivotal victory was New York's granting of women's suffrage in 1917. The result was a sufficient number of members of Congress with female voters to induce Congress in 1919 to approve the Nineteenth Amendment, which was ratified the following year. Although early arguments for women's suffrage tended to emphasize universal suffrage, the arguments gradually shifted to reforms that women voters might help bring about. That included the promotion of peace, as well as the prohibition of alcoholic beverages, which became part of the Constitution through the Eighteenth Amendment (1919) only to be repealed by the Twenty–First Amendment (1933).

A major difference between the struggles for voting rights by blacks and women is that, once women won their right to vote by constitutional amendment, that right was actually honored. By contrast, most African Americans were kept from registering and voting in the South for the first six decades of the Twentieth Century, before ultimately regaining their right to vote in the "Second Reconstruction."

D.   THE SECOND RECONSTRUCTION

The period from the end of World War II through the 1960s is sometimes referred to as the "Second Reconstruction," due to the major gains in civil rights that occurred during this period. While the Supreme Court mostly allowed the disenfranchisement of African Americans in the late Nineteenth and early Twentieth Centuries, it did intervene to stop the White Primary. The decisions in *Smith v. Allwright*, 321 U.S. 649 (1944) and other cases (discussed in Chapter 9.B) contributed to black registration more than tripling (from around 250,000 to 775,000) between 1940 and 1947. The military service of approximately one million black men during World War II helped generate support for the movement to reenfranchise African Americans in the South. Nevertheless, literacy tests, poll taxes, voter registration practices—and sometimes methods as crude as threats and violence—prevented blacks from registering, let alone voting, through much of the South. It became clear that federal intervention was necessary, and

state and local authorities in the South had a vested
interest in keeping blacks from voting.

Congress enacted modest voting rights legislation
in 1957 and 1960, and the Civil Rights Act of 1964
also contained some provisions designed to advance
voting rights. These laws led to some victories, with
the percentage of voting-age blacks registered in the
South having reached 38% by 1964. But the burden
of obtaining relief rested with the U.S. government,
and piecemeal litigation was largely ineffectual in
the face of white Democrats' intransigent resistance
to allowing blacks to vote. A pivotal moment in the
struggle for voting rights was "Bloody Sunday,"
March 7, 1965, when future Congressman John
Lewis and other voting rights marchers were
viciously attacked by state police as they crossed the
Edmund Pettus Bridge in their attempted march
from Selma to Montgomery, Alabama. The following
week, President Lyndon B. Johnson employed the
"We Shall Overcome" slogan of Martin Luther King,
Jr. and other civil rights leaders during a speech to
Congress urging enactment of a stronger voting
rights law. In August, President Johnson signed the
Voting Rights Act of 1965 (VRA) into law.

The VRA effectively dismantled the system of
mass disenfranchisement that had developed since
the first Reconstruction. Among its key provisions
were the following:

- *Section 2* essentially restated the Fifteenth
  Amendment's prohibition on race discrimination
  in voting. It was not of great immediate
  importance, but became very important as a

means of stopping vote dilution after it was amended in 1982.

- *Section 4* prohibited literacy tests and other tests and devices in covered jurisdictions. Under the original VRA, covered jurisdictions were states and localities that conditioned registration or voting on a test, and in which less than half the voting age population voted in 1964. This formula was designed to cover the places where black disenfranchisement was most pronounced: Alabama, Georgia, Louisiana, Mississippi, South Carolina, Virginia, and much of North Carolina. Other state and local jurisdictions were added through the 1970 and 1975 amendments to the VRA.

- *Section 5* required covered jurisdictions to obtain "preclearance" of any new voting rules or practices from either the U.S. Attorney General or the federal district court in Washington, D.C. It was designed to prevent states and localities from adopting new barriers to voting once old ones had been removed, as had been common practice before 1965.

Almost immediately, the VRA succeeded in increasing black registration and participation. In Alabama, for example, black registration rose from 19.3% to 51.6% in two years, while in Mississippi it increased from 6.7% to 59.8%. Overall, black registration increased from 29.3% to 52.1% in the seven covered states between 1965 and 1967. Bernard Grofman, MINORITY REPRESENTATION AND THE QUEST FOR VOTING EQUALITY (1992).

Sections 4 and 5 of the VRA were originally enacted as temporary provisions, but were renewed in 1970, 1975, 1982, and 2006. With each renewal, Congress attempted to strengthen the VRA. In 1970, its reach grew through an extension of the Section 4 coverage formula, while the ban on literacy tests was made applicable nationwide. Congress made the ban on literacy tests permanent in 1975, while requiring assistance for certain language minorities (specifically, those whose primary language is Spanish or an Asian, Native American, or Native Alaskan language). In 1982, Congress expanded Section 2's protection against minority vote dilution, while reauthorizing Sections 4 and 5 for 25 years. Congress reauthorized these provisions for another 25 years in 2006, while imposing a higher standard on jurisdictions seeking preclearance of voting changes. In *Shelby County v. Holder,* 133 S. Ct. 2612 (2013), however, the Supreme Court struck down Section 4's coverage formula, effectively ending Section 5 preclearance. The VRA and its amendments are discussed at greater length in Chapter 6.

E. EXPANSION OF THE FRANCHISE AND RECENT CONTROVERSIES

1. AGE RESTRICTIONS

One of the most important developments since the VRA's enactment was the expansion of the franchise to people 18 and over. The VRA was amended in 1970 to prohibit states from setting a lower voting age, and a divided Supreme Court partly upheld this provision in *Oregon v. Mitchell*, 400 U.S. 112 (1970). There was, however, no opinion for a majority. Four justices upheld the lowering of the voting age under the Fourteenth Amendment, while the fifth, Justice Black, concluded that Congress had the power to set a minimum age for federal but not state elections—despite the fact that Article 1, Section 2 and the Seventeenth Amendment tie congressional voting qualifications to state legislative voting qualifications. The Twenty–Sixth Amendment to the Constitution, ratified in 1971, resolved the question by providing that states may not set age limits lower than 18.

2. DURATIONAL RESIDENCY REQUIREMENTS

Until the late Twentieth Century, it was common for states to deny voting rights to citizens newly arrived in the state. A one-year durational residency requirement was typical. In *Pope v. Williams*, 193 U.S. 621 (1904), the Supreme Court upheld a one-year waiting period for those seeking to vote, reasoning that voting was a "privilege" on which the state was entitled to legislate. In 1970, the VRA was amended to prohibit states from requiring citizens to reside in the state or to register more than 30 days before a presidential election. This still allowed states to set longer durational residency requirements for other elections, though the cost and inconvenience of doing so is usually prohibitive. In *Dunn v. Blumstein*, 405 U.S. 330 (1972), the Court struck down a requirement of one year's residency in a state, and three months' residency in a county. The Court subsequently upheld a 50–day durational residency and registration requirement in *Marston v. Lewis*, 410 U.S. 679 (1973). Durational residency requirements of 30 days or fewer are now the norm, due mostly to the 1970 VRA amendments.

3.   NONCITIZENS

Aliens were often allowed to vote during the Eighteenth Century but, in the early Nineteenth Century, states moved to make citizenship a requirement for voting. In the late Nineteenth Century, there was a temporary reversal of this trend but, by 1926, all states denied the vote to noncitizens. In *Sugarman v. Dougall*, 413 U.S. 634 (1973), the Court stated that citizenship is a permissible basis for denying voting rights, given a state's "broad power to define its political community." Although this is dictum, lower courts have upheld the denial of votes to noncitizens under the Fourteenth Amendment. See, e.g., *Skafte v. Rorex*, 553 P.2d 830 (Colo. 1976). Some local jurisdictions allow noncitizens to vote in their elections.

4.   PRISONERS AND FELONS

All but two states deny the vote to people who are currently incarcerated, and many others deny the vote to those who are on parole or probation. Roughly one-third of states deny the franchise to some or all of those who have completed their punishment, unless they obtain reinstatement of voting rights. The Supreme Court upheld the disenfranchisement of felons who have completed their sentences, including probation and parole, in *Richardson v. Ramirez*, 418 U.S. 24 (1974). The Court relied on Section 2 of the Fourteenth Amendment, which reduces the representation of states that deny the vote to male citizens "except for participation in rebellion, or other crime"—language that the Court understood to mean that states were permitted to deny the vote to citizens convicted of a crime. But in *Hunter v. Underwood*, 471 U.S. 222 (1985), the Court held that an Alabama felony disenfranchisement law, adopted in 1901 with the intent of disenfranchising blacks, violated the Equal Protection Clause. More recently, there have been several challenges to felony disenfranchisement under Section 2 of the VRA, but so far federal courts of appeal have rejected these challenges. There have, however, been some successful efforts to relax state felony disenfranchisement laws through the political process.

5. ELECTION ADMINISTRATION REFORM

Since the 2000 presidential election, there has been unprecedented attention to the "nuts and bolts" of election administration. That includes voting equipment, voter identification, voter registration, provisional ballots, absentee and early voting, polling place operations, recounts, and contests. All these topics have been the subject of legislation and litigation since 2000. Perhaps the most controversial issue to emerge is whether voters should be required to present government-issued photo identification (like a driver's license). Supporters argue that a photo ID requirement is needed to prevent voter fraud and increase public confidence. Opponents argue that strict identification laws will impede racial minorities, poor people, and other eligible citizens from voting. Other prominent subjects of controversy include voter registration practices, the period for early voting, and the counting of provisional ballots. These topics are addressed in detail in Chapter 7.

CHAPTER 3

THE CONSTITUTIONAL RIGHT TO VOTE

A. CONSTITUTIONAL TEXT AND STRUCTURE

The U.S. Constitution does not expressly confer a general right to vote, but instead leaves the regulation of elections to the states and Congress. Qualifications for voting in congressional elections are tied to qualifications for voting in state legislative elections under Article I, Section 2 of the original Constitution and the Seventeenth Amendment. The Elections Clause, in Article I, Section 4 of the Constitution, gives states the authority to regulate the "Times, Places, and Manner" of holding congressional elections, while authorizing Congress to "make or alter such Regulations." Under the original structure of the Constitution, then, the setting of qualifications and the regulation of elections was left to the states, with Congress authorized to make or alter rules for the conduct of congressional elections.

Since the late Nineteenth Century, the Supreme Court has declared the right to vote "fundamental" because it is "preservative of all rights." The Court first characterized voting as a fundamental right in *Yick Wo v. Hopkins*, 118 U.S. 356 (1886). While that case did not involve voting, the Court has repeated its statement that voting is a fundamental right many times. The idea is that the vote—and by extension, representation in government—is essential to ensure that all our other interests are protected.

The primary source of the fundamental right to vote is the Fourteenth Amendment. Other provisions of the Constitution provide additional protection for the vote:

- *The Fifteenth Amendment* (1870) prohibits the denial or abridgement of the vote based on race, color, or previous condition of servitude.

- *The Nineteenth Amendment* (1920) prohibits denial or abridgement of the vote on account of sex.

- *The Twenty–Fourth Amendment* (1964) prohibits the denial or abridgement of the vote in federal elections based on the failure to pay a poll tax or other tax.

- *The Twenty–Sixth Amendment* (1971) prohibits the denial or abridgement of the vote on account of age to citizens 18 and over.

Note that these constitutional amendments prohibit the exclusion of people from voting on certain grounds, but do not confer an affirmative right to vote on all citizens.

Despite the specific clauses regarding voting and the longstanding characterization of the right to vote as fundamental, the Court has not always treated voting as a fundamental right. Ironically, at the same time that the Supreme Court declared the right to vote "fundamental" in *Yick Wo*, white

Democrats in the South were employing practices designed to ensure the mass disenfranchisement of African Americans (as discussed in Chapter 2). These practices persisted until the 1960s. Even today, the Constitution is not understood to prohibit all barriers to voting. Part C discusses Supreme Court precedent on which restrictions on the franchise are permissible and which are not.

B.   RESTRICTIONS ON WHO MAY VOTE

In what circumstances may the vote be denied to people who fail to satisfy certain qualifications or requirements? In reviewing restrictions on who may register and vote, a key question is the appropriate level of constitutional scrutiny. The Supreme Court has said that *strict scrutiny* is the appropriate standard for reviewing some restrictions on voting. This standard requires the government to show that its restrictions are *narrowly tailored to serve a compelling government interest.* In other cases, the Court has applied a less searching level of scrutiny. In still other cases, the Court has not been clear about the level of scrutiny it is applying. Sections 1 through 3 below address restrictions that were used to keep blacks from voting—literacy tests, gerrymandering, and poll taxes. Section 4 considers exclusions based upon a supposed lack of sufficient interest or "stake" in election results.

1.   LITERACY TESTS

The Supreme Court has never held literacy tests categorically unconstitutional, although the Voting

Rights Act of 1965 (VRA) suspended literacy tests in covered jurisdictions, and that ban was made permanent and extended nationwide by later amendments to the VRA. In a case that preceded enactment of the VRA, *Lassiter v. Northampton County Board of Elections*, 360 U.S. 45 (1959), the Court held that literacy tests were constitutional if used in a race-neutral fashion.

Plaintiff in *Lassiter* was a black citizen of North Carolina whose application for registration was rejected because she refused to submit to a literacy test as required by state law. In upholding this state requirement against a facial challenge, Justice Douglas' opinion for the Court relied on Article I, Section 2 and the Seventeenth Amendment, which tie the qualifications for voting in congressional elections to qualifications for voting in state legislative elections. The opinion went on to say that literacy and illiteracy were race-neutral requirements for voting.

At the same time, *Lassiter* recognized the potential for a facially neutral test to be used in a racially discriminatory way, in violation of the Fifteenth Amendment. It cited with approval a lower court decision finding a literacy test to be a device for racial discrimination, given the discretion vested in registrars. In the case of North Carolina's literacy test, by contrast, there was no assertion that the requirement that voters "be able to read and write any section of the Constitution of North Carolina in the English language" was being used to discriminate on the basis of race.

2.   GERRYMANDERING

In *Gomillion v. Lightfoot*, 364 U.S. 339 (1960), the Court struck down city boundaries that had been redrawn so as to exclude African American voters, thus preventing them from voting in city elections. In 1957, the Alabama legislature redrew the boundaries of the city of Tuskegee, altering the city's shape "from a square to an uncouth twenty-eight-sided figure." Plaintiffs alleged that the redrawn boundaries were designed to disenfranchise black citizens, citing evidence that the new boundaries removed from the city all but four or five of its 400 black voters, without removing even one white voter. Justice Frankfurter's opinion for the Court held these allegations sufficient to make out a constitutional claim. If proven, they would show that the new boundaries were "solely concerned with segregating white and [black] voters by fencing [black] citizens out of town so as to deprive them of their pre-existing municipal vote." Such a showing would suffice to establish a violation of the Fifteenth Amendment's prohibition on racial discrimination in voting.

3.   POLL TAXES

In *Harper v. Virginia State Board of Elections*, 383 U.S. 663 (1966), the Court struck down a $1.50 poll tax for voting in state elections under the Equal Protection Clause of the Fourteenth Amendment. The poll tax was one of the devices that white Democrats used to keep blacks—as well as poor whites—from voting during the period after

Reconstruction. The Twenty–Fourth Amendment (ratified in 1964) prohibited poll taxes in federal elections, but a few states still used them for state and local elections until *Harper*.

In contrast to *Gomillion*, the opinion in *Harper* did not rest on racial discrimination under the Fifteenth Amendment. Instead, Justice Douglas' majority opinion concluded that it was impermissible under the Fourteenth Amendment to condition voting on a citizen's economic status, reasoning that: "Wealth, like race, creed, or color, is not germane to one's ability to participate intelligently in the electoral process." The Court distinguished *Lassiter* on the ground that the literacy test—unlike the poll tax—had some relation to the "intelligent use of the ballot."

Harper is an important case in the development of the constitutional doctrine on the level of scrutiny applicable to restrictions on voting. Justice Douglas' opinion for the majority cites *Yick Wo* for the proposition that voting is a fundamental right because it is preservative of all rights. It goes on to say that restrictions on voting must be "carefully and meticulously scrutinized," quoting *Reynolds v. Sims*, 377 U.S. 533 (1964) (discussed in Chapter 4.A). At the end of the opinion, the Court states that classifications that invade or restrain fundamental rights must be "closely scrutinized and carefully confined" under the Equal Protection Clause. Although the multi-tiered levels of constitutional scrutiny used today were not yet developed, the standard applied in *Harper* is a precursor of what we now know as strict scrutiny.

Justice Black and Justice Harlan both dissented in *Harper*. Justice Black thought that it was constitutionally permissible for a state to impose a poll tax, urging adherence to the Court's prior decision in *Breedlove v. Suttles*, 302 U.S. 277 (1937), which had upheld a poll tax imposed on men but not women and minors. Justice Harlan, joined by Justice Stewart, noted that property qualifications had historically been imposed as a condition of voting, but that all but four states had already gotten rid of the poll tax. While acknowledging that poll taxes were not in accord with then-prevailing "egalitarian notions of how modern democracy should be organized," Justice Harlan thought it was up to legislative bodies to get rid of such restrictions on voting.

4. EXCLUSIONS BASED ON LACK OF AN INTEREST

A more complicated analysis applies to laws that exclude people from voting based on a lack of interest or "stake" in the community. An early case striking down a prohibition on voting by those believed to lack a sufficient interest is *Carrington v. Rash*, 380 U.S. 89 (1965). A Texas statute prohibited members of the armed forces who moved into the state during the course of their service from voting in any Texas election, as long as they remained in military service. Carrington was a U.S. Army sergeant who had moved to Texas, where he owned a home and had started a business. He was stationed in New Mexico, commuting to his Army job from El Paso. Although he resided in Texas, he was ineligible to vote in state elections under the statute.

Texas defended the statute by arguing that it was entitled to prevent the votes of military personnel from "overwhelm[ing]" the local civilian community, and to prevent "transients" from infiltrating these elections. Justice Stewart's opinion for the Court reasoned that a state could not "[f]ence out" bona fide residents for fear of their presumed political views. Nor could the state rely on an imprecise categorical rule excluding people in military service as a way of avoiding the administrative burden of determining whether people were in fact bona fide residents. Justice Harlan dissented, on the ground that the state could rationally decide to protect state and local politics from military voting strength by delaying their right to vote until they had left the service.

State and local jurisdictions have limited authority to deny the vote to other residents who are seen as lacking the requisite interest in government decisions. In *Kramer v. Union Free School District No. 15*, 395 U.S. 621 (1969), the Court struck down a state law restricting voting in school district elections to those who either (1) owned or leased taxable real property in the district, or (2) had children in the public schools. Plaintiff was a bachelor who lived at his parents' home in the district; he paid no rent and had no children.

Chief Justice Warren's opinion for the *Kramer* majority struck down the state restriction on voting in school district elections. It held that the statute must be subjected to "close and exacting examination" because it denied the franchise to people otherwise qualified by age and citizenship. The Court rejected the state's argument that the statute was designed to limit voting to those "primarily interested" in school district decision. Using the language of strict scrutiny, the Court concluded that the statute's exclusion was not "necessary to promote a compelling state interest." Specifically, the Court found that the classification "permit[ted] inclusion of many persons who have, at best, a remote and indirect interest in the school meeting decisions" while "exclud[ing] others who have a distinct and direct interest in the school board meeting decisions." Justice Stewart, joined by Justices Black and Harlan, dissented on the ground that "close scrutiny" was inappropriate, given that Kramer and others like him were fully able to participate in elections for state legislature, the body that had adopted the statute.

State and local governments may not constitutionally impose lengthy waiting periods on residents, like the one-year durational residency requirement struck down in *Dunn v. Blumstein*, 405 U.S. 330 (1972) (discussed in Chapter 2.E). But they may require that voters be bona fide residents of the relevant state or local jurisdiction. That is true even when the governmental entity exercises some authority over people who live outside its boundaries. An example is *Holt Civic Club v. City of*

Tuscaloosa, 439 U.S. 60 (1978). Plaintiffs in *Holt Civic Club* challenged a rule that denied the vote to people who lived within the "police jurisdiction" of Tuscaloosa, which extended three miles outside the city's boundaries. Under Alabama law, the police jurisdiction was subject to the city's criminal laws as well as the jurisdiction of its municipal courts, and businesses in the police jurisdiction paid city taxes (about half what they would have paid if within the city's boundaries). The Court upheld the exclusion of people outside the city but within its police jurisdiction, reasoning that a government entity's decisions invariably affect people outside of its borders. Justice Brennan dissented. While acknowledging that the vote could be denied to nonresidents, he argued that citizens within the police jurisdiction should be considered residents.

Can *Kramer* and *Holt Civic Club* be reconciled? Recall that *Kramer* struck down the denial of the vote to certain residents, on the ground that many of those excluded had an interest in the decisions made by their local school boards. On the other hand, *Holt Civic Club* appears to view the interests of those residing outside city limits as irrelevant to their claim of voting rights. In fact, police jurisdiction residents arguably had a *greater* interest in city affairs than did non-taxpaying, childless adults in school district decisions. Perhaps these decisions can be explained by the need for a bright-line rule—i.e., residents are generally eligible to vote, while non-residents are generally not. Alternatively, these decisions may be understood as reflecting an understanding of what it means to be a full member of the political community. On this reading, the right to participate in school board decisions is integral to community membership. By contrast, those living outside city limits had voluntarily excluded themselves from the political community, and therefore had a lesser claim to participation in community decisionmaking. See James A. Gardner, *Liberty, Community and the Constitutional Structure of Political Influence: A Reconsideration of the Right to Vote*, 145 U. PA. L. REV. 893 (1997).

Race-based restrictions on who may vote are, of course, explicitly forbidden by the Fifteenth Amendment. But does this prohibit any consideration of race or ethnicity in deciding who may vote? In *Rice v. Cayetano*, 528 U.S. 495 (2000), the Court considered this question in an unusual context. The case involved a Hawaiian state agency, the Office of Hawaiian Affairs (OHA). The OHA was responsible for administering programs for "Hawaiians," a term defined by state statute to include only people who descended from the aboriginal Hawaiians living on the islands in 1778 when Europeans first arrived. Under Hawaii's constitution, only "Hawaiians" (as defined by statute) were eligible to vote for OHA trustees. The Court understood ancestry to be a proxy for race and struck down Hawaii's limitation on voting under the Fifteenth Amendment, stating that: "There is no room under the Amendment for the concept that the right to vote in a particular election can be allocated based on race." *Rice* thus viewed the Fifteenth Amendment as erecting an absolute prohibition against denying the vote in public elections based on race, including ancestry.

CHAPTER 4

REPRESENTATION AND DISTRICTING

In the preceding chapter, the focus was on election laws and practices that prevent people from voting, sometimes referred to as "vote denial." But being able to cast a vote is not the same as casting a meaningful vote, which depends on each person's vote being aggregated with those of other like-minded citizens. We now shift our focus to practices that weaken the certain groups of voters, commonly known as "vote dilution."

There are many types of vote dilution claims, but they can generally be divided into two categories. *Quantitative* vote dilution claims focus on the number of people in different legislative districts. *Qualitative* vote dilution claims, by number, have to do with the quality of representation different groups of voters receive, rather than the raw numbers of people in particular districts. This chapter focuses on quantitative vote dilution, while the next two chapters focus on two types of qualitative vote dilution claims: partisan gerrymandering (Chapter 5) and minority vote dilution (Chapter 6).

The most important example of quantitative vote dilution claims are challenges to the malapportionment of legislative bodies. Malapportionment exists when districts with different populations have the same representation. Until the 1960s, for example, one district might have ten times the population of a neighboring district, even though both had one representative in the legislature. People in larger districts—which tended to be in urban and suburban areas—were effectively underrepresented. By contrast, people in rural districts were overrepresented, sometimes enjoying a majority of representatives in the legislature even though they were a minority of the overall population.

For a long time, malapportionment was considered to be a nonjusticiable "political question," one that was left to the political branches of government and thus deemed beyond the power of federal courts to decide. But in *Baker v. Carr*, 369 U.S. 186 (1962), the Court reversed course to hold malapportionment claims justiciable. In the succeeding years, it issued a series of decisions— collectively known as the "one person, one vote" line of cases—requiring that each legislative district's representation correspond to its population. We discuss the political question doctrine in Part A and the one person, one vote cases in Part B. In Part C, we discuss the criteria (in addition to population equality) that may be used in drawing districts.

A. THE POLITICAL QUESTION DOCTRINE

Not all questions involving politics are "political questions." Instead, this term refers to questions that are deemed "nonjusticiable" because they are for the political branches of the government, not the federal judiciary, to resolve. The roots of the political question doctrine extend back to *Marbury v. Madison*, 5 U.S. 137 (1803), in which the Court said that there were some "[q]uestions in their nature political," and therefore inappropriate for resolution by the federal judiciary.

An important early case was *Luther v. Borden*, 48 U.S. 1 (1849), which arose from the Dorr Rebellion in Rhode Island (discussed in Chapter 2.A). The plaintiffs sought to obtain a judicial decree establishing which of two rival state governments was the legitimate one. They argued that the old Charter government, which limited voting to real property owners, was in violation of the Republican Guarantee Clause contained in Article IV, Section 4 of the U.S. Constitution, which states: "The United States shall guarantee to every State in the Union a Republican form of Government. . . ." The Supreme Court declined to entertain this question. It based its decision on concern that a federal judicial decision would infringe on state sovereignty, as well as the authority of the political branches of the federal government to decide which state government to recognize. The Court again declined to entertain a challenge to a state government under the Republican Guarantee Clause in *Pacific States Telephone & Telegraph Co. v. Oregon*, 223 U.S. 118 (1912). To this day, it remains the law that claims under the Republican Guarantee Clause are political questions, not justiciable in federal courts.

Until the 1960s, challenges to the malapportionment of legislative bodies were deemed nonjusticiable political questions as well. The most famous explanation of why appears in Justice Frankfurter's plurality opinion in *Colegrove v. Green*, 328 U.S. 549 (1946), which challenged the malapportionment of Illinois' congressional districts. Justice Frankfurter's plurality opinion stated that the case was beyond the competence of the federal judiciary to resolve, because it was "of a peculiarly political nature." The opinion noted that Congress had the authority to correct the problem, by virtue of its power to "make or alter" the regulations governing congressional elections, under the Elections Clause (contained in Article I, Section 4 of the Constitution). The most often cited statement from this opinion is Justice Frankfurter's statement that: "Courts ought not to enter this political thicket." To do so, the plurality opinion observed, would embroil the court in controversies best left to the political process. Even today, the idea that courts should stay out of the "political thicket" is invoked by those who believe in judicial restraint when it comes to laws regulating elections and politics.

Justice Frankfurter did not believe that federal courts should stay out of *all* matters involving elections and politics. In fact, he wrote the majority opinion in *Gomillion v. Lightfoot*, 364 U.S. 339 (1960) (Chapter 3), which allowed a Fifteenth Amendment challenge to a state law that redrew city boundaries to exclude black voters. Justice Frankfurter's opinion in *Gomillion* distinguished *Colegrove*, on the ground that malapportionment claims challenge only the *dilution* of voting strength, while redrawn city boundaries resulted in the affirmative *denial* of black citizens' votes. In addition, *Gomillion* involved discrimination against a racial minority, expressly prohibited by the Fifteenth Amendment, while *Colegrove* did not.

The turning point in the Supreme Court's political question jurisprudence was *Baker v. Carr*, 369 U.S. 186 (1962). That case arose from a challenge to the malapportionment of the state legislature of Tennessee. Like many other states, Tennessee's legislative districts had not been redrawn since the turn of the Twentieth Century. In the intervening six decades, the state had experienced enormous growth of its population, as well as the movement of people within the state. Yet all proposals to redraw state legislative boundaries failed. Plaintiffs claimed that the resulting malapportionment of the state legislature denied them equal protection, in violation of the Fourteenth Amendment. Justice Brennan's opinion for the Court held that their equal protection claim was not a political question. According to the Court, Republican Guarantee Clause cases like *Luther v. Borden* did not foreclose cases challenging malapportionment under the Equal Protection Clause.

The *Baker* Court redefined the political question doctrine. It set forth the following list of factors to be considered in determining whether a nonjusticiable political question exists:

Prominent on the surface of any case held to involve a political question is found [1] a textually demonstrable constitutional commitment of the issue to a coordinate political department; or [2] a lack of judicially discoverable and manageable standards for resolving it; or [3] the impossibility of deciding without an initial policy determination of a kind clearly for non judicial discretion; or [4] the impossibility of a court's undertaking independent resolution without expressing lack of the respect due coordinate branches of government; or [5] an unusual need for unquestioning adherence to a political decision already made; or [6] the potentiality of embarrassment from multifarious pronouncements by various departments on one question.

In later cases, the first two factors—a textual commitment of an issue to one of the political branches, and the absence of judicially manageable standards—have emerged as the most important ones in assessing whether a nonjusticiable political question exists. Also significant is what was omitted from *Baker*'s list of factors. Conspicuously absent from this list is respect for state sovereignty or federalism. Although federalism had been an important element of the political question doctrine in *Luther v. Borden* and other political question cases, *Baker* redefined the doctrine to eliminate federalism as a consideration.

Justice Frankfurter, joined by Justice Harlan, wrote a vigorous dissent excoriating the majority for "revers[ing] a uniform course of decision established by a dozen cases . . . [,] a massive repudiation of the experience of our whole past. . . ." Urging adherence to *Colegrove* and other cases in which the Court had declined to entertain malapportionment challenges, Justice Frankfurter argued that the Equal Protection Clause furnished "no clearer guide" for judicial decisionmaking than the Republican Guarantee Clause. It was a huge mistake, in his view, for the federal judiciary to embroil itself in questions of how to draw legislative district lines.

The *Baker* majority was not specific about the constitutional standard by which malapportionment claims should be judged. Instead, the Court stated that "[j]udicial standards under the Equal Protection Clause are well developed and familiar," while leaving the determination of the precise standard for adjudicating malapportionment claims to future cases. In succeeding years, the Court decided a series of cases defining the constitutional standard of "one person, one vote." We now turn to this line of cases.

B.   ONE PERSON, ONE VOTE

1.   THE EQUAL POPULATION RULE

In cases following *Baker*, the Court held that congressional, state legislative, and local legislative districts must be drawn on an equal population basis after each decennial census. The first major "one person, one vote" case was *Gray v. Sanders*, 372 U.S. 368 (1963). This was a challenge to Georgia's "county unit" system for counting votes in Democratic primaries. Under this system, candidates for statewide office competed on a county-by-county basis. The candidate who won the greatest number of counties would win the election, even if that candidate got fewer votes statewide than another candidate. Justice Douglas' opinion for the Court held that the county unit system violated the Equal Protection Clause, declaring that the "conception of political equality . . . can mean only one thing—one person, one vote."

The following year, the Court decided *Wesberry v. Sanders*, 376 U.S. 1 (1964). It ruled that the malapportionment of *congressional* districts within a state violated Article I, Section 2 of the Constitution. *Wesberry* arose from Georgia, in which the most populous congressional district (consisting of Fulton County) was two to three times as large as some other districts. Justice Black wrote the majority opinion, which held that Article I, Section 2's requirement that U.S. House Representatives be chosen "by the People of the several States" meant that each person's vote be worth as much as that of others. Although the text of the Constitution does not mandate equally populated House districts, the Court rested its opinion on originalist grounds, concluding that the intent of the Framers was that "in allocating Congressman the number assigned to each State should be determined solely by the number of the State's inhabitants." The Court thus held that the one person, one vote rule applies to congressional districts.

Justice Harlan dissented in *Wesberry*, arguing that Article I, Section 2 provided no basis for requiring that congressional districts within a state be of equal population. According to Justice Harlan, the majority misunderstood the Constitutional Convention debates, which were focused on how to apportion congressional seats *among* the states, not how to draw congressional districts *within* each state. That determination, Justice Harlan contended, was left to states in the first instance by the Elections Clause in Article I, Section 4, which gives states the power to prescribe the "Manner" of conducting congressional elections. In addition, Justice Harlan restated Justice Frankfurter's argument, made in *Colegrove* and his *Baker* dissent, that separation of powers required that malapportionment be left to the political branches rather than the judiciary.

Four months after *Wesberry*, the Court decided *Reynolds v. Sims*, 377 U.S. 533 (1964), probably the most important of the one person, one vote cases. *Reynolds* held that the malapportionment of *state legislative bodies* violates the Equal Protection Clause. The case arose from Alabama, which had population disparities of up to 16 to 1 in the state house and 41 to 1 in the state senate. Companion cases arising from other states (Colorado, Delaware, Maryland, New York, and Virginia) were decided the same day.

Chief Justice Warren's majority opinion in *Reynolds* employed the rhetoric of individual rights in support of its conclusion that the Equal Protection Clause required equally populated state legislative districts. He asserted that legislators

"represent people, not trees or acres" and that "to
the extent a citizen's right to vote is debased, he is
that much less a citizen." Thus, the majority opinion
concluded that each citizen should have "an equally
effective voice in the election of members of his state
legislature." Because "fair and effective
representation for all citizens" is the purpose of
legislative apportionment, a system that denies
"equal participation by all voters" violates the Equal
Protection Clause.

In the course of holding that both houses of the
state legislature must be apportioned on a
population basis, the majority rejected an analogy to
the U.S. Senate. Under the Constitution, each state
has two senators regardless of population. According
to the *Reynolds* majority, there were special
concerns with state sovereignty underlying this
allocation of representation in the U.S. Senate. The
United States was originally formed by thirteen
sovereign states. The establishment of a bicameral
federal legislature, with one chamber apportioned
by population and the other with equal
representation to each state, was part of the
compromise under which the several states gave up
some of their sovereignty to form the Union. In
contrast to the states, counties and other political
subdivisions had never been sovereign entities.
Accordingly, there was no comparable interest in
apportioning either house of a bicameral state
legislature by county, or on any basis other than
equal population.

While the *Reynolds* opinion used the language of individual rights, some commentators believe that equal representation of different *groups* is what really underlies *Reynolds*. In many states, urban and suburban areas had districts with larger populations while rural districts were generally less populated, due to population shifts in the preceding decades. The net effect was to distort representation, by according greater representation to people living in underpopulated rural areas. *Reynolds* put this in individualistic terms, saying that one is no more or less a citizen if "he lives in the city or on the farm," but the real problem, on this view, is that certain groups of citizens enjoy greater representation than their numbers warrant.

Reynolds may also be understood as an application of process-based (or representation-reinforcement) constitutional theory, by promoting fair political competition and preventing the entrenchment of incumbents. There was little incentive for incumbent legislators to redraw district lines in a way that corresponded with population shifts. In fact, they had a positive disincentive to redraw the lines, given that most members of the state legislature benefited from the perpetuation of malapportionment. In Alabama, for example, just a quarter of the population resided in districts which collectively controlled a majority of seats in the state legislature. Accordingly, it was very unlikely that the problem of malapportionment would fix itself. For exponents of the *Carolene Products* theory of judicial review (see Chapter 1.D), this provides a strong argument for judicial intervention. Because self-interested legislatures could not be relied on to correct this defect in the political process, the argument goes, the Court was justified in clearing the channels for political change.

Justice Harlan dissented in *Reynolds*, as he had in *Wesberry*. He thought that the Fourteenth Amendment imposed no obligation on states to draw equally populated state legislative districts. Justice Harlan objected in particularly strong terms to the Court's failure to ground its reasoning in the language of the Fourteenth Amendment, the understanding of its framers, or the political practices of states since its adoption. He also reiterated the argument that malapportionment was "not amenable to the development of judicial standards." In the end, this worry turned out to be unfounded. Whatever its faults, the one person, one vote cases provided a rule that was relatively easy to administer—namely, that single-member legislative districts must be of equal population.

Of *Reynolds'* companion cases, the most noteworthy is *Lucas v. 44th General Assembly of Colorado*, 377 U.S. 713 (1964). Chief Justice Warren's majority opinion in *Lucas* relied on *Reynolds* to strike down Colorado's malapportioned state senate districts. In contrast to the other cases decided that day, the Colorado districts had been adopted through an initiative approved by the electorate, but the Court found this difference insufficient to sustain their constitutionality. The Court reasoned that constitutional rights may not be infringed by a majority acting through direct democracy, any more than by the state legislature.

Justices Clark and Stewart both wrote dissents in *Lucas*. Justice Clark emphasized that the people of Colorado had actually approved of the challenged state legislative districting scheme through the initiative process. This fact seemingly belied the claim that this scheme was designed to benefit incumbent state legislators, at the expense of a majority of the electorate—a claim that could at least plausibly be made with respect to the other companion cases. Given the electorate's awareness of apportionment problems and their approval of the challenged scheme, Justice Clark argued, that there was no justification for federal judicial intervention. If we understand the one person, one vote rule in representation-reinforcement terms, there is some force to this argument. Why should courts intervene to "fix" the state's political process, after all, if a majority of a state's voters have given it their approval? There might be some justification for intervention if a scheme adopted by initiative diluted the voting strength of a minority group, but there was no evidence of such dilution in *Lucas*. To the contrary, as the *Lucas* majority acknowledged, a majority of voters *in every county* had approved Colorado's apportionment initiative.

Justice Stewart's dissent in *Lucas* (joined by Justice Clark) accused the majority of "convert[ing] a particular political philosophy into a constitutional rule"—and, in so doing, rendering most state legislative bodies unconstitutional.

Justice Stewart also emphasized that what constitutes a rational plan is likely to vary from state to state. He criticized the Court for failing to take into account the distinctive characteristics of each state and instead imposing a one-size-fits-all rule: that both houses of the state legislature in all fifty states must be apportioned on an equal population basis.

2.   APPLICATION AND EXTENSION OF THE RULE

Five important questions have emerged since *Wesberry*, *Reynolds*, and the other cases that initially articulated the one person, one vote rule. The first question is how much equality the Constitution requires or, stated conversely, how much of a departure from precise numerical equality is permissible. The second is how to measure numerical equality, specifically who should be counted and who may be left out. The third question is whether the equal population rule extended to other entities—such as local government entities and special purpose bodies—in addition to Congress and state legislatures. The fourth is whether one person, one vote applies to democratic processes other than candidate elections, such as super-majority requirements, nomination petitions, and direct democracy. The fifth question, one that is still alive today, is whether the principle of "fair and effective representation," stated in *Reynolds*, extends to other practices that dilute the votes of certain groups.

a. The Degree of Equality Required

The first round of one person, one vote cases established that districts must be of at least approximately equal population, but they did not establish the degree of equality that must obtain. Put another way, they did not settle the question of how much departure from precise numerical equality is constitutionally permitted. In cases that followed, the answer turned out to be different for challenges to *congressional* malapportionment than for challenges to *state legislative* malapportionment, with greater deviation being allowed under the latter than the former.

Recall that Article I, Section 2 is the textual source for the equal population rule for congressional districts under *Wesberry*, while the Equal Protection Clause is the textual source of the equal population rule for state legislative districts under *Reynolds*. For congressional districts, the Court has required that districts "as nearly as practicable" be of precisely equal population. Applying this standard, the Court in *Kirkpatrick v. Preisler*, 394 U.S. 526 (1969), struck down a Missouri congressional redistricting plan in which the most populous district was 3.13% above the ideal and the least populous district 2.84% below it. And in *Karcher v. Daggett*, 462 U.S. 725 (1983), the Court struck down a New Jersey congressional plan in which the difference in population between the largest and smallest district was less than one percent (0.6984% to be exact). Justice Brennan's majority opinion said that "there are no *de minimis* population variances, which could practically be avoided, but which nonetheless meet the standard of Art. I, § 2, without justification." The *Karcher* Court went on to explain, however, that the state should still be given a chance to defend departures from precise equality, by showing that they are "necessary to achieve some legitimate state objective." Among the considerations that might justify a departure are compactness, adherence to municipal boundaries, preserving the core or pre-existing districts, and avoiding contests between incumbents. It further said that any criteria that are "nondiscriminatory" are legitimate. But *Karcher* affirmed the district court's conclusion that the state had failed to meet its burden of showing that the population deviations were necessary to achieve any legitimate objective.

The Court further clarified the standard for congressional districts in *Tennant v. Jefferson County Commission*, 133 S. Ct. 3 (2012). That case involved a "minor" deviation (0.79%) between the largest and smallest districts. Such a deviation, *Tennant* held, need only be justified by a "legitimate" state objective. The Court found there to be legitimate state interests in preserving local boundaries, avoiding contests between incumbents, and minimizing shifts between old and new districts.

The Court has been more tolerant of population deviations in state and local redistricting plans, as opposed to congressional redistricting plans. An example is *Mahan v. Howell*, 410 U.S. 315 (1973).

The Court upheld a Virginia state plan in which the largest district was 6.8% larger than the ideal, and the smallest district 9.6% under the ideal, for a total deviation of 16.4%.

Justice Rehnquist's opinion for the *Mahan* Court held that challenges to state districting plans under the Equal Protection Clause should not be judged under the "more stringent standards" that applied to congressional plans under Article I, Section 2. The equal protection test focuses not on "necessity" but instead on what the state may "rationally consider" in pursuing its chosen policies. *Mahan* concluded that Virginia's interest in adhering to political subdivision lines justified the deviation, although it suggested that the 16.4% total maximum deviation "may well approach tolerable limits."

Likewise, in *Gaffney v. Cummings*, 412 U.S. 735 (1973), the Court upheld a Connecticut state house plan with a total maximum deviation of 7.83%. The state justified the deviations in the plan as an attempt to ensure a plan that would roughly approximate the political strengths of the two major parties. Justice White's opinion for the Court accepted this justification.

After *Gaffney*, it was generally presumed that state and local plans with a total deviation over 10% required justification, while those with a deviation under 10% did not. That understanding was disrupted by the decision in *Cox v. Larios*, 542 U.S. 947 (2004). In that case, the Court summarily affirmed a district court judgment striking down a plan with a total maximum deviation of 9.9%. The district court had found that the departure was the result of partisanship on the part of the Democratic Party, which controlled the process, and was therefore discriminatory. The Supreme Court summarily affirmed. A summary affirmance does not necessarily indicate agreement with the district court's reasoning. Still, the Court's decision eliminates the presumption that a deviation under 10% provides a safe harbor for state legislative plans. Most lower courts have understood *Larios* as requiring plaintiffs to show that a plan is unfair or discriminatory if the deviation is in this range.

b. Measurement of Equal Population

Reynolds speaks of both equal population and equal voters. But not everyone who lives in a district is a voter. Many people are not eligible to vote, among them children, noncitizens, people with criminal convictions (in some places), and people who are incarcerated (almost everywhere). Moreover, many people who are eligible to vote do not in fact vote.

In determining whether districts are equally populated, it can make a big difference whether to count the total population, the voting-age population, the citizen-voting-age population, the voting-eligible population, registered voters, or actual voters. That is because some places will have many more noncitizens, children, and other nonvoters than others. Which measure is most appropriate is likely to depend on whether one thinks the rule is designed to protect all people within the jurisdiction (regardless of whether they can vote), only those who vote, or perhaps some but not all of those who reside in the jurisdiction but do not vote.

The usual practice is for those drawing legislative maps to consider *total population* in determining whether districts are equally populated. That does not, however, mean that the use of total population is constitutionally required. To the contrary, in *Burns v. Richardson*, 384 U.S. 73 (1966), the Court upheld a Hawaii plan that used registered voters to determine population equality. Conversely, in *Garza v. County of Los Angeles*, 918 F.2d 763 (9th Cir. 1990), the majority rejected a one person, one vote argument challenging a court-drawn plan, in which districts were of equal total population but (due to the large number of noncitizens in some areas) had very different numbers of voting-age citizens from one district to another.

Recently, the question of how to count prisoners has generated considerable controversy. The traditional practice is to consider prisoners to be residing where they are incarcerated, rather than where they lived before incarcerated or where they plan to go after being released. This is largely due to the U.S. Census counting people at their "usual residence" (i.e., where they live and sleep most of the time). The traditional method of counting enhances the representation of communities where prisons are located, which tend to be rural. This can have a substantial impact on representation given that there are approximately 2.3 million people incarcerated nationwide—a number larger than the population of each of the fifteen smallest states. So far, lower courts have rejected constitutional challenges to the practice of counting prisoners where they are incarcerated. However, some states have passed legislation to consider prisoners residents of the place where they lived before incarceration rather than where they are incarcerated.

c. Localities and Special–Purpose Entities

The early one person, one vote cases established the applicability of the equal population rule to congressional and state legislative districts. But what about *local* bodies and governmental entities that perform specialized functions?

Local bodies are generally subject to the equal population rule if their members are elected on a districted basis. The first case to extend the equal population rule to local bodies was *Avery v. Midland County*, 390 U.S. 474 (1968), which involved a five-member county commissioners court. One member was selected at large by voters from the entire county, while the other four members were selected from districts, the smallest of which had a population of 414 and the largest of which had a population of 67,906. Justice White's majority opinion held that the applicability of the one person, one vote rule did not depend on whether the commissioners court's functions were labeled legislative, as opposed to administrative, executive, or judicial. The Court acknowledged that this body had functions that could be deemed to fall in each of these categories. What was dispositive, in the Court's view, was that this body had "power to make a large number of decisions having a broad range of impacts on all the citizens of the county," including the setting of tax rates and issuance of bonds. Likewise, in *Board of Estimate of City of New York v. Morris*, 489 U.S. 688 (1989), the Court struck down a New York City body that included one seat for the president of each of the five boroughs—despite the fact that the boroughs have very different populations.

On the other hand, in *Sailors v. Board of Education of Kent County*, 387 U.S. 105 (1967), the Court upheld a system in which a five-member *county* school board was chosen not by an election of county voters, but by delegates selected by *local* school boards. Each local school board would select one delegate, regardless of the local school district's population. *Avery* distinguished *Sailors* based on the administrative nature of the county school board's decisions and the "essentially appointive form of the scheme employed." The distinction between *Sailors* and *Morris* is not obvious, but it may be the fact that *local* school boards (not the county board) were the primary unit of government in *Sailors*, while New York City (not the five boroughs) was the primary unit of government in *Morris*. The boroughs are generally understood as component parts of New York City, not as autonomous entities, in contrast to local school boards.

While local government entities are generally bound by the one person, one vote rule, certain special purpose governmental entities are not. The leading cases on this subject are *Salyer Land Co. v. Tulare Lake Basin Water Storage District*, 410 U.S. 719 (1973) and *Ball v. James*, 451 U.S. 355 (1981). In *Salyer Land*, the Court upheld a California statute that limited voting for water storage district boards to landowners, apportioning votes according to the assessed value of land owned. Water storage districts had authority over the acquisition, diversion, storage, and distribution of water— including fixing charges for its use. In upholding the allocation of voting rights based on the value of land owned, Justice Rehnquist's opinion for the Court rested on the water storage district's limited authority. The district did not, according to the majority, exercise " 'normal governmental' authority," and its actions disproportionately affected those who owned land. In dissent, Justice Douglas noted that the water storage district in question had actually made decisions with a major impact on non-landowners. He noted in particular a decision not to store water in a lake, which appeared to have benefited the largest landowner in the district—but resulted in flooding of the homes of some residents who did not own land.

It is not obvious that a water storage district exercises less control over the lives of residents than a county commissioner's court, New York City's board of estimate, or a local school board. The distinction seems to be that the water storage district was a sort of business enterprise, created by and mostly serving agricultural landowners. This point is made more explicit in *Ball v. James*, which upheld a one acre, one vote system for the board of a water reclamation district. Although this district was originally a private association of farmers, it eventually became a public entity under Arizona law for tax reasons. But as Justice Stewart's majority opinion acknowledged, the district in *Ball* served many more people—almost half of Arizona's population—than the one in *Salyer Land*. In addition, the Arizona district had become one of the largest suppliers of electric power in the state, with most of its costs met through the sale of power. *Ball* nevertheless held that this large and important district was not subject to one person, one vote, because its functions were of a "narrow, special sort." More specifically, it said that the water reclamation districts were "essentially business enterprises, created by and chiefly benefiting a specific group of landowners." These landowners were subject to the district's taxing power, and the district's decisions had a disproportionate effect upon them. This is probably the best explanation why the special purpose districts in *Salyer Land* and *Ball v. James*, unlike most other state and local bodies, are exempt from the one person, one vote rule.

d. Other Democratic Processes

The one person, one vote rule applies not only to the districts of multi-member bodies, but also to some other democratic processes. One of them is the "county unit" system for conducting statewide primary elections struck down in *Gray v. Sanders*, 372 U.S. 368 (1963), in which the candidate winning a majority of *counties* (rather than a majority of votes) would be declared the winner. The Court has also applied the rule to the procedures for qualifying new political parties.

In *Moore v. Ogilvie*, 394 U.S. 814 (1969), the Court struck down an Illinois state law governing the qualification of independent candidates. The law required 25,000 qualifying signatures, including 200 in each of at least 50 of the state's 102 counties. The evidence showed that 93.4% of voters resided in the 49 most populated counties. The Court found that Illinois' law discriminated against residents of more populous counties and in favor of those in rural counties, in violation of the Fourteenth Amendment.

On the other hand, the one person, one vote rule does not prevent states from imposing supermajority requirements. In *Gordon v. Lance*, 403 U.S. 1 (1971), for example, the Court upheld a West Virginia requirement that, in a referendum to approve tax increases or bonded indebtedness, 60% of those voting give their approval. Nor does the Constitution prevent states from imposing separate majority-vote requirements for different subgroups affected by a referendum. In *Town of Lockport v. Citizens for Community Action at the Local Level*, 430 U.S. 259 (1977), the Court upheld a New York law requiring that a new county charter could only take affect if approved by separate majorities of city dwellers and non-city dwellers in the county.

e. "Fair and Effective Representation"

Reynolds' equal protection holding was at least partly based on the idea that people should have an "equally effective voice" in elections, so as to ensure "fair and effective representation for all citizens." Is there a greater principle underlying the one person, one vote cases? If so, should the Court accord heighted to election practices that dilute the representation of certain groups?

Since the one person, one vote cases were decided, there have been numerous attempts to apply the idea of "fair and effective representation" to alleged inequities in the way that elections are conducted, including redistricting. The one person, one vote cases focus on the diminution of some people's voice in government, in a way that is easily quantifiable (i.e., the population of districts). It is more difficult to quantify other ways in which some citizens' votes may be diluted. An example is partisan gerrymandering—a redistricting plan alleged to advantage one political party at the expense of another (discussed in Chapter 5). Another example is the alleged dilution of the voting strength of a racial minority group (Chapter 6). Those who support such constitutional claims often advert to *Reynolds'* apparent endorsement of the idea that the Constitution requires "fair and effective representation."

C. DISTRICTING CRITERIA

Before moving to the subject of partisan gerrymandering and minority voting rights, it is helpful to be familiar with the criteria that may be used in drawing district lines. When redistricting a state or local jurisdiction, there are many different ways of drawing equally populated districts. In some jurisdictions, the criteria to be used are spelled out by law, usually the state constitution. In other jurisdictions, the entity responsible for redistricting—typically the state legislature, for congressional and state legislative districts—has great discretion. That entity may therefore determine for itself what criteria to follow in drawing district lines.

Among the criteria that may be taken into consideration in drawing district boundaries are:

- *Compactness.* This criterion focuses on the shape of the district. A district shaped in a circle is compact, while an irregularly shaped district with multiple tentacles or appendages is not.

- *Contiguity.* A district is contiguous if one can travel from one point in the district to any other, without entering another district. The main complication that arises is whether a district is contiguous if two parts are separated by water, as is necessary in the case of an island. Districts connecting across water are generally considered contiguous, so long as district lines do not cross. Another question is whether "Figure 8" districts, which connect at a point, are contiguous. If contiguity is required by state law, the answer will depend on how that law is written and interpreted.

- *Communities of interest.* This term is generally understood to mean a group of people that shares some common interest, such as those defined by politics, culture, or religion. As with other redistricting criteria, there is no uniform definition of a community of interest, but some jurisdictions require it to be considered.

- *Political boundaries.* Some states require that lines be drawn so as to avoid breaking up local governmental entities like counties, municipalities, wards, and precincts, and requiring that whole governmental units be joined together when possible or practicable.

- *Geographic boundaries.* Another criterion is to draw districts so as to avoid crossing important geographic markers, like mountain ranges or rivers. This may be justified by the interest in making it relatively easy for candidates and others to travel through the district. It may also be related to the preservation of communities of interest.

- *Census tracts.* These are geographic groupings defined by the U.S. Census Bureau, generally consisting of 1,200 to 8,000 people with an optimum size of 4,000. Keeping census tracts together may be justified by the interest in administrative convenience. It may also help keep communities of interest together.

- *Nesting.* This means putting two or more districts of the *lower* chamber of the state legislature wholly within each district of the *upper* chamber. For example, each senate district might contain three whole house districts. In addition to making the map look "cleaner" it may promote administrative convenience by reducing the number of ballot formats that must be created.

- *Partisanship.* Districts may be drawn so as to favor one party over another or, on the other hand, to avoid favoritism for any party by drawing plans that roughly correspond to the political makeup of the jurisdiction as a whole. A plan strongly favoring one major party over the other is a partisan gerrymander, discussed further in the next chapter. Alternatively, partisan fairness—that is, a rough correspondence between each party's popular support and its share of seats—may be a criterion for drawing district lines.

- *Incumbency.* As with partisanship, plans may be drawn either to maximize the advantage of incumbents, or to avoid any favoritism for incumbents. The two major parties will sometimes agree (some would say collude) to draw a map that maximizes the number of safe seats that both parties control. Such a plan effectively insulates incumbent legislators from competition, arguably making them less accountable to voters.

- *Competitiveness.* This is the flip side of plans that are drawn to favor a political party or incumbents generally. A plan may be drawn to promote competitive districts, ones that contain roughly the same number of voters from both major parties. This gives both parties a chance to win the district. The asserted benefits of competitive districts include sensitivity to changes in the electorate's political views and an incentive for candidates to appeal to the median voter. In the aggregate, this may encourage moderation and diminish partisan polarization.

- *Minority Protection.* Redistricting plans may be drawn to enhance the representation of a minority group defined by race, ethnicity, language, religion, or some other characteristic. The most important example of a law that requires minority representation to be taken into account is the Voting Rights Act of 1965 (VRA), as amended, which protects racial minorities' opportunity to elect their candidates of choice. This criterion is the principal focus of Chapter 6.

Criteria that focus on the characteristics of particular districts and the people they include are known as "formal" criteria. This category includes compactness, contiguity, preserving communities of interest, nesting, and keeping political subdivisions, geographic boundaries, and census tracts together. Other criteria are "results-oriented," in that they look to the expected consequences of drawing district lines in a particular way. Examples of results-oriented criteria are favoritism toward one party over the other, promotion of proportional representation of the parties, protection of safe seats for incumbents, enhancing competitive elections, and protection of minority representation.

There are limited federal legal requirements on the criteria, aside from equal population, that should be considered in drawing district lines. Federal law requires that each state elect its representatives in the U.S. House through single-member districts. 2 U.S.C. § 2c. But with the important exception of the Voting Rights Act (Chapter 6), there is little federal statutory law governing the criteria to be used in drawing district lines.

There are, however, *state* legal requirements on how congressional and state legislative districts should be drawn. These vary widely. Among the requirements that appear in state laws are compactness, contiguity, preservation of communities of interest, adherence to political subdivision boundaries, and nesting of state house districts within state senate districts. Some states require a greater degree of population equality in state legislative districts than the U.S. Constitution requires. Some state requirements are stated in negative terms. For example, the people of Florida in 2010 adopted an initiative constitutional amendment prohibiting districts from being drawn with "the intent to favor or disfavor a political party or an incumbent."

In some cases, courts are called upon to draw district lines. Suppose, for example, that the state legislature is controlled by one party and the governor is of the other major party, and the two sides cannot agree on a plan after the new census data comes out. The one person, one vote rule requires new districts to be drawn after each census to conform to population shifts. Thus, the old district lines—usually drawn a decade before—can no longer be used without violating the Constitution. If no new plan has been drawn, then a lawsuit may be brought alleging a violation of the one person, one vote rule, and the court may wind up drawing a new plan. Where state law does not prescribe criteria to be used, state courts sometimes articulate their own. An example is *Legislature of California v. Reinecke*, 507 P.2d 626 (Cal. 1973), in which the California Supreme Court mostly adopted a set of criteria proposed by special masters, which included contiguity, compactness, adherence to county boundaries, adherence to geographic boundaries, preserving communities with common social and economic interests, nesting, and adherence to census tracts.

Supreme Court precedent requires federal courts to respect state law regarding the criteria to be used in drawing district lines. That includes not only the requirements set forth in the state constitution, but also state *judicial* determinations. In *Scott v. Germano*, 381 U.S. 407 (1965), the Court held that federal courts should defer to parallel state proceedings. The Court restated and amplified this holding in *Growe v. Emison*, 507 U.S. 25 (1993), expressly rejecting the district court's conclusion that it need only defer to the state legislature and not the state judiciary. *Growe* stated that federal courts should not generally obstruct state redistricting. Thus, it is ordinarily up to the states to draw new redistricting plans, even where there is a constitutional violation. Federal courts will generally draw district lines only if state institutions (including state courts) cannot or will not act in time.

CHAPTER 5
PARTISAN GERRYMANDERING

A. WHAT IS GERRYMANDERING?

It is often said that, if elections are when voters choose their leaders, redistricting is when leaders choose their voters. This is not far from the truth. Typically, congressional and state legislative redistricting in the United States is handled by state legislatures, usually through a statute that it passes and then must be signed by the Governor. Other states delegate responsibility for drawing districts to a commission that is controlled by one party or the other. In a few states, districting is handled by a commission with some degree of independence from partisan politics. Throughout U.S. history, partisan politicians have used their power to draw district lines so as to benefit themselves and their parties. Gerrymandering refers to the practice of drawing electoral districts or other boundaries so as to advantage one group voters while disadvantaging another.

There are different types of gerrymanders but they can generally be divided into three categories. The term is most often used to describe a *partisan gerrymander*, a plan that advantages one major political party while disadvantaging the other. This is typically accomplished by concentrating (or "packing") as many of the other side's voters into as few districts as possible, while dividing (or "cracking") the other party's voters in the remaining districts to minimize the number in which the other party has an effective majority. A second form of gerrymander, related but distinct, is the *bipartisan gerrymander* (sometimes called an "incumbent gerrymander" or "sweetheart gerrymander"). In a bipartisan gerrymander, electoral districts are drawn to protect incumbents of *both major parties* from competition. A *racial gerrymander* advantages a group of voters defined by race or ethnicity. An example is the 28–sided figure into which the boundaries of Tuskegee were redrawn to exclude black voters, struck down in *Gomillion v. Lightfoot*, 364 U.S. 339 (1960) (Chapter 3.B). The Supreme Court has also held some majority-minority districts unconstitutional, where race was the predominant factor in their creation (Chapter 6.B). The focus of this chapter is on partisan and bipartisan gerrymanders.

It can be very difficult to determine whether a particular plan should be deemed a partisan or bipartisan gerrymander. Part of the difficulty is conceptual. Must a plan have the *intent* of benefiting a particular group in order to be considered a gerrymander? Or is it sufficient that the plan have the *effect* of giving an advantage to a group? There is no consensus on this question.

Furthermore, both effect and intent are hard to measure. If effect is the standard, how much of a beneficial impact on the dominant party is required to establish a violation? There are, moreover, different ways of assessing the effect of a redistricting plan on incumbents or parties. On the other hand, intent is an imperfect standard as well. It is notoriously difficult to ascertain intent or purpose, especially when it comes to multi-member bodies like a state legislature. Moreover, an intent to benefit the party in power is almost always one of the factors motivating a redistricting plan. How much of a partisan (or incumbent-protective) intent is too much? Intent thus presents problems of measurement comparable to effect.

One possible effects-based focuses on *proportionality* between the number of districting favoring each party and that party's share of the total vote. For example, if a party enjoys 40% of the statewide vote, proportionality would mean that it would get 40% of the seats in the state legislature. This raises the question of how much deviation from proportionality is acceptable. In addition, it is not necessarily possible to determine in advance whether a particular plan will yield proportional results.

Another proposed effects-based test considers whether there is *symmetry*. Under this standard, a party may receive a "bonus" for winning more than half the seats, so long as the other party would receive a similar bonus for winning the same share. For example, the symmetry standard would be satisfied if Republicans won 60% of the seats with 55% of the vote, so long as Democrats would also get 60% of the seats if they won 55% of the vote. As explained in the next section, a majority of the Supreme Court has not accepted proportionality, symmetry, or any other test for determining whether there has been an unconstitutional partisan gerrymander.

There have been many different proposals for dealing with the problem of gerrymandering have. These proposals can generally be broken down into two categories. The first is to impose *substantive standards* on redistricting, such as criteria that the legislature must consider (or must not consider) in drawing district lines. For example, Florida has adopted state constitutional amendments that prohibit legislative districts from being drawn to "favor or disfavor a political party or an incumbent." These amendments also require that districts be "as nearly equal in population as practicable," "compact," and "where feasible, utilize existing political and geographical boundaries."

The other means by which to curb gerrymandering is through *procedural requirements*. The most common proposal is to assign responsibility for redistricting to an independent commission instead of the state legislature. California took this approach through a 2008 initiative. That initiative created a citizens' redistricting commission consisting of five Democrats, five Republicans, and four people of neither major party. The citizens commission was originally given responsibility over state legislative redistricting. Another initiative, adopted in 2010, gave the commission power over congressional redistricting as well.

Whatever one's views on the propriety of such redistricting reforms, the way district lines are drawn can have a significant impact on the electoral fortunes of political parties, incumbents, and challengers. Most states still vest responsibility for drawing districts in the legislature or other partisan actors. This arrangement triggers the question whether courts should intervene, to ensure that the districts are fair. Proponents of judicial intervention typically rely on *Reynolds'* assertion of the ideal of "fair and effective representation," arguing that partisan or bipartisan gerrymanders do not afford such equality. As we shall see, however, the U.S. Supreme Court has not been receptive to such claims—although it has not shut the door completely to them either.

B.   CONSTITUTIONAL LIMITS ON GERRYMANDERING

1.   GERRYMANDERING AND POPULATION EQUALITY

It is possible to draw districts that are equal in population, yet strongly favor one political party or incumbents generally. In fact, the early cases challenging gerrymanders on constitutional grounds involve the one person, one vote rule, discussed in Chapter 4.

In *Gaffney v. Cummings*, 412 U.S. 735 (1973), the Court rejected an equal protection challenge to Connecticut state legislative districts. After concluding that the districts were sufficiently close to population equality, Justice White's opinion for the Court considered evidence that the plan was drawn with the intent of approximating the two major parties' support in the statewide electorate. It concluded that consideration of this factor did not violate equal protection, reasoning that those drawing a plan need not be blind to the political consequences of their efforts. Aside from striking down plans that "fence[] out" a particular political or racial group, the Court explained, "we have not ventured far or attempted the impossible task of extirpating politics from what are essentially political processes of the sovereign States" in drawing district lines. It also stated that the judiciary's interest is at its "lowest ebb" when a state purports to allocate power to parties in accordance with their voting strength.

The Court's next significant encounter with an alleged political gerrymander was in *Karcher v. Daggett*, 462 U.S. 725 (1983). Justice Brennan's majority opinion held that New Jersey's congressional redistricting plan violated the one person, one vote rule under Article I, Section 2 due to a tiny disparity in population (0.6984% between the largest and smallest district). As discussed in Chapter 4, the Court has been much less tolerant of population deviations with respect to congressional districts than state legislative districts, holding that Article I, Section 2 imposes a more stringent requirement of exactitude than the Equal Protection Clause. Particularly germane to the question of partisan gerrymandering was Justice Stevens' concurring opinion, asserting that population equality was an insufficient basis for determining the constitutionality of redistricting plans. Instead,

Justice Stevens asserted, courts should look to "[1] whether the plan has a significant adverse impact on an identifiable political group, [2] whether the plan has objective indicia of irregularity, and then, [3] whether the State is able to produce convincing evidence that the plan nevertheless serves neutral, legitimate interests of the community as a whole." Rather than looking exclusively to deviations from mathematical population equality, Justice Stevens urged that the Court should also consider such factors as non-compact district shapes, failure to follow established the boundaries of political subdivisions, and the process by which the plan was adopted. Without exhaustively applying these factors to the case at hand, Justice Stevens concluded that they strengthened his determination that New Jersey's plan was unconstitutional.

2.   GERRYMANDERING AND JUSTICIABILITY

a. *Davis v. Bandemer*

In *Davis v. Bandemer*, 478 U.S. 109 (1986), the Court held that partisan gerrymandering claims are justiciable. *Bandemer* was an equal protection challenge, brought by Democrats to the Republican-controlled redistricting of Indiana's state legislature. In an opinion written by Justice White, the Court first concluded that this claim was justiciable—i.e., that it was not a political question (see Chapter 4). There was, however, no majority opinion on the merits of the equal protection claim. On that question, the Court was divided into three groups.

Justice White's plurality opinion (joined by Justices Blackmun, Brennan, and Marshall), upheld the plan under a standard that required plaintiffs to prove "both *intentional discrimination* against an identifiable political group and an actual *discriminatory effect* on that group" (emphasis added). Explaining this standard, Justice White asserted that it should not generally be difficult to show that the legislature intended the likely political consequences of the plan it drew. The main question, then, was what was required to show an actual discriminatory effect on a particular political group. It should not be enough, Justice White thought, to shows it is more difficult for members of one group to elect their representatives of choice, because those members may still enjoy some influence on the political process. Rather, Justice White concluded, plaintiffs must show that "the electoral system is arranged in a manner that will consistently degrade a voter's or a group of voters' influence on the political process as a whole." While the meaning of this standard was not precisely clear, lower courts understood it to impose a high burden on plaintiffs. Justice White's plurality opinion concluded that the plaintiffs in *Bandemer* had not met this standard.

The second group in *Bandemer* consisted of Justices Powell and Stevens, who joined the portion of Justice White's opinion holding partisan gerrymandering claims justiciable, but *dissented* from the Court's rejection of Indiana Democrats' equal protection claim. Justice Powell's dissenting opinion relied on Justice Stevens' concurrence in

Karcher, advocating a multi-factor test that looked to the shape of districts, adherence to the boundaries of political subdivisions, the procedures used in adopting the plan, and the legislative history showing the legislature's goals. Applying this standard, Justices Powell and Stevens would have found the Equal Protection Clause violated based on evidence that the districts disregarded political subdivisions, that Democrats were excluded from the process, and that the plan had a partisan purpose.

The third group in *Bandemer* consisted of Justice O'Connor, joined by Justice Rehnquist and Chief Justice Burger. These justices concurred in the judgment rejecting plaintiffs' claim, but would have done so on the ground that it raised a nonjusticiable political question.

Justice O'Connor's concurring opinion argued that the recognition of partisan gerrymandering claims would ultimately lead toward a requirement of proportional representation, which she thought to be at odds with U.S. history, tradition, and political institutions. She also thought that judicial intervention was unnecessary, because partisan gerrymandering is an inherently self-limiting enterprise. Recall that a partisan gerrymander seeks to maximize the number of seats the party in power controls. This is generally accomplished by packing as many of the other major party's voters into as few districts as possible, thus leaving the dominant party with a majority of the remaining districts. But the more districts the dominant party attempts to secure for itself, the narrower its margins are likely to be in those districts. Thus, Justice O'Connor contended, an overly aggressive partisan gerrymander "can lead to disaster for the legislative majority." In reading Justice O'Connor's opinion, it is helpful to recall that she was the only justice on the Court who had actually served in the legislature, as a state senator and ultimately state senate majority leader in Arizona.

Under *Bandemer*, partisan gerrymandering claims were justiciable, but there was no majority opinion on the constitutional standard for evaluating these claims. Justice White's plurality opinion offered a fairly strict standard, while Justice Powell's dissenting opinion offered a more lenient one. The lower courts generally applied the standard set forth in Justice White's plurality opinion. Far from leading to a requirement of proportional representation, the courts almost without exception rejected partisan gerrymandering claims, causing one casebook to label *Bandemer* "an invitation to litigation without much prospect of redress." Samuel Issacharoff, Pamela S. Karlan & Richard H. Pildes, THE LAW OF DEMOCRACY (rev. 2d ed. 2002).

b. *Vieth v. Jubelirer*

The Court next took up the issue of partisan gerrymandering in *Vieth v. Jubelirer*, 541 U.S. 267 (2004), a challenge to Pennsylvania's congressional districts, which were alleged to favor Republicans at the expense of Democrats. Yet again, there was no opinion on the merits that commanded a majority of the Court. As in *Bandemer*, the justices in *Vieth* can be divided into three groups.

The first group consisted of Justice Scalia, who wrote the plurality opinion (joined by Chief Justice Rehnquist and Justices O'Connor and Thomas). These four justices believed that partisan gerrymandering claims were a nonjusticiable political question, and would therefore have overruled *Bandemer*'s contrary holding. Justice Scalia's plurality opinion in *Vieth* explained that there was a long history of political gerrymanders in the U.S., and that the Constitution provides a remedy: Under Article I, Section 4, Congress may "make or alter" the rules for conducting congressional elections, including U.S. House districts. Justice Scalia's plurality opinion proceeded to assert that post-*Bandemer* experience had demonstrated the lack of judicially discoverable and manageable standards for partisan gerrymandering claims. It rejected the "intent plus effect" standard for which plaintiffs argued, as well as the alternative standards proposed by the dissenting justices.

The second group in *Vieth* consisted only of Justice Kennedy, concurring in the result. Justice Kennedy agreed with the plurality that plaintiffs' partisan gerrymandering claim should be rejected, but did not wish to foreclose the possibility of relief in some future case. While Justice Kennedy thought there were "weighty arguments for holding cases like these to be nonjusticiable," he was unwilling to take that step. Justice Scalia's plurality opinion asserted that Justice Kennedy should be understood as a reluctant vote against justiciability, but that was not in fact Justice Kennedy's position. To the contrary, Justice Kennedy expressly stated: "I would . . . reject the plurality's conclusions as to nonjusticiability." Unfortunately, Justice Kennedy—although the swing justice in *Vieth*—did not specify what standard he thought should govern. He rejected the standards proposed by plaintiffs and the dissenters, while holding out hope that "a standard might emerge" in some future case.

Justice Kennedy's opinion also suggested that the First Amendment might provide a more suitable textual basis for partisan gerrymandering claims than the Fourteenth Amendment, reasoning that First Amendment concerns arise "where an apportionment has the purpose and effect of burdening a group of voters' representational rights." But he did not provide much detail on what would be required to prove such a claim.

The third group in *Vieth* consisted of the four dissenters: Justices Stevens, Souter, Ginsburg, and Breyer. These justices agreed that partisan gerrymandering claims were justiciable, though there was not consensus among them on the precise standard that should govern such claims. In fact, there were three separate opinions on that question.

Justice Stevens' dissent asserted that questions of partisan gerrymandering raised "the same constitutional concern" as claims of racial gerrymandering and would therefore have applied a standard similar to that in the *Shaw v. Reno* line of cases (discussed in Chapter 6.B). Specifically, Justice Stevens' standard would require plaintiffs to show that "the legislature allowed partisan considerations to dominate and control the lines drawn, forsaking all neutral principles."

The second dissent, by Justice Souter (joined by Justice Ginsburg), argued for a multi-factor test requiring plaintiff to show: (1) membership in a cohesive political group, such as a political party; (2) the legislature's disregard for traditional districting criteria like contiguity, compactness, respect for political subdivisions, and adherence to geographic boundaries; (3) correlations between these deviations and the distribution of plaintiff's political group; (4) the existence of a hypothetical district with less deviation from traditional districting criteria; and (5) defendants' intentional manipulation of districts to pack or crack plaintiff's political group.

The final dissent, by Justice Breyer, would have looked to the plan as a whole rather than to a particular district, inquiring into whether it showed "the *unjustified* use of political factors to entrench a minority in power" (original emphasis). He explained that the unjustified entrenchment meant that one political group's hold on power was due to "partisan manipulation" rather than some other factor.

Justice Scalia responded to the *Vieth* dissenters by arguing that their failure to agree on a constitutional standard demonstrated the absence of any judicially discernible and manageable standard, thus supporting the plurality's conclusion that partisan gerrymandering claims were nonjusticiable political questions. Justice Breyer took issue with this assertion. He suggested that the more thorough discussion that comes with separate statements could ultimately lead to development of a constitutional standard by the Court.

c. *LULAC v. Perry*

There is still no standard for assessing partisan gerrymandering claims that has garnered support from a majority of justices on the Court. Its most recent partisan gerrymandering decision was *League of United Latin American Citizens v. Perry*, 548 U.S. 399 (2006) (*LULAC*). In that case, plaintiffs challenged the Republican-controlled legislature's mid-decade redrawing of Texas' congressional districts, allegedly to favor Republicans and harm Democrats. A majority of justices, in an opinion by Justice Kennedy, held that the claim was justiciable. But on the merits, the Court was even more splintered than it had been in *Vieth*. On one side of the Court, Justices Scalia and Thomas adhered to their position in *Vieth* that partisan gerrymandering claims were nonjusticiable political questions. On the other side of the Court, Justices Stevens, Souter, Ginsburg, and Breyer, adhered to their positions in *Vieth*, dissenting from the rejection of plaintiffs' partisan gerrymandering claim.

The swing justices in *LULAC* were Justice Kennedy and two justices who had joined the Court since *Vieth*: Chief Justice Roberts and Justice Alito. Justice Kennedy rejected plaintiffs' argument that a plan should be presumed invalid when it is drawn in the middle of the decade, rather than right after the census as is customary in most states. He also rejected plaintiffs proposal that a plan be deemed unconstitutional if partisanship is the "sole" motivation, as well as the "symmetry" standard proposed in an amicus brief (see Part A above). But as in *Vieth*, Justice Kennedy's opinion in *LULAC* does not specify the standard that should apply to partisan gerrymandering claims. Chief Justice Roberts (joined by Justice Alito) agreed with Justice Kennedy that plaintiffs had not provided an adequate standard, while taking no position on whether partisan gerrymandering claims are justiciable, on the ground that the issue had not been argued.

Where does the law of partisan gerrymandering stand after *Vieth* and *LULAC*? This is not an easy question to answer, given the absence of any majority opinion. It is clear that partisan gerrymandering claims are justiciable. To the extent there was any doubt on the question after *Vieth*, it was dispelled by *LULAC*. It is equally clear, however, that there was not a majority for any constitutional standard in either *Vieth* or *LULAC*. So what law should litigants and lower court justices apply to partisan gerrymandering claims? Perhaps the best view is that the standard articulated in *Bandemer* remains the law, because one cannot replace something (*Bandemer*) with nothing (*Vieth*). See Daniel Hays Lowenstein, Vieth*'s Gap: Has the Supreme Court Gone from Bad to Worse on Partisan Gerrymandering?*, 14 CORNELL J. L. & PUB. POL'Y 367 (2005). The plurality opinion in *Bandemer* articulated an intent-plus-effect standard for partisan gerrymandering. That opinion represents the narrowest grounds for the result in that case. Thus, in the absence of any consensus on the Court in later cases, it may be viewed as the law on the subject, although the matter is not free from doubt. An alternative view is that the lack of a majority opinion in *Bandemer*, *Vieth*, or *LULAC* means that there is no law from the Supreme Court on the subject, leaving lower courts free to develop their own constitutional standard.

Whatever the current law on the subject, most commentators believe it unlikely that the Supreme Court, as currently constituted, will hold any plan to be an unconstitutional partisan gerrymander. While technically leaving the door open to such claims, it is unlikely to allow anyone to pass through.

CHAPTER 6

MINORITY REPRESENTATION

The struggle for racial minorities to gain the full measure of their constitutionally protected voting rights was a lengthy one, as set forth in Chapter 2. In fact, that struggle continues to this day. The Fourteenth Amendment guaranteed equal protection of laws and the Fifteenth Amendment expressly prohibited the denial or abridgement of the vote on account of race. Yet from the end of Reconstruction through most of the Twentieth Century, African Americans were systematically denied voting rights throughout the states of the former Confederacy.

The Voting Rights Act of 1965 (VRA) ended the system of mass disenfranchisement that had kept southern blacks from registering and voting. The first generation of VRA enforcement focused on putting an end to literacy tests, poll taxes, and other practices that were used to deny racial minorities the vote (i.e., vote denial). But over time, advocates of minority voting rights came to believe that the access to the ballot box was necessary but not sufficient to achieve equality in the political process. Thus, the second generation of VRA enforcement focused on practices—most notably at-large elections and redistricting schemes—that diluted racial, ethnic, and language minorities' voting strength (i.e., vote dilution). In the 1990s, however, the Supreme Court imposed limits on VRA enforcement, through the *Shaw v. Reno* lines of "racial gerrymandering" cases, under which districts are subject to strict scrutiny if race is the predominant factor in their creation. As explained below, the combined effect of the VRA and racial gerrymandering cases is to create a sort of "Goldilocks" effect: race must be taken into consideration in drawing districts, at least in some cases (under the VRA) but not too much (under *Shaw* and its progeny).

Part A discusses the requirements of the VRA, focusing on its two most important provisions: *Section 5*, which requires certain covered jurisdictions to obtain preclearance of voting changes, but was effectively nullified by the Supreme Court's decision in *Shelby County v. Holder*, 133 S. Ct. 2612 (2013); and *Section 2*, which prohibits practices that result in the denial or abridgement of minority voting rights. Part B discusses *Shaw* and the other racial gerrymandering cases, which limited the intentional creation of majority-minority districts.

A. THE VOTING RIGHTS ACT

1. SECTION 5

a. The Preclearance Process

Section 5 of the VRA requires certain "covered jurisdictions" to obtain advance permission from either the U.S. Attorney General or the U.S. District Court in Washington, D.C., before implementing any voting changes. This requirement, referred to as "preclearance," grew out of the experience with recalcitrant southern officials in the years preceding 1965, the year of the VRA's enactment. Under previous federal laws, the burden was on the United States government to go to court and prove that existing election practices in each offending county discriminated against black voters. This was costly and time consuming. In addition, some federal district judges in the South were resistant to providing relief. And even when the government succeeded in obtaining a federal court injunction against practices used to keep blacks from voting, southern election officials came up with ingenious new ways of disenfranchising them. For these reasons, the rates of black registration and participation increased only slightly in many parts of the South before 1965.

Sections 4 and 5 of the VRA were designed to deal with the intransigence that had rendered case-by-case litigation largely ineffectual. Section 4 designated certain states and counties "covered" jurisdictions, based on two criteria: (1) the use of a test or device for voting, such as a literacy test; and (2) fewer than 50% of voting-age residents registered or voting in the 1964 presidential election. This formula was designed to include those portions of the South with the worst voting problems (Alabama, Georgia, Louisiana, Mississippi, South Carolina, Virginia, and much of North Carolina). The coverage formula was later augmented to include other jurisdictions. In addition to defining the covered jurisdictions, Section 4 temporarily suspended literacy tests in covered jurisdictions, a ban that was later extended nationwide and made permanent.

Section 5 requires that covered jurisdictions obtain preclearance from the Attorney General of federal court in Washington, D.C. before giving effect to any new voting qualifications or procedures. In *South Carolina v. Katzenbach*, 383 U.S. 301 (1966), the Court upheld Sections 4 and 5 against a constitutional challenge brought by the state of South Carolina. Reviewing the record of discrimination against black voters in the covered jurisdictions, the Court concluded that Sections 4 and 5 fell within Congress' power to enforce the Fifteenth Amendment. Once implemented, they had an almost immediate impact in stopping vote denial, thus opening up registration lists and polling places across the South to black voters who had been disenfranchised since the end of the Nineteenth Century.

Once African Americans were allowed to vote in the South, attention turned to other practices that were used to diminish the strength of their votes— that is, to vote dilution. Prominent among the devices used to weaken black voting strength were at-large elections. In an at-large system, all voters throughout a jurisdiction vote for all members of a multi-member body, rather than voting for a representative serving a particular district. For example, in 1966, the state of Mississippi amended its state laws to provide that county boards of supervisors could be elected at large by all qualified voters in a county. Before this amendment,

Mississippi counties were divided into five districts with each district electing one member to the board. After the amendment, by contrast, all voters throughout the county would vote for all supervisorial positions. The effect of this change was to keep blacks from electing a representative of their choice to county boards. Suppose that blacks constituted 40% of the voting population of a county and whites 60% of the voting population. One would expect blacks to win two seats on the board, if the districts were drawn proportionally. But with an at-large election, blacks would be denied any seats on the board, given the high degree of racial polarization among the electorate.

In *Allen v. State Board of Elections*, 393 U.S. 544 (1969), the Court held that Section 5 requires preclearance of the move from districted elections to an at-large system. Chief Justice Warren's opinion for the majority rejected Mississippi's argument that Section 5 only applied to state rules regarding who may register and vote. Instead, the Court held that Section 5 applies to "the subtle, as well as the obvious, state regulations which have the effect of denying citizens the right to vote because of their race." The Court relied on the language of Section 5 stating that "any voting qualification or prerequisite to voting, or standard, practice, or procedure with respect to voting" must be precleared. *Allen* went on to explain that the right to vote may be affected by dilution and not just by denial of the vote. The Court also held that other voting changes (making an office appointive rather than elective, imposing new requirements for getting on the ballot as an independent candidate, and changing the procedures for write-in votes) were subject to Section 5, and thus must be precleared before taking effect. Justice Harlan dissented from the Court's holding on at-large elections, though he agreed that the other changes were subject to Section 5.

The Court's decision in *Allen* had a major impact on voting rights enforcement, by making questions of vote dilution—and not just vote denial—subject to Section 5 preclearance. Very few jurisdictions sought preclearance of voting changes before *Allen*. After 1969, however, the number of preclearance requests increased dramatically. In addition to at-large elections, new redistricting plans were subject to preclearance under the logic of *Allen*. This meant that redistricting plans could not take effect unless and until they received preclearance from either the U.S. Attorney General or the U.S. District Court in Washington, D.C.

Under *Presley v. Etowah County Commission*, 502 U.S. 491 (1992), however, changes to the decisionmaking authority of elected officials were not subject to Section 5. *Presley* concerned a resolution taking away responsibilities from individual county commissioners, after a black commissioner (Presley) had been elected. Justice Kennedy's opinion for the Court concluded that this change to county governance was not a voting change. Therefore, it was not subject to Section 5 preclearance.

Prior to *Shelby County*, the U.S. Attorney General received thousands of preclearance requests each year. Responsibility for preclearance was delegated to the Assistant Attorney General for Civil Rights and handled by the Voting Rights Section of the Civil Rights Division of the U.S. Department of Justice. The vast majority of preclearance requests were granted.

In practice, state and local jurisdictions covered by Section 5 almost always chose to seek preclearance from the Attorney General (administrative preclearance) rather than the D.C. federal district court (judicial preclearance). It was usually less costly and time-consuming to seek administrative preclearance as opposed to judicial preclearance. If a state or local jurisdiction was denied administrative preclearance, it could then seek judicial preclearance from the D.C. federal district court. In effect, then, covered jurisdictions could "appeal" the Attorney General's *denial* of preclearance to the federal district court. On the other hand, if administrative preclearance was *granted* by the Attorney General, that decision was not subject to judicial review by anyone objecting to the change. *Morris v. Gressette*, 432 U.S. 491 (1977). While covered jurisdictions usually sought administrative preclearance before *Shelby County*, they sometimes chose judicial preclearance, especially when they thought they have a better shot at getting preclearance through that route.

What if there were a delay in obtaining judicial preclearance for a new redistricting plan? That issue arose in Texas after the 2010 Census, and came before the Supreme Court in *Perry v. Perez*, 132 S. Ct. 934 (2012). Recall that, under the one person, one vote rule established in *Wesberry* and *Reynolds*, congressional and state legislative districts must be redrawn every decade to conform to new U.S. Census data. If a state fails to redraw its districts, it is in violation of the Constitution. A state or federal court may then be asked to draw a new redistricting plan. In Texas, the Republican-controlled state legislature passed legislation redrawing state legislative and congressional district lines after the 2010 Census, as required by the one person, one vote rule. The state then chose to seek judicial preclearance rather than administrative preclearance, presumably because it was concerned that the U.S. Attorney General (who was part of the administration of President Obama, a Democrat) would deny preclearance. As of 2012, preclearance had not yet been granted. A federal district court in Texas drew new districts, to prevent a one person, one vote violation.

The question before the Court in *Perry v. Perez* was whether the federal district court had accorded sufficient deference to the redistricting plans drawn by the state legislature, which had not yet been precleared. In a *per curiam* opinion, the Court held that the federal district court had *not* afforded sufficient deference to the state legislature's plans. *Perry* held that a district court is required to defer to the un-precleared redistricting plans, *unless* there is a "reasonable probability" that they will not be precleared. The Court went on to define "reasonable probability" as a "not insubstantial" challenge under Section 5. In other words, if there *was* a substantial Section 5 challenge, then a federal court did not have to defer to the challenged aspect of the legislature's plan. On the other hand, if there was *no* substantial Section 5 challenge to the plan, then the federal court had to defer to the plan, despite the fact that it had not yet been precleared.

b. The Legal Standard for Preclearance

Under what circumstances should Section 5 preclearance be granted? The text of the statute provides that a voting change should be precleared if it "neither has the purpose nor will have the effect of denying or abridging the right to vote on account of race or color. . . ." Thus, Section 5 includes both a *purpose* prong and an *effects* prong. The effects prong looks to whether the voting change has a *retrogressive* effect—that is, whether it makes minority voters worse off than they were before the change. The purpose prong looks to whether there is any racially discriminatory purpose behind the voting change. We shall examine the effects prong first, then the purpose prong.

(1) Retrogressive Effect

Section 5's effects prong looks to whether the voting change being challenged has a retrogressive effect on racial minorities, making them worse off than they were before. In other words, a voting change must be *nonretrogressive* in order to be precleared. The nonretrogression standard originated in *Beer v. United States*, 425 U.S. 130 (1976), which involved councilmanic districts in the city of New Orleans. At the time, approximately 45% of New Orleans' total population and 35% of its registered voters were African American. Yet until 1970, there were no African Americans on the New Orleans City Council, which included five members elected from districts and two members elected at large. After the 1970 Census, the districts were redrawn to create two districts with a black majority of the total population, one of which had a black majority (52.6%) of registered voters. The U.S. Attorney General denied preclearance under Section 5, prompting the city to seek judicial preclearance.

In *Beer*, the Supreme Court concluded that the post–1970 councilmanic districts satisfied the requirements of Section 5. Examining the legislative history of Section 5, Justice Stewart's majority opinion held that its objective was to stop voting changes that would "lead to a *retrogression* in the position of racial minorities with respect to their effective exercise of the electoral franchise" (emphasis added). Thus, a voting change that enhanced the position of racial minorities did not violate Section 5. *Beer* went to say that the application of the nonretrogression test to the facts before it was straightforward. The Court reasoned that black voters were necessarily better off than before, given that the number of majority-black districts had increased. Justice Marshall (joined by Justice Brennan) dissented, arguing that the proper question was whether "in absolute terms" the voting change had a negative effect on racial minorities.

There are two significant components to the standard articulated in *Beer*. The first is that the effect of a voting change is to be assessed in *relative* terms—that is, in comparison with the benchmark that existed before the change—rather than in absolute terms. The second, less obvious component of *Beer*'s holding concerns the assessment of retrogression when it comes to legislative districts. The Court measured retrogression in terms of the number of districts in which the racial minority group was in the majority. Such districts are commonly referred to as "majority-minority" districts. Under *Beer*, then, the application of the retrogression test to redistricting plans was relatively straightforward: Simply count up the number of majority-minority districts. If there is a reduction, then the plan is retrogressive. If there is no reduction, then the plan is not retrogressive.

This was the general understanding of the nonretrogression standard before the Supreme Court's decision in *Georgia v. Ashcroft*, 539 U.S. 461 (2003). In that case, the Court considered Georgia's state senate redistricting plan. Until 2000, blacks were a majority of the voting-age population in 10 of the state's 56 senate districts. After the 2001 redistricting, blacks were a majority of the voting-age population in 11 districts—an increase of one. Nevertheless, the Attorney General opposed preclearance on the ground that the percentage of black *registered voters* had dropped below 50% in three senate districts. Note that this plan was drawn by Democrats and, at least at the time, perceived to benefit Democrats. It avoided the concentration of reliably Democratic black voters into just a few districts, instead spreading them out in a way that Democrats thought likely to help their overall electoral prospects. For this reason, many black politicians in Georgia—including voting rights hero Rep. John Lewis—supported the plan at the time.

The Court held that Georgia's plan should have been precleared, even though it reduced the number of districts in which blacks were a majority of registered voters. The most important aspect of Justice O'Connor's opinion for the Court is its holding that retrogressive effect should not be assessed merely by counting up the total number of majority-minority districts and comparing it to the previous plan (commonly referred to as the "benchmark" plan). The ultimate question, instead, was whether there was retrogression with respect to the "effective exercise of the electoral franchise."

Georgia v. Ashcroft went on to explain that, in applying this test, it is appropriate to consider "substantive representation" (how well the plan achieves racial minorities' policy goals) as well as "descriptive representation" (how well the plan "mirrors" the electorate). Retrogression thus could not be measured simply by counting up the number of "safe" minority districts, in which minorities can control the outcome. Courts were also required to consider "coalitional" districts in which minorities can elect their preferred candidate in conjunction with voters of another race, and "influence" districts in which racial minorities can "play a substantial, if not decisive, role in the electoral process." According to *Georgia v. Ashcroft*, a plan that reduced the number of "safe" districts while increasing the number of "coalitional" or "influence" districts might still satisfy Section 5.

Justice Souter (joined by Justices Stevens, Ginsburg, and Breyer) dissented in *Georgia v. Ashcroft*. While the dissenters agreed that a reduction in the number of majority-minority districts did not necessarily make a plan retrogressive, they argued that the majority's new test was too hard to administer. To satisfy Section 5's effects prong, Justice Souter argued, it was not sufficient that minority voters have some "influence"—a standard the dissenters thought too amorphous. Rather, the state or local jurisdiction must show that the new plan will yield election results for racial minorities at least as favorable as those under the old plan.

Georgia v. Ashcroft was important in clarifying the distinction between descriptive and substantive representation, as well as categorizing three different types of districts—safe, coalitional, and influence districts—that arguably serve racial minorities' interests. Its holding, however, was reversed by the 2006 Voting Rights Act Reauthorization Act (VRARA). In addition to extending Section 5 for another 25 years, the 2006 Act modified the effects test, explicitly to overrule *Georgia v. Ashcroft*. This amendment, known as the "*Georgia v. Ashcroft* fix," provides that a voting change violates Section 5 if it has the effect of diminishing racial minorities "ability . . . to elect their preferred candidates of choice." 42 U.S.C. § 1973c(b). It is clear that this language forecloses a covered jurisdiction from substituting "influence" districts from "safe" majority-minority districts. It is less clear whether "coalition" (or "crossover") districts, in which racial minorities constitute less than a majority but can elect their preferred candidate by combining their votes with like-minded others, may be considered. The House Report accompanying the 2006 amendments suggests that such districts should be considered in determining retrogression, while the Senate Report states that only "majority-minority" districts may be considered. See Nathaniel Persily, *The Promise and Pitfalls of the New Voting Rights Act*, 117 YALE L.J. 174 (2007).

(2) Discriminatory Purpose

Section 5 also prohibits covered jurisdictions from giving effect to voting changes with the "*purpose* . . . of denying or abridging the right to vote on account of race or color" (emphasis added). This requirement encompasses *any* discriminatory purpose. That had been the prevailing understanding of Section 5's purpose prong throughout the 1990s, providing a basis for a number of preclearance denials by the Attorney General. In *Reno v. Bossier Parish School Board*, 528 U.S. 320 (2000) (*Bossier Parish II*), however, the Court interpreted Section 5 to prohibit not just any discriminatory purpose, but only a *retrogressive* purpose—that is, a purpose of making racial minorities worse off than they were before.

Congress amended Section 5 in 2006 to overrule *Bossier Parish II*. As amended, Section 5's purpose prong is expressly defined to "include any discriminatory purpose." 42 U.S.C. § 1973c(c). Regulations subsequently promulgated by the U.S. Department of Justice rely on the Supreme Court's opinion in *Village of Arlington Heights v. Metropolitan Housing Development Corp.*, 429 U.S. 252 (1977), for the factors that should be considered in determining whether a discriminatory purpose exists. They include (1) whether the impact of the action bears more heavily on one race than another; (2) the historical background of the action; (3) the sequence of events leading to the action; (4) departures from ordinary procedures; (5) substantive departures from the normal factors considered; and (6) the legislative or administrative history, including contemporaneous statements by decisionmakers. 28 C.F.R. § 51.57(e).

c. The Constitutionality of Preclearance

Section 5 imposed an unusual burden on covered state and local jurisdictions, requiring them to obtain advanced permission before giving effect to any voting changes. After all, local and state entities do not usually need to get the federal government's permission before changing their laws or practices. Nevertheless, the Supreme Court long held this extraordinary burden on covered state and local entities justified by the extraordinary history of voting discrimination in covered jurisdictions.

In *South Carolina v. Katzenbach*, 383 U.S. 301 (1966), the Court held that Section 5 was a permissible exercise of Congress' enforcement power under the Fifteenth Amendment. It relied on Chief Justice Marshall's statement in *McCulloch v. Maryland*, 17 U.S. 316 (1819): "Let the end be legitimate, let it be within the scope of the constitution, and all means which are appropriate, which are plainly adapted to that end, which are not prohibited, but consist with the letter and spirit of the constitution, are constitutional." This language has long been understood to confer broad power on Congress, and to require deferential review by courts. The Court later upheld other provisions of the original VRA and its amendments in *Katzenbach v. Morgan*, 384 U.S. 641 (1966), and *Oregon v. Mitchell*, 400 U.S. 112 (1970). In *City of Rome v. United States*, 446 U.S. 156 (1980), it reaffirmed *South Carolina v. Katzenbach*'s holding that Section 5 falls within Congress' Fifteenth Amendment enforcement power.

In a subsequent line of cases, however, the Court imposed significant limits on Congress' power to enforce constitutional rights. The first case in this line of "new federalism" cases was *City of Boerne v. Flores*, 521 U.S. 507 (1997), which struck down provisions of the Religious Freedom Restoration Act on the ground that they exceeded Congress' power to enforce the Fourteenth Amendment. *Boerne* articulated a new requirement that there be "congruence and proportionality" between the constitutional right and the means chosen by Congress to enforce it. Later cases struck down various federal statutes purporting to enforce constitutional rights under the congruence and proportionality standard. But these cases were careful to distinguish *South Carolina v. Katzenbach* and other decisions involving the VRA, given the strong record of voting discrimination and the fact that Section 5 was enacted pursuant to Congress' Fifteenth Amendment power.

In *Lopez v. Monterey County*, 525 U.S. 266 (1999), the Court upheld the application of Section 5's preclearance requirement, expressly rejecting a California county's argument that Congress lacked the power to enact this requirement under the Fifteenth Amendment. Other cases suggested that Congress has broader power under the Fourteenth Amendment to remedy discrimination against a suspect class, *Nevada Department of Human Resources v. Hibbs*, 538 U.S. 721 (2003), and to protect fundamental rights, *Tennessee v. Lane*, 541 U.S. 509 (2004). These cases were thought to support the constitutionality of Section 5, given that it protects a suspect class (racial minorities) with respect to a fundamental right (voting).

After the VRA was amended and reauthorized for another twenty-five years in 2006, there were several lawsuits challenging the constitutionality of Section 5 preclearance. These cases asserted that racial discrimination in voting, though widespread in 1965, had largely dissipated in the succeeding decades. They also argued that the coverage formula in Section 4(b) was no longer justified, given improvements in covered states.

The Court entertained a challenge to Section 5 in *Northwest Austin Municipal Utility District Number One v. Holder*, 557 U.S. 193 (2009) (*Northwest Austin*), but avoided the constitutional merits. After reviewing the history of Section 5, including its reauthorizations in 1970, 1975, 1982, and 2006, Chief Justice Roberts' majority opinion noted that the VRA imposes "current burdens" that must be justified by "current needs." It also observed that conditions had improved dramatically in the South, largely due to the VRA's efficacy. Nevertheless, the Court avoided the question whether Section 5 is unconstitutional, by construing the VRA to allow the plaintiff utility district to "bail out" of coverage. Section 4(b) of the VRA provides that a covered "State or political subdivision" may apply to a federal court to be excused from coverage. Another provision of the VRA, however, Section 14(c)(2), defines a political subdivision to mean a "county or parish," or "any other subdivision of a State that conducts registration for voting." Although the plaintiff utility district was not a county or parish and did not conduct voter registration, eight justices agreed that it could still apply to bail out of Section 5 coverage.

Only Justice Thomas reached the constitutional merits in *Northwest Austin*. His opinion, concurring in the judgment and dissenting in part, would have struck down Section 5 as exceeding Congress' Fifteenth Amendment enforcement power.

In *Shelby County v. Holder*, 133 S. Ct. 2612 (2013), the Supreme Court held that the coverage formula used for Section 5 preclearance is unconstitutional. Section 4(b) contains the coverage formula used to determine which jurisdictions must seek preclearance under Section 5. Coverage of some jurisdictions—including Alabama, where Shelby County is located—derived from elections data going back to 1964. Shelby County argued that this formula was irrational, because it no longer corresponded to current conditions. A 5–4 majority of the Supreme Court agreed.

Chief Justice Roberts' opinion for the *Shelby County* majority relied on the principle of "equal sovereignty." It said that this principle must be considered when a federal law accords disparate treatment to different states. Quoting *Northwest Austin*, the majority reiterated that preclearance imposes "current burdens" that must be justified by "current needs." While acknowledging that the coverage formula was rational when first enacted in 1965, the majority concluded that it is no longer rational. The Court cited data collected by Congress when it reauthorized the VRA in 2006, showing that minority registration and voting have increased dramatically in covered jurisdictions. Accordingly, the Court held Section 4(b)'s coverage formula unconstitutional on its face. Justice Thomas concurred, joining the majority opinion in its entirety while also restating his view from *Northwest Austin* that Section 5 is unconstitutional as well.

Justice Ginsburg dissented in *Shelby County* joined by Justices Breyer, Sotomayor, and Kagan.

The dissenters thought that Congress' decision to maintain the pre-existing coverage formula was amply justified by the evidentiary record. According to the dissent, this record showed that covered jurisdictions—including Alabama—still had worse problems with voting discrimination than other parts of the country. Justice Ginsburg called special attention to evidence that minority voters still face "second-generation barriers," or vote dilution, in covered jurisdictions.

In sum, *Shelby County* held the coverage formula in Section 4(b) unconstitutional. Technically, the Court did not rule on the constitutionality of Section 5. However, the practical effect of the decision is to end Section 5 preclearance, unless and until Congress enacts a new coverage formula.

2. SECTION 2

In its original form, Section 2 of the VRA tracked the Fifteenth Amendment, prohibiting the denial or abridgement of the right to vote on account of race or color. Because its language mirrored the Constitution, Section 2 was much less significant than Sections 4 and 5 in stopping practices used to disenfranchise African Africans in the early years of the VRA. While Section 5 required covered jurisdictions to preclear voting changes, minority voters or the U.S. government have the burden of suing to obtain relief for voting discrimination under Section 2.

After 1982, however, Section 2 became a potent means of stopping practices used to dilute the votes of racial minorities—most notably, at-large elections and redistricting plans that weakened their voting strength. That was because of amendments to Section 2, adding a "results" test in response to *City of Mobile v. Bolden*, 446 U.S. 55 (1980), which required proof of discriminatory intent for a constitutional claim. To understand the significance of the 1982 amendments, it is first necessary to discuss the constitutional standard as it developed in cases up to *Bolden*. We shall then examine the "results" test and subsequent cases construing it. The most important of these cases is *Thornburg v. Gingles*, 478 U.S. 30 (1986), which established the test for minority vote dilution under Section 2 that remains in effect.

a. The Constitutional Standard for Vote Dilution

In a series of cases after the VRA's enactment, the Court defined the constitutional standard applicable to claims that a racial minority group's voting strength is diluted. These cases concerned redistricting plans with multi-member districts or at-large election systems.

In *Whitcomb v. Chavis*, 403 U.S. 124 (1971), the Court rejected a challenge to Indiana's multi-member state legislative districts. Eight the state's 31 senatorial districts and 25 of its 39 house districts were represented by two or more legislators, each elected by all the voters in that district. Plaintiffs alleged that this system diluted the votes of African Americans in the Indianapolis area. Specifically, they alleged that the multimember voting district effectively weakened blacks' voting strength by preventing them from electing their preferred candidates. Justice White's opinion for the majority rejected this claim. The majority concluded that the mere fact that a racial minority group had been outvoted did not establish that the challenged scheme invidiously discriminated against them in violation of the Equal Protection Clause. Multi-member districts were not, therefore, categorically unconstitutional.

Two years later, however, the Supreme Court struck down a different multi-member districting scheme in *White v. Regester*, 412 U.S. 755 (1973). The district court in *White* had determined that multi-member state house districts in two Texas counties discriminated against minority voters. Specifically, the district court had found discrimination against African American voters in Dallas County and Mexican American voters in Bexar County.

Justice White again wrote for the majority. He defined the plaintiffs' burden as showing that racial minorities "had less opportunity than did other residents . . . to participate in the political processes and to elect legislators of their choice." As we shall see, this language was adopted almost verbatim into the 1982 amendments to Section 2. Under the *White* standard, multi-member districts were not categorically unconstitutional, and racial minorities had no constitutional right to proportional representation. Rather, the Court followed the district court in examining the "totality of circumstances." It affirmed the district court's conclusion that African American and Mexican American voters had effectively been excluded from the political process in the two counties. The relevant circumstances included the absence of racial minorities from the legislature, the history of minorities being excluded from party primaries, racist campaign tactics, and "cultural and economic realities" such as low income and high unemployment rates. This evidence was sufficient, *White* concluded, to prove unconstitutional voting discrimination.

Taken together, *Whitcomb* and *White* established that multi-member districts are not inherently unconstitutional, but may violate the Constitution under some circumstances. Both decisions were somewhat vague on the showing required to prove a constitutional violation. Specifically, it was unclear whether discriminatory purpose, as opposed to a discriminatory effect, had to be proven. While both decisions used the term "invidious discrimination," they did not specifically impose a requirement of discriminatory purpose or intent.

Some lower courts gave additional content to the "totality of circumstances" test articulated in *White*. The most important was *Zimmer v. McKeithen*, 485 F. 2d 1297 (5th Cir. 1973), *aff'd sub nom. East Carroll Parish School Board. v. Marshall*, 424 U.S. 636 (1976) (per curiam). In *Zimmer*, the Fifth Circuit held that plaintiffs could prevail by showing *either* discriminatory purpose *or* an effect of "minimiz[ing] or cancel[ling] out the voting strength" of racial minorities. *Zimmer* also defined a set of factors to be considered in determining whether there was unconstitutional vote dilution, including racial minorities' lack of access to the process for slating candidates, legislators' lack of responsiveness to minorities' interests, a tenuous state interest for at-large elections or multi-member districting, and the existence of past discrimination.

In *City of Mobile v. Bolden*, 446 U.S. 55 (1980), the Court clarified that discriminatory intent, not just discriminatory effect, is required to establish unconstitutional vote dilution. *Bolden* challenged the city of Mobile's system for electing its city commissioners. All three commissioners were elected at large by the entire city electorate. Given the high degree of racial polarization in Mobile— with whites voting for white candidates and blacks voting for black candidates—no black had been elected to the commission, even though blacks were approximately 35% of the city population. There was no majority opinion in *Bolden*. Writing for a plurality of four justices, Justice Stewart's opinion concluded that proof of a racially discriminatory purpose was required to show a violation of either the Fourteenth or Fifteenth Amendment. Justices Blackmun and Stevens wrote separate opinions concurring in the judgment, while Justices Brennan, White, and Marshall dissented.

The *Bolden* plurality's requirement prompted great concern among voting rights lawyers, who worried that it would bring vote dilution litigation to a virtual standstill. Fortunately for them, the preclearance requirements of Sections 4 and 5 were due to expire in 1982, providing an opportunity to amend Section 2. Congress lacks the power to overrule a Supreme Court interpretation of the Constitution, but it can amend statutes. That is precisely what Congress chose to do, amending Section 2 to make it easier for racial minorities to prove vote dilution.

Just after the 1982 VRA amendments were signed into law, the Court handed down another decision applying the discriminatory purpose standard. In *Rogers v. Lodge*, 458 U.S. 613 (1982), the Court struck down an at-large election system for the board of commissioners in Burke County, Georgia. That system had not been adopted with a discriminatory purpose, but the lower courts found that it had been *maintained* for such a purpose. Justice White's opinion for the Court affirmed that this system violated the Constitution, relying on blacks' lack of success in electing their preferred candidates, racially polarized voting, a history of discrimination, the socioeconomic status of blacks, and elected officials' lack of responsiveness to the black community. *Rogers* thus suggested that the constitutional test for discriminatory purpose was not really that different from *White*'s totality of circumstances test. But the enactment of the 1982 amendments effectively mooted that question, replacing the *Bolden–Rogers* standard with a "results" test.

b. The 1982 Amendments to Section 2

Congress amended Section 2 of the VRA in 1982, in direct response to *Bolden*. The amended language prohibits any voting practice that "*results* in the denial or abridgement" of the vote on account of race, not merely those that have a racially discriminatory purpose. It also provides that a violation of this results test is to be determined by assessing whether, based on the "totality of circumstances," the challenged practice gives racial minorities "less opportunity to participate in the political process and elect representatives of their choice." This language was taken directly from *White*. At the same time, the 1982 amendments expressly provide that they should not be understood to require proportional representation for racial minorities: "nothing in this section establishes a right to have members of a protected class elected in numbers equal to their proportion of the population."

The 1982 amendments followed a sometimes heated debate over minority vote dilution in Congress between 1981 and 1982. A version of the "results" language was part of the version of the bill approved by the House with little debate. The question whether to move to a results test was much more contentious in the Senate. Senators Edward Kennedy and Charles Mathias, Jr. introduced the bill in the Senate. They encountered stiff opposition to this amendment from conservative Republicans Strom Thurmond, Chair of the Judiciary Committee, and Orrin Hatch, Chair of the

Subcommittee on the Constitution. The main argument against the results test is that it would turn into a mandate for proportional representation, or "quotas." Some officials in the Reagan Administration's Justice Department agreed. One of them was a young lawyer named John Roberts, later to become Chief Justice of the Supreme Court, who wrote memos arguing against the proposed results test.

Ultimately, the Senate agreed to a compromise proposed by moderate Republican Robert Dole. The Dole compromise kept the "results" language, while adding the proviso that it was not to be understood as a mandate for proportional representation. It also added the new language on "totality of circumstances," which Senator Dole expressly stated was designed to codify language from *White v. Regester*, 412 U.S. 755 (1973). Senator Hatch and some other conservatives continued to oppose the results test, even with the Dole compromise language. Among his arguments was that there was no "core value" with reference to which violations of Section 2 could be measured. For a more detailed account of the legislative history, see Thomas M. Boyd & Stephen J. Markman, *The 1982 Amendments to the Voting Rights Act: A Legislative History*, 40 WASH. & LEE L. REV. 1347 (1983).

After the 1982 amendment to Section 2, a minority vote dilution claims required a showing of discriminatory results, not discriminatory intent. But there was considerable uncertainty about what this meant in practice—and, in particular, what evidence was required to prove an impermissible result. The amended language explicitly says that the statute should not be understood to mandate proportional representation. But how could one determine whether there was a discriminatory result, other than by reference to the standard of proportional representation? The text of Section 2 was of little help. In particular, its statement that a violation should be assessed by looking to racial minorities' ability to participate in the process and elect legislators of choice did not offer much in the way of guidance to courts.

There was some legislative history purporting to provide additional guidance on how Section 2 should be applied. The U.S. Senate Judiciary Committee's report on the legislation offered a list of "typical factors" probative of a Section 2 violation:

1. the extent of any history of official discrimination in the state or political subdivision that touched the right of the members of the minority group to register, to vote, or otherwise to participate in the democratic process;

2. the extent to which voting in the elections of the state or political subdivision is racially polarized;

3. the extent to which the state or political subdivision has used unusually large election districts, majority vote requirements, anti-single shot provisions, or other voting practices or procedures that may enhance the

opportunity for discrimination against the minority group;

4. if there is a candidate slating process, whether the members of the minority group have been denied access to that process;

5. the extent to which members of the minority group in the state or political subdivision bear the effects of discrimination in such areas as education, employment and health, which hinder their ability to participate effectively in the political process;

6. whether political campaigns have been characterized by overt or subtle racial appeals;

7. the extent to which members of the minority group have been elected to public office in the jurisdiction.

The Senate Report also referred to two additional factors mentioned in prior cases:

[8] whether there is a significant lack of responsiveness on the part of elected officials to the particularized needs of the members of the minority group.

[9] whether the policy underlying the state or political subdivision's use of such voting qualification, prerequisite to voting, or standard, practice or procedure is tenuous.

These factors are drawn from the constitutional vote dilution cases preceding *Bolden*, most notably *White* and *Zimmer*. As we shall see, they played an important role in subsequent Section 2 litigation.

c. *Thornburg v. Gingles*

Because the language of Section 2 was not crystal clear, it was left to the Supreme Court to provide a standard for vote dilution claims under the amended Section 2. The Court did so in *Thornburg v. Gingles*, 478 U.S. 30 (1986), articulating three preconditions for vote dilution claims under Section 2 that remain in effect today.

The challenge confronted in *Gingles* was to develop a test for assessing vote dilution that would give content to the less-than-precise language of the statute. On the one hand, it was clear from the text and legislative history that Congress meant courts to apply a "results" test, rather than an intent test. On the other hand, the text and legislative history made equally clear that the amended Section 2 should not be understood as a mandate for proportional representation.

Gingles involved a challenge to a multi-member state legislative districting plan in North Carolina. The district court had concluded that five of the districts violated Section 2, and the Court affirmed as to all but one of them. Justice Brennan wrote the majority opinion in *Gingles*, although there were portions of his opinion that were only for a plurality. The majority opinion defined the "essence" of a Section 2 claim to be that "a certain electoral law, practice, or structure interacts with social and historical conditions to cause an inequality in the opportunities enjoyed by black and white voters to elect their preferred representatives." The district court in *Gingles* had focused mostly on these factors in concluding that North Carolina's scheme violated Section 2. The Supreme Court recited these factors, but took a different approach.

The most important portion of the *Gingles* majority opinion is its articulation of three "preconditions" that must be satisfied in a Section 2 vote dilution case:

> First, the minority group must be able to demonstrate that it is sufficiently large and geographically compact to constitute a majority in a single-member district. . . . Second, the minority group must be able to show that it is politically cohesive. . . . Third, the minority must be able to demonstrate that the white majority votes sufficiently as a bloc to enable it—in the absence of special circumstances, such as the minority candidate running unopposed—usually to defeat the minority's preferred candidate.

The three *Gingles* preconditions are often referred to as "compactness," "political cohesiveness," and "majority bloc voting" respectively. The last two are sometimes conflated under the heading "racial polarization." These three preconditions provide the basic framework for all the Section 2 vote dilution litigation that followed. Their development in subsequent case law is discussed at greater length below, in subsection d.

One advantage of the approach taken by the *Gingles* Court is that it provides a more manageable inquiry, in comparison to the nine Senate factors. While not exactly a bright-line test, the *Gingles* preconditions focus the judicial inquiry. This test also helps thread the needle between requiring discriminatory purpose and mandating proportional representation—both of which Congress explicitly sought to avoid. Under the *Gingles* test, intervention is limited to places where a *compact* majority-minority district may be drawn.

In addition, the *Gingles* test puts the question of racial polarization at the center of the judicial inquiry in a Section 2 case. The Court explained that it was necessary to inquire into racial polarization, to determine whether the strength of racial minorities votes was really being weakened by the challenged system. If there is no racial polarization, then racial minorities may be able to elect their candidate of choice, even when they constitute a minority of the voting population within a particular district. But if a high degree of racial polarization exists, then a minority group that does not control the district is unlikely to elect their preferred candidate of choice. Thus, by requiring a showing of racial polarization, the second and third preconditions limit judicial intervention to cases in which racial minorities are most likely to need it, in order to elect their candidates of choice.

That said, there was considerable disagreement among the justices in *Gingles* on how racial polarization should be measured. The plurality

portion of Justice Brennan's opinion asserted that
plaintiffs need only show a *correlation* between race
and voting patterns (i.e., that blacks vote one way
and whites vote another), and did not need to prove
causation (i.e., that the voting pattern was caused
by race). In effect, Justice Brennan's test would
require only a *bivariate* analysis, looking at just two
variables: the race of voters and the share of the
vote received by candidates. If there was a
sufficiently strong correlation between race and vote
share, then racial polarization existed, even if the
vote patterns might be explained by factors other
than race (such as party or ideological preferences).

Justice O'Connor's opinion concurring in the
judgment, also for four justices, took a different
approach. While Justice O'Connor agreed that racial
polarization was an important part of the Section 2
inquiry, she criticized the majority for departing
from the factors developed by the Fifth Circuit in
Zimmer and restated in the Senate Report. And in
contrast to the *plurality* portion of Justice
Brennan's opinion, Justice O'Connor thought that
courts should consider *why* voters of different races
prefer different candidates—or, as she put it,
whether "divergent racial voting patterns may be
explained in part by causes other than race," such
as the different interests of minority and
nonminority voters. This approach suggests a
multivariate analysis, which would look not only to
race and voting patterns, but also to other factors
that might explain differences in how different
racial groups vote. In other words, evidence that
racial voting patterns are explainable by factors

other than race was, on Justice O'Connor's test, relevant to a Section 2 claim. She thought that the majority's contrary test would lead to a requirement of proportional representation for minority voters.

Justice White was the one justice who joined Justice Brennan's majority opinion in *Gingles*, yet declined to join the portion of Brennan's opinion (Part III.C) concerning evidence of racially polarized voting. Justice White explained that he disagreed with the plurality's conclusion that the "race of the *candidate* is irrelevant" (emphasis added) to the Section 2 inquiry. In the plurality's view, the race of the voters was all that mattered. Thus, under the plurality's test, racial polarization would exist if black voters supported a white Republican candidate, while white voters supported a white Democratic candidate. Justice White thought the failure to consider the race of candidates led to an improper focus on interest-group politics rather than racial discrimination. On this point, Justice White was in agreement with Justice O'Connor's concurrence, which also declined to adopt Justice Brennan's position that the candidate's race was irrelevant to the Section 2 inquiry. There were therefore five votes in *Gingles* for the proposition that the race of the candidate may sometimes be relevant.

d. Refinement of the *Gingles* Standard

Gingles set the standard by which Section 2 vote dilution cases should be evaluated, but left many important questions unresolved. There have been a large number of Section 2 vote dilution cases in the ensuing years, raising too many questions to itemize here. But the most important post-*Gingles* issues can be broken down into three categories. The first concerns the definition of the first *Gingles* precondition, whether the minority group is "sufficiently large and geographically compact." The second question concerns the proof of racial polarization (which as noted above encompasses both the "political cohesiveness" and "majority bloc voting" preconditions). The third concerns totality of circumstances test—specifically, whether proof of the three preconditions is *sufficient* to prove a Section 2 violation, or whether evidence on the Senate factors (and if so, how much) is required.

(1) "Sufficiently Large and Geographically Compact"

Recall that the first *Gingles* precondition looks to whether the minority group is "sufficiently large and geographically compact to constitute a majority in a single-member district." The basic idea is that racial minorities must be concentrated into a particular part of the relevant jurisdiction, so that it is possible to draw a majority-minority district that is reasonably compact (i.e., not too bizarre in its shape). One of the questions that arose in cases after *Gingles* is what it means for a district to be compact. Another is how numerous racial minorities must be within the relevant portion of the jurisdiction, and what measure of population to use in determining whether the minority group is large enough.

In early cases, compactness was not a great obstacle to Section 2 vote dilution claims, but it became more significant later on. *Gingles* itself does not define "compactness," and there are different ways of measuring it in the social science literature. Some states have their own definition, looking for example to the sum of perimeters of district boundaries or the degree to which the population is dispersed. (For more on compactness, see the discussion of districting criteria in Chapter 4.C.)

Compactness became very important in the 1990s, given the limitations that the Court imposed on the creation of majority-minority districts in the racial gerrymandering line of cases. As explained in Part B below, *Shaw v. Reno*, 509 U.S. 630 (1993), held that a bizarrely shaped majority-black district in North Carolina violated the Equal Protection Clause. Subsequent cases struck down other majority-minority district in which race was the predominant factor.

In *League of United Latin American Citizens v. Perry*, 548 U.S. 399 (2006) (*LULAC*), the Court incorporated some of the *Shaw* analysis into the first *Gingles* precondition, while adding a new element which some have referred to as "cultural" compactness. Justice Kennedy wrote the portion of the opinion in *LULAC* on the Section 2 claim. (Another portion of this case, having to do with partisan gerrymandering, was discussed in Chapter 5.B.) Latino voters in and around Laredo, Texas argued that their rights under Section 2 had been violated when the state legislature redrew a congressional district (CD 23) to split the Latino population, which was on the verge of gaining a controlling majority. Specifically, the redrawn lines dropped Latinos from 57.5% to 46% of the citizen-voting-age population. Although Latinos in the Laredo area had not yet elected their preferred candidate of choice, the majority concluded that they had an opportunity to do so.

Even more important, the *LULAC* majority rejected the state's argument that a Latino-majority district created in a *different* part of the state (CD 25) compensated for the elimination of CD 23. To defend the elimination of a compact district (CD 23) on this ground, the Court held, the state must demonstrate that it was under an obligation to create the *new* district. Texas could not make this showing, however, because Latinos in the area covered by the newly created CD 25 were not "compact." To the contrary, there was a 300–mile gap between two disparate Latino communities in this new district, "and a similarly large gap between the needs and interests of the two groups." Specifically, CD 25 included Latinos in the Austin area who tended to be more affluent, and Latinos living near Texas' southwestern border who were poorer and less educated. The Court's analysis in *LULAC* thus seems to incorporate a new element into the compactness precondition: A racial minority group must share certain "needs and interests" to be considered compact under the first *Gingles* precondition. Compactness looks to a racial group's needs and interests, as well as geography.

In addition to compactness, the first precondition requires courts to consider whether the racial minority group is "sufficiently large." It took a long time for the Supreme Court to answer the question of how numerous racial minorities must be to meet the first precondition. In *Bartlett v. Strickland*, 556 U.S. 1 (2009), the Court held that there must be a *numerical majority* (i.e., more than 50%) of racial minorities within a compact district. The question in *Bartlett* was whether black voters had a claim under Section 2, when they were less than 50% of a compact district but were still likely to control the outcome by combining their votes with those of like-minded white voters (sometimes called "crossover" voters). The Court concluded that Section 2 did not come into play in these circumstances. Writing for a plurality of the Court, Justice Kennedy understood *Gingles* reference to "a majority in a single-member district" to mean a *numerical majority*. If minority voters could make a Section 2 claim when less than a majority of a single-member district, it would open the door to many more Section 2 claims. The two other justices in the majority, Justices Scalia and Thomas, concurred on the broader ground that Section 2 should not be understood to authorize vote dilution claims at all, an argument made at greater length in Justice Thomas' concurring opinion in *Holder v. Hall*, 512 U.S. 874 (1994). Because Justice Kennedy's opinion furnishes the narrower ground for decision, it may be understood as stating the holding of the case. Thus, after *Bartlett*, racial minorities must constitute a numerical majority of a single-member district to satisfy *Gingles*.

But a majority of what? The total population, voting-age population (VAP), citizen-voting-age population (CVAP), citizen-voting-eligible population (CVEP), or registered voters? In some parts of the country, there are major differences between these numbers. Some areas include large number of noncitizens who are not eligible to vote. A place with a large number of Latino immigrants, for example, will generally have a much lower percentage of Latinos among its *citizen*-voting-age population, than among its total population and voting-age population. Some places have larger numbers of minors, who are ineligible to vote, than others. The percentage of people incarcerated or ineligible due to past felony convictions may also vary dramatically from place to place. For all these reasons, it can make a big difference which measure of population is used in determining whether the first *Gingles* precondition is satisfied. The Supreme Court has not spoken clearly on this question, although *LULAC v. Perry*, 548 U.S. 399 (2006), appeared to assume that citizen-voting-age population was the proper measure. Most lower courts have taken the same position, at least in challenges brought by Latino voters in places with a large number of noncitizens and others ineligible to vote.

(2) Racial Polarization

As discussed above, the second *Gingles* precondition requires the racial minority group to show that it is politically cohesive. The third requires them to show that whites vote as a bloc so as usually to defeat minority-preferred candidates. Together, these preconditions are referred to as "racial polarization." The basic idea is that white voters tend to vote one way, while minority group members vote the other.

The second prong has spawned relatively little litigation, because it is usually not difficult to show that racial minorities vote as a bloc. One complication that does sometimes arise is whether two different racial or ethnic minority groups—such as Latinos and African Americans—may form a coalition that may jointly be deemed to meet this requirement. The Court assumed without deciding that two distinct groups could combine to make a Section 2 claim in *Growe v. Emison*, 507 U.S. 25 (1993), but rejected the claim for lack of sufficient evidence of political cohesion. Some lower courts have accepted claims by coalitions of minority groups, while others have rejected such claims. Conversely, there are some circumstances in which a minority group is not politically cohesive. Cuban Americans and Mexican Americans, for example, tend to have very different voting preferences, even though both may be considered Latinos. So too, different Native American tribes may not be politically cohesive.

The other component of racial polarization, majority bloc voting, has produced considerable litigation. One question that sometimes arises is how polarized voting must be in order to satisfy this requirement. The Supreme Court has never defined a numerical threshold, but has instead adhered to the *Gingles* formulation that white bloc voting must be sufficient to "usually defeat the minority's preferred candidate." This question is of considerable current importance, given evidence that polarized voting has become less pronounced in some parts of the country.

Another major issue is whether courts should consider the reasons *why* the white majority opposes minority-preferred candidates. Is it enough to show that white voters regularly oppose minority preferred candidates? Or must it be shown that white voters opposed those candidates *for racial reasons*, as opposed to political or ideological ones? This goes back to the debate between Justice Brennan and Justice O'Connor in *Gingles*. The lower courts have divided over this question. Some have said that the fact of racially polarized voting is what matters, not the reasons for it. See *Lewis v. Alamance County*, 99 F.3d 600 (4th Cir. 1996). Others have looked to causes of racially polarized voting other than race, as evidence that may defeat a claim of white bloc voting. The most notable example is the Fifth Circuit's opinion in *LULAC v. Clements*, 999 F.2d 831 (5th Cir. 1993) (en banc), in which the court held that "nonracial causes of voting preferences" such as party affiliation should be considered.

(3) Totality of Circumstances

Gingles focused the Section 2 vote dilution inquiry on three preconditions, but left open the question whether other factors—such as those identified in the Senate Report—should also be considered. Lower courts divided over this question after *Gingles*. In *Johnson v. De Grandy*, 512 U.S. 997 (1994), the Court put the issue to rest, holding that satisfaction of the three *Gingles* precondition was necessary to prevail on a vote dilution claim, but not sufficient. The ultimate question is whether, based on the totality of circumstances, racial minorities have been denied the ability effectively to participate in the political process and elect their representatives of choice. Among the circumstances that should be considered, *De Grandy* further held, is whether racial minorities enjoy proportional representation in the relevant body. Thus, proportional representation is not required by Section 2, nor is its existence a "safe harbor" that automatically shields defendant from liability; but if a racial minority group is proportionally represented, that fact cuts against its vote dilution claim.

e. Extension and Limitation of *Gingles*

Recall that the *Gingles* test was designed for challenges to at-large and multimember districting schemes alleged to dilute racial minorities' right to vote. The remedy typically sought in such cases is the creation of single-member districts, usually a majority-minority district, from which the group may elect its preferred candidate of choice. *Gingles* left open the question whether its test would also apply to single-member districting schemes alleged to dilute minorities' voting rights. Since then, however, the Court has applied the *Gingles* test in challenges to single-member districting schemes too. See *Johnson v. DeGrandy*, 512 U.S. 997 (1994); *LULAC v. Perry*, 548 U.S. 399 (2006).

The Court has also applied Section 2 to non-legislative election schemes alleged to dilute racial minorities' voting strength. In *Chisom v. Roemer*, 501 U.S. 380 (1991), the Court held that Section 2 applies to Louisiana's scheme for electing its state supreme court justices, which was alleged to dilute African American voters' rights. It reached this holding even though Section 2 uses the term "representatives"—which might be taken to include legislators but not judges—rather than a broader term like "candidates." On the other hand, Section 2's test does not necessarily apply in exactly the same way to non-legislative elections. In *Houston Lawyers' Association v. Attorney General of Texas*, 501 U.S. 419 (1991), for example, the Court held that the state's interest in maintaining the link between its judges' jurisdiction and voters in that area was a factor to be considered among the "totality of circumstances," in determining whether Section 2 had been violated.

The Supreme Court has declined to apply Section 2 to governance schemes, as opposed to representational schemes, that are alleged to weaken racial minorities' influence. In *Holder v. Hall*, 512 U.S. 874 (1994), for example, the Court considered a challenge to a single-commissioner form of government used in a rural Georgia county, in which African Americans were almost 20% of the county population. Under this system, blacks were unable to elect their preferred candidate. Plaintiffs therefore sought to replace the single-commissioner system with a multi-member commission, to which racial minorities could expect to elect at least one member. Justice Kennedy's plurality opinion rejected their claim, citing the absence of a satisfactory "benchmark" of fair representation against which to evaluate the system. Justice Thomas concurred in the judgment, joined by Justice Scalia, on much broader grounds. He called for a "systematic reassessment" of the Court's Section 2 jurisprudence, arguing against the theory of vote dilution adopted in cases since *Gingles* on the ground that they are inimical to "the ideal of a color-blind Constitution."

B.   RACIAL GERRYMANDERING

1.   BACKGROUND

Sections 2 and 5 of the VRA had a profound effect in increasing the representation of racial minorities. This was especially true in the post–1990 round of redistricting. The 1982 amendments to Section 2, as construed in *Gingles*, resulted in the abolition of many at-large election systems and the creation of majority-minority districts from which racial minorities could elect their candidates of choice. In addition, the U.S. Department of Justice vigorously enforced Section 5 of the VRA in the 1990s. This was partly due to the influence of career lawyers committed to increasing minority representation. In addition, officials in President George H.W. Bush's administration had an incentive to compel the creation of majority-minority districts, sometimes even districts with a large supermajority of African Americans and Latinos. While this may seem counterintuitive, concentrating these reliably Democratic voters in a few districts tends to help Republicans in the aggregate, by making surrounding districts more white and more conservative.

The end result of the more robust enforcement of Sections 2 and 5 was a pronounced increase in minority representation after 1990. The number of African Americans serving in Congress increased from 25 to 38, while the number of Latinos increased from 10 to 17. Similar changes, also prompted by VRA enforcement, occurred at the state and local levels. The compelled creation of majority-minority districts ultimately prompted a reaction from the Supreme Court, which took the form of a new equal protection doctrine imposing limits on the consideration of race in drawing district lines. The cases articulating this doctrine are commonly referred to as the racial gerrymandering cases, or the *Shaw* cases, after the first case in this line, *Shaw v. Reno*, 509 U.S. 630 (1993) (*Shaw I*).

Prior to *Shaw v. Reno*, the Court had upheld the purposeful use of race to create majority-minority districts against a constitutional challenge. In *United Jewish Organizations, Inc. v. Carey*, 430 U.S. 144 (1977), the state of New York drew districts that divided Brooklyn's Hasidic community to create supermajority-black (65%) state senate and assembly districts. This was done to satisfy the Justice Department's preclearance demands. A divided Court upheld the plan. In a portion of the opinion that spoke for a plurality of three justices, Justice White wrote that the intentional use of race to create these districts was consistent with the Fourteenth and Fifteenth Amendments, because the districts were drawn to enhance the opportunity for minority representation and not to minimize or cancel out whites' voting strength. Justice Stewart, joined by Justice Powell, concurred on similar grounds, concluding that there was no purpose or effect to discriminate against white voters. Justice Brennan's opinion suggested even broader constitutional latitude for "benign" race-conscious policies adopted pursuant to the VRA. A clear majority in *United Jewish Organizations* thus saw no constitutional problem with the purposeful use of race to create districts in which minorities could elect their preferred candidate.

2.   *SHAW V. RENO*

The Court took a very different approach in the 1990s, starting with *Shaw v. Reno*, 509 U.S. 630 (1993) (*Shaw I*). Plaintiffs in *Shaw I* challenged two majority-black congressional districts in North Carolina, a state that had not elected a single African American to Congress between 1900 and 1990, even though the state's population was approximately 20% black. Both districts had a rather odd shape under the 1991 redistricting plan. One of the congressional districts (CD 1) was described as looking like a "bug splattered on a windshield," the other (CD 12) as "snake-like," winding along I–85 from one part of the state to another "until it gobble[d] in enough enclaves of black neighborhoods" to create a black majority. In truth, the unusual shape of these districts was the consequence of two factors: first, North Carolina's attempt to satisfy the Department of Justice's demand for two black-majority districts, as a condition of Section 5 preclearance; second, the desire of the state legislature's Democratic majority to protect the seats of *white* Democrats in Congress. The shape of the two black-majority districts was thus attributable to the legislature's desire to satisfy the Justice Department while protecting white incumbents in other districts.

Plaintiffs in *Shaw* challenged these two districts on the ground that they violated the Equal Protection Clause by excessively relying on race. Justice O'Connor's opinion for the majority in *Shaw I* allowed these claims to proceed, reversing the lower court's order dismissing them. This was, the Court recognized, a new kind of equal protection claim, analytically distinct from ones recognized before. In support of this new claim, the majority relied on two lines of cases. The first was the line of cases including *Gomillion v. Lightfoot*, 364 U.S. 339 (1960) (Chapter 3), which struck down racially gerrymandered city boundaries designed to exclude blacks. The other was the line of "colorblindness" cases applying strict scrutiny to race-conscious affirmative action programs. The *Shaw* Court imported the affirmative action cases' concern with racial essentialism into its analysis of race-conscious districting.

Focusing on the "bizarre" shape of the district, the Court concluded that plaintiffs had stated a claim by alleging that the plan was "so extremely irregular on its face that it can only be viewed as an effort to segregate the races for purposes of voting, without regard for traditional district principles and without sufficiently compelling justification." This suggests that strict scrutiny applies in at least some cases where legislative districts are drawn for racial purposes. The *Shaw I* opinion used highly charged language to describe the use of race in redistricting, drawing a comparison to "political apartheid," labeling the message sent by such districts "pernicious," and saying that racial gerrymandering threatens to "balkanize" us into competing factions. The new constitutional injury that the Court recognized in *Shaw I* has been characterized as an "expressive harm." Richard H. Pildes & Richard A. Niemi, *Expressive Harms, "Bizarre Districts," and Voting Rights: Evaluating Election–District Appearances After* Shaw v. Reno, 92 MICH. L. REV. 483 (1999). The idea is that the meaning or message conveyed by these districts, especially the appearance that all other values were subordinated to race, created a constitutional injury. In later cases, the Court signaled its agreement with the idea that such districts work an "expressive harm."

Four justices (Justices White, Blackmun, Stevens, and Souter) dissented in *Shaw I*, each of them writing a separate opinion. Justice White's dissent (joined by Justices Blackmun and Stevens) would have adhered to the position taken in his *United Jewish Organizations* opinion to conclude that plaintiffs had stated no cognizable claim. He emphasized that white voters in North Carolina had not shown a discriminatory purpose or effect, criticizing the majority's comparison of North Carolina's districts to apartheid and segregation. Justice Stevens' dissent recognized that there was a constitutional duty to "govern impartially," but concluded that the purpose of the challenged districts was not to enhance the power of the majority at the expense of a minority "and thereby to strengthen the unequal distribution of power."

3.   POST–*SHAW* CASES

It was clear from *Shaw I* that the use of race in drawing districts sometimes triggers strict scrutiny. But *Shaw I* left open some significant questions about when race may and may not be considered in drawing district lines. Two of these questions are especially important. The first question is when strict scrutiny applies. Did *any* use of race in drawing districts trigger strict scrutiny, requiring that they be narrowly tailored to a compelling interest? Was it the bizarre shape of the districts that triggered strict scrutiny? Or did strict scrutiny only come into play if there was an *excessive* use of race? If so, how much was too much?

The second open question was what could justify the use of race, in cases where strict scrutiny applied. At the conclusion of the *Shaw I* opinion, the

Court stated its holding as follows: "that [plaintiffs] have stated a claim under the Equal Protection Clause by alleging that the North Carolina General Assembly adopted a reapportionment scheme so irrational on its face that it can be understood only as an effort to segregate voters into separate voting districts because of their race, and *that the separation lacks justification*" (emphasis added). *Shaw I* did not answer the question what sort of justification would suffice to meet strict scrutiny. The most important aspect of this question was whether and when compliance with the VRA was a compelling state interest that could justify the use of race.

The Court provided guidance on these questions in subsequent cases arising from the post–1990 redistricting cycle. On the first question, the Court clarified that strict scrutiny applies when race is the *predominant factor* in drawing district lines in *Miller v. Johnson*, 515 U.S. 900 (1995), which arose from Georgia's post–1990 congressional redistricting. The district challenged in *Miller* was not as oddly shaped as the ones in *Shaw*, but the Court nevertheless held that it was subject to strict scrutiny. Again, the vote was 5–4. Justice Kennedy's majority opinion held that the ultimate question was whether "race was the predominant factor motivating the legislature's decision to place a significant number of voters within or without a particular district." This required plaintiffs to show that race was subordinated to other districting criteria, like compactness, contiguity, and respect for political subdivisions. Applying this standard,

Justice Kennedy concluded that race was the predominant factor in drawing the challenged district and, accordingly, that strict scrutiny applied. The Court later applied this standard in *Shaw v. Hunt*, 517 U.S. 899 (1996) (*Shaw II*), to hold that North Carolina's CD 12 was subject to strict scrutiny and to strike down that district by another 5–4 vote.

Turning to the second question, the Court's pronouncements after *Shaw II* were less clear as to what could justify a plan in which race was the predominant factor. In *Miller*, the Court rejected the state of Georgia's attempt to justify its majority-black district on the ground that the Justice Department had required it as a condition of Section 5 preclearance. The Court assumed that compliance with the VRA could sometimes justify the use of race in drawing a district. But it rejected the argument that compliance with the Justice Department's demand was sufficient. Rather, courts had an independent obligation to examine the basis for the Section 5 objection. The *Miller* majority went on to say that the Justice Department's apparent policy of maximizing majority-black districts was not required by Section 5. Accordingly, compliance with its demand was not a compelling interest that satisfied strict scrutiny.

The Court clarified what must be shown to satisfy strict scrutiny in two cases decided in 1996. In *Bush v. Vera*, 517 U.S. 952 (1996), the Court struck down three Texas congressional districts by another 5–4 vote, again without a majority opinion. Justice

O'Connor's lead opinion (joined by only two other justices) assumed that compliance with the VRA could be a compelling interest, but concluded that the districts were not narrowly tailored to this interest. In addition, Justice O'Connor took the unusual step of writing a separate concurring opinion, speaking only for herself. That opinion took the position that compliance with Section 2 of the VRA *is* a compelling interest. Combined with the four dissenting justices, that made a majority for the proposition that compliance with the VRA can be a compelling interest. But Chief Justice Rehnquist's opinion for the majority in *Shaw II* clarified that merely avoiding VRA litigation is *not* a sufficient justification. The state must have a "strong basis in evidence" for believing it is violating the VRA, not just reason to believe it will be sued.

The final and perhaps most important case in the *Shaw* line is *Easley v. Cromartie*, 532 U.S. 234 (2001). That case also concerned North Carolina's CD 12, as redrawn in 1997, after the decision in *Shaw II*. This district court had initially granted summary judgment for plaintiffs, concluding that the new CD 12—which now had less than a majority (47%) of African Americans—violated the *Shaw* doctrine. The Court unanimously remanded and ordered the district court to hold a trial on the reasons for drawing the districts. After a trial, the district court again held the new CD 12 unconstitutional. And again, the Supreme Court reversed. This time, Justice O'Connor—who wrote *Shaw I* and was part of the majority in all the subsequent cases noted above—switched sides, joining Justice Breyer's majority opinion in *Easley* (along with Justices Stevens, Souter, and Ginsburg).

The *Easley* majority concluded that politics, not race, was the predominant factor in drawing the challenged district. While race was a consideration, the Court rejected the district court's conclusion that race was predominant. That conclusion was based upon the district's shape, its splitting of political subdivisions, and its high percentage of African Americans. The *Easley* majority found this evidence insufficient to prove that race was the predominant factor, given other evidence showing that political considerations played a role in the district's boundaries. Where there was a high degree of correlation between race and political affiliation, as in North Carolina, plaintiffs had the burden of showing that the legislature's political objectives could have been achieved in ways that were "comparably consistent with traditional districting principles" and would have "brought about significantly greater racial balance."

Easley's clarification of the predominant factor standard gave states a relatively easy way around a *Shaw* violation: Show that political factors rather than racial ones were the main justification for the challenged district. It may be significant that the redrawn CD 12 was not a majority-minority district, although it was one from which blacks (in combination with white crossover voters) could elect their preferred candidate of choice. It is probably even more significant that this district was not drawn under compulsion of a denial of preclearance.

By the time *Easley* was decided, the Justice Department, chastened by the prior cases in the *Shaw* line, was not as demanding in terms of requiring majority-minority districts.

Whether because of *Easley* or because of the Justice Department's less vigorous enforcement of the VRA, *Shaw* litigation dramatically declined in the post–2000 redistricting cycle. None of these claims were successful at the statewide level. Jocelyn Benson, *A Shared Existence: The Current Compatibility of the Equal Protection Clause and Section 5 of the Voting Rights Act*, 88 NEB. L. REV. 124 (2009). So long as a state or locality can point to a non-racial, political justification for drawing lines in a particular way, it is likely to prevail. That does not mean that the *Shaw* doctrine is no longer significant. As noted above, the Court incorporated a *Shaw*-like analysis into its analysis of a claim under Section 2 of the VRA in *LULAC v. Perry*, 548 U.S. 399 (2006). That decision upheld a challenge to the elimination of a compact Latino opportunity district, rejecting the argument that a non-compact Latino district was an adequate substitute. This can be seen as adopting *Shaw*'s underlying concern with racial essentialism.

Moreover, there remains a tension between the VRA—which sometimes require race to be considered in drawing district lines—and the *Shaw* doctrine, which limits consideration of race in drawing district lines. Taken together, the VRA and *Shaw* cases impose a "Goldilocks" obligation on those responsible for drawing district lines, requiring them to engage in some—but not too much—consideration of race.

CHAPTER 7

ELECTION ADMINISTRATION AND REMEDIES

Lawsuits regarding the administration of elections have become commonplace. This development can be traced to the disputed presidential election between George W. Bush and Al Gore in 2000. In *Bush v. Gore*, 531 U.S. 98 (2000), the Supreme Court concluded that the manner in which Florida was conducting its recount of punch-card ballots violated the Equal Protection Clause. This decision effectively sealed Bush's victory. Congress subsequently enacted the Help America Vote Act of 2002 (HAVA), which sought to address some of the problems that came to light in Florida and other states. Since then, the United States has seen controversies regarding a number of election administration issues, many of which have become the subjects of litigation. The subjects that have spawned disagreement include voting equipment, voter registration, voter identification, provisional ballots, absentee and early voting, recounts, and contests. The Supreme Court has had occasion to consider some of these issues, most notably in its decision upholding Indiana's voter identification law, *Crawford v. Marion County Election Board*, 553 U.S. 181 (2008), which addressed the constitutional standard for assessing laws that impose burdens on voting.

Election administration in the U.S. has two distinctive features, which are important to be aware of when studying the law in this area. First, American election administration is extremely decentralized in comparison with other countries. Most of the governing law comes from the states, not Congress, and much authority resides in the hands of thousands of counties and municipalities scattered across the country. This decentralization, along with the absence of data by which to measure election performance, makes it extremely difficult to determine how well election administration is functioning in various jurisdictions. See Heather Gerken, THE DEMOCRACY INDEX: WHY OUR ELECTION SYSTEM IS FAILING AND HOW TO FIX IT (2009). Second, U.S. election administration is distinctive in its partisanship. Most states' chief election officials (usually the Secretary of State) are elected in partisan elections; in most of the remaining states, chief election officials are appointed by partisan elected officials. Many county and municipal election officials are likewise affiliated with one of the major parties. This creates an apparent (if not actual) conflict of interest between election officials' responsibility to administer elections evenhandedly and their interest in helping their party.

This chapter does not attempt to describe the multitude of state laws and policies governing election administration, nor can any course in Election Law attempt to cover all this material. Instead, it provides an overview of the federal law governing election administration, while summarizing important features of state election laws and the remedies available in challenge challenges to election administration practices. Part A addresses the still-developing federal constitutional law governing election administration. Part B discusses the three most important federal statutes in this area: the Voting Rights Act, National Voter Registration Act, and Help America Vote Act. Part C summarizes the key features of state election administration. Part D discusses remedies available for election errors, including pre-election litigation and post-election litigation seeking to overturn the declared result.

A. CONSTITUTIONAL REQUIREMENTS

1.   THE 2000 ELECTION LITIGATION

Before 2000, there was relatively little constitutional litigation surrounding election administration. That has changed dramatically, largely as the result of the Florida 2000 election and the Supreme Court decision that effectively resolved that election, *Bush v. Gore*, 531 U.S. 98 (2000). Understanding this episode is therefore critical to understanding the constitutional law in the area of election administration.

a. The Electoral College

The United States does not elect its President through a direct popular election. Instead, Article II and the Twelfth Amendment to the U.S. Constitution prescribe that the President be elected through an indirect system, popularly known as the Electoral College. The Constitution allocates to each state a number of electors, equal to the sum total of its U.S. Representatives and Senators, giving the state legislature the power to determine how those electors shall be chosen. The Twenty–Third Amendment accords to Washington, D.C. a number of presidential electors, which may not exceed those of the least populous state (currently three), with Congress empowered to select the method of appointment. All the states and Washington, D.C. choose their electors through popular election, with 48 states and D.C. allocating their electors on a winner-take-all basis to the candidate with the most votes. The remaining two states (Maine and Nebraska) award their presidential electors by congressional district, with a presidential candidate getting an electoral vote for each district he or she wins and the statewide winner receiving the two remaining electoral votes from the state. There is no single meeting of all states' electors. Instead, the electors from each state meet in their state capital on a prescribed date (41 days after Election Day), and their votes are transmitted to Congress where they are counted in joint session. The candidate who receives the greatest number of electoral votes becomes President.

b. The Protest and Contest

The 2000 presidential election turned on the winner of the State of Florida, in which then-Governor George W. Bush and then-Vice President Al Gore were locked in a very close race. Narrowly trailing on election night, Gore called Bush to concede, but later called back to retract his concession after realizing that the race was too close to call. The initial count had Bush ahead by 1,784 votes out of almost six million votes cast for President. Most voters in Florida used punch-card voting systems, in which voters used a stylus to punch out a perforated "chad" in the paper ballot. For a significant number of punch-card ballots, no vote had been counted for President. Gore hoped that he might be able to exceed Bush's vote total, if enough of these ballots could ultimately be validated through the recount process. Accordingly, he filed an election "protest" under Florida law, asking for manual recounts in four counties. These recounts had not been completed by Florida's deadline, but Gore was successful in securing an extension from the unanimous Florida Supreme Court, based on its interpretation of state law.

Bush sought review of the Florida Supreme Court's decision, arguing it violated Article II, Section 1, Clause 1 of the U.S. Constitution, which requires that states appoint their presidential electors "in such manner as *the legislature* thereof direct" (emphasis added). Bush argued that the Florida Supreme Court had erroneously relied on the Florida Constitution in its ruling that extended the recount, when it should have relied exclusively on statutes enacted by the Florida legislature. In *Bush v. Palm Beach County Canvassing Board*, 531 U.S. 70 (2000), the U.S. Supreme Court remanded in a unanimous *per curiam* opinion, instructing the Florida Supreme Court to clarify the basis for its ruling. The Court cited Article II and *McPherson v. Blacker*, 146 U.S. 1 (1892), which had upheld a

Michigan statute allocating presidential electors by congressional district. Although the issue was not squarely presented in *McPherson*, there is some language in that opinion suggesting that a state constitution may not "circumscribe the legislative power" over the selection of presidential electors. *Bush v. Palm Beach Canvassing Board* did not decide whether state constitutions may circumscribe the state legislative power over presidential electors. Instead, it remanded for the Florida Supreme Court to make clear the precise grounds for its decision. On the same day that the U.S. Supreme Court heard argument in *Bush v. Gore*, 531 U.S. 98 (2000), described below, the Florida Supreme Court issued an opinion reaching the same result, but this time basing its reasoning entirely on Florida statutory law, not the state constitution. *Palm Beach County Canvassing Board v. Harris*, 772 So. 2d 1273 (Fla. 2000).

Gore still trailed Bush narrowly at the time of the extended deadline set by the Florida Supreme Court. As a result, he filed an election "contest" which sought a selective manual recount of "undervotes" (ballots on which no vote for was recorded) in two counties. Again, the Florida Supreme Court sided with Gore, this time by a 4–3 margin. In addition to ordering that certain recounts completed after its previous deadline be included in vote totals, it ordered a manual recount of all undervotes throughout the state, not just those in the counties originally requested by Gore. The Florida Supreme Court held that the "clear intent of the voter," a standard prescribed by

Florida law, should be applied in these recounts. It did not prescribe a more detailed standard for which ballots should be counted. Again, Bush immediately sought review of the Florida Supreme Court's ruling.

c. *Bush v. Gore*

On December 9, 2000, the U.S. Supreme Court issued an order in *Bush v. Gore*, 531 U.S. 1046 (2000), staying the Florida Supreme Court's mandate. This order prevented the recount from proceeding. Although the order did not explain the basis for the stay, Justice Scalia (who was part of the majority) issued an unusual concurring opinion, asserting that it would "cast[] a cloud upon . . . the legitimacy of [Bush's] election" if the recount were allowed to proceed. Justice Stevens dissented from the stay order, joined by Justices Souter, Ginsburg, and Breyer. Justice Stevens asserted that: "Preventing the recount from being completed will inevitably cast a cloud over the legitimacy of the election."

Three days later, on the evening of December 12, 2000, the U.S. Supreme Court issued an unsigned *per curiam* opinion holding that Florida's recount process violated the Equal Protection Clause of the U.S. Constitution. 531 U.S. 98 (2000). There were five justices in the majority and four dissenters (Justices Stevens, Souter, Ginsburg, and Breyer), each of whom wrote separately. In addition, Chief Justice Rehnquist, who joined the *per curiam* opinion, wrote a separate concurring opinion concluding that Florida's recount violated Article II of the U.S. Constitution as well.

(1) The Equal Protection Holding

The *per curiam* opinion expressed the views of the five justices in the majority (Chief Justice Rehnquist, and Justices Scalia, O'Connor, Kennedy, and Thomas). After setting forth the procedural history of the case, the *per curiam* opinion described the problems that had emerged with the punch-card voting system used in Florida, noting that an "unfortunate number of ballots" were not completely punched through. The Court explained that, although the U.S. Constitution does not confer a right to vote for President, all states now appoint their electors through a popular vote. Once the state decides to allow its citizens to vote for President, their right to vote is "fundamental" and subject to the requirements of the Equal Protection Clause. The Court was less than precise in defining these requirements. It stated the general principle that "equal weight" should be accorded to each vote, and "equal dignity" to each voter, and, later, that: "Having once granted the right to vote on equal terms, the State may not, by later arbitrary and disparate treatment, value one person's vote over another." But the Court did not precisely define the constitutional standard applicable to equal protection violations concerning the counting of votes.

Instead, the Court focused on the particular features of Florida's recount that it thought problematic. Those problems included: (1) the lack of "specific rules designed to ensure uniform treatment" of ballots, (2) consequent differences in how ballots were treated among different counties, (3) differences in how ballots were treated within counties, from one recount team to another, (4) the Florida Supreme Court's "ratification" of this differential treatment of similar ballots, (5) the fact that recounts in three counties (Miami–Dade, Palm Beach, and Broward) were not limited to undervotes, but extended to overvotes as well, (6) the inclusion of a partial total from one county (Miami–Dade), without assurance that the final certification would reflect a complete total, and (7) the Florida Supreme Court's failure to specify who would recount ballots, resulting in the creation of "ad hoc teams" at the county level with no training in counting ballots.

The majority opinion in *Bush v. Gore* cited just four equal protection cases in support of its ruling on the merits: *Harper v. Virginia Board of Elections*, 383 U.S. 663 (1966) (Chapter 3.B), which struck down the poll tax, and three one person, one vote cases, including *Reynolds v. Sims*, 377 U.S. 533 (1964) (Chapter 4.B). The Court was not clear on the level of scrutiny being applied. Its citation to *Harper* and the one person, one vote cases may be understood as suggesting some form of heightened scrutiny, as was applied in those cases. On the other hand, the Court's reference to "*arbitrary* and disparate" treatment implies rational basis review.

The scope of the Court's equal protection holding, and thus its implications for other disparities in the administration of elections, was likewise unclear. This resulted in a vigorous and still-continuing debate over its relevance to subsequent election administration disputes. Some interpret the opinion narrowly, focusing on the Court's statement that "the recount process, in its features here described, is inconsistent with the minimum procedures necessary to protect the fundamental right of each voter in the special instance of a statewide recount under the authority of a single state judicial officer." See Daniel Hays Lowenstein, *The Meaning of* Bush v. Gore, 68 OHIO ST. L.J. 1007 (2007). Others have read it to prohibit inter-jurisdictional disparities in how votes are treated, similar to the one person, one vote cases that *Bush v. Gore* cites. Still others have understood *Bush v. Gore* to condemn excessive discretion vested in local officials, and the resulting opportunities for partisan officials to favor their preferred candidate. See Edward B. Foley, *The Future of* Bush v. Gore?, 68 OHIO ST. L.J. 925 (2007); Daniel P. Tokaji, *Leave It to the Lower Courts: Judicial Intervention in Election Administration*, 68 OHIO ST. L.J. 1065 (2007). While the U.S. Supreme Court has not relied on *Bush v. Gore* in subsequent cases, the dispute over the majority opinion's meaning has played out in a number of lower court decisions, discussed below.

(2) The Remedy

Perhaps the most controversial aspect of the majority opinion was the remedy. After concluding that Florida's recount process violated the Equal Protection Clause, the Court considered whether it would be possible to conduct a constitutional recount.

After noting the practical difficulties in conducting a recount in accordance with the requirements of equal protection and due process, the majority turned to the so-called "safe harbor" date contained in the Electoral Count Act of 1887, 3 U.S.C. § 5. This federal statute requires that, if a state provides for a final determination of its electors (including resolution of contests) six days before the presidential electors meet, Congress must honor the state's choice of electors when it counts electoral votes. In 2000, the safe harbor date was December 12, the very same day that the opinion in *Bush v. Gore* came down.

The *Bush v. Gore* majority interpreted a previous opinion of the Florida Supreme Court to find that the Florida legislature intended to avail itself of this safe harbor. That meant that all post-election litigation must be resolved by December 12, as a matter of state law. It was impossible for Florida to conduct a recount that met constitutional standards within the timeframe prescribed by state law. The Court thus reversed the Florida Supreme Court's recount order outright, rather than remanding to allow a recount pursuant to uniform standards. The effect was to end the election in Bush's favor.

(3) The Article II Issue

Chief Justice Rehnquist joined the *per curiam* majority opinion, but also wrote a separate concurring opinion, joined by Justices Scalia and Thomas. That opinion identified an alternative constitutional ground on which, these three justices believed, the Florida Supreme Court's decision was in error.

Chief Justice Rehnquist concluded that the recount ordered by the Florida Supreme Court violated the requirement in Article II, Section 1, Clause 2 of the Constitution that presidential electors be appointed by each state "in such Manner as the *Legislature* thereof may direct" (emphasis added). Quoting *McPherson v. Blacker*, 146 U.S. 1 (1892), Chief Justice Rehnquist emphasized that Article II "leaves it to the legislature exclusively to define the method" of choosing presidential electors. He thought that the Florida Supreme Court had improperly supplanted the Florida legislature's role. Specifically, Chief Justice Rehnquist took issue with the Florida Supreme Court's interpretation of Florida statutes regarding the certification deadline, an "error in vote tabulation," and a "legal vote," concluding that "[n]o reasonable person" would interpret these provisions in the way that the Florida Supreme Court majority had.

Calling the Florida Supreme Court's interpretation of state election law "peculiar" and "absurd," Chief Justice Rehnquist determined that it had violated Article II by failing to honor the state legislature's directions on how presidential elections should be conducted. In addition, Chief Justice Rehnquist wrote that the Florida Supreme Court's order jeopardized the Florida legislature's desire to avail itself of the safe harbor provided by 3 U.S.C. § 5.

(4) The Dissents

Justices Stevens, Souter, Ginsburg, and Breyer each wrote separate dissenting opinions disagreeing with various aspects of the majority and concurring opinions. The four dissenting justices are best understood as falling into two groups.

One group consisted of Justices Stevens and Breyer, both of whom agreed with the majority that there was an equal protection problem with the manner in which Florida's recount was being conducted, but disagreed with the majority's remedy. Rather than ending the recount—and effectively ending the election—as the majority did, Justices Souter and Breyer would have remanded to the Florida Supreme Court. This would have allowed the possibility of a recount being conducted with uniform standards, in conformity with the requirements of the U.S. Constitution. Justice Breyer thought that it was up to Florida's courts to decide whether state law mandated that election controversies be resolved by the safe harbor date, and whether there was time to recount in time for the Electoral College meeting six days later. In addition, Justice Breyer opined that the Constitution and Electoral Count Act give Congress rather than the courts the primary role in resolving close presidential elections.

The other two dissenters, Justices Stevens and Ginsburg, did not believe there was any constitutional problem with the manner in which Florida's recount had been conducted. Justice Stevens' dissenting opinion took particular issue with the majority for its "unstated lack of confidence in the impartiality and capacity of the state judges who would make the critical decisions if the vote count were to proceed," believing that this decision undermined public confidence "in the judge as an impartial guardian of the rule of law."

(5) The Aftermath

The decision in *Bush v. Gore* effectively ended the 2000 presidential election. The next evening, Gore officially conceded. However, disputes over the meaning of the *Bush v. Gore* and, more broadly, the application of the Fourteenth Amendment election administration have persisted. In fact, there has been a marked increase in election litigation since 2000. Election litigation has risen from a pre–2000 average of 94 cases per year, to a post–2000 average of 242.5 cases per year. Richard L. Hasen, *The 2012 Voting Wars, Judicial Backstops, and Resurrection of* Bush v. Gore, __ GEO. WASH. L. REV. __ (forthcoming 2013).

The following discussion traces two lines of constitutional cases in the area of election administration: (1) burdens on voting, such as voter identification requirements, and (2) unequal treatment of voters, such as the use of different types of voting technology.

2.   BURDENS ON VOTING

a. Voter Identification

Voter identification has been the most hotly contested—and one of the most heavily litigated—election administration issue since *Bush v. Gore.* There is no generally applicable voter identification requirement under federal law. Many states, however, have adopted laws requiring voters to present some form of identification when they register or vote. The strictest of these laws require voters to show government-issued photo identification, such as a driver's license. Proponents of these laws (mostly Republicans) argue that they are needed to prevent voting fraud, while opponents (mostly Democrats) argue that they will reduce participation, especially by racial minorities, poor people, college students, and elderly voters. Photo identification requirements have been adopted in several states, including Georgia, Indiana, Texas, Tennessee, and Wisconsin. There have been several cases challenging voter identification laws, including cases under the Voting Rights Act of 1965 (discussed in Chapter 6) and state constitutions, as well as the U.S. Constitution.

The Supreme Court has decided two cases regarding state voter identification laws. The first was *Purcell v. Gonzalez*, 549 U.S. 1 (2006), involving an Arizona state law requiring voters to show either one form of photo identification or two forms of non-photo identification. In *Purcell*, the Supreme Court issued a brief *per curiam* opinion, vacating an injunction against Arizona's law that had been issued by the Ninth Circuit. While not ruling on the merits, the Supreme Court suggested that lower courts should be cautious in issuing injunctions against state election laws shortly before Election Day. The Court relied on the "voter confusion and consequent incentive to remain away from the polls" that court orders may induce. In addition, the Court suggested that real or perceived voter fraud, which voter identification laws are supposedly designed to combat, might cause legitimate voters to refrain from voting.

The Supreme Court's other decision regarding voter identification, *Crawford v. Marion County Election Board*, 553 U.S. 181 (2008), is more significant. In that case, the Court upheld Indiana's photo identification law against a facial challenge. There were six votes on the Court to uphold the law, but no opinion commanded a majority. The justices split into three groups of three. Justice Stevens wrote the lead opinion, which was joined by Chief Justice Roberts and Justice Kennedy. Justice Scalia concurred in the judgment and wrote a separate opinion, joined by Justices Thomas and Alito. Justice Souter (joined by Justice Ginsburg) and Justice Breyer both wrote dissenting opinions.

Justice Stevens' opinion noted that some burdens on voting, like the poll tax struck down in *Harper*, are subject to heightened scrutiny because they are "invidious," while other voting rules are subject to a more deferential standard. Justice Stevens referred approvingly to the "balancing approach" set forth in *Anderson v. Celebrezze*, 460 U.S. 780 (1983), and refined in *Burdick v. Takushi*, 504 U.S. 428 (1992) (both discussed in Chapter 9.D). These cases require courts to consider the "character and magnitude" of the alleged burden on voting, against the "precise interests put forward by the State." Under the *Anderson–Burdick* standard, "severe" burdens on voting are subject to strict scrutiny, meaning that they must be narrowly tailored to serve a compelling state interest. On the other hand, "reasonable, nondiscriminatory restrictions" are subject to less searching review, and may generally be justified by "the State's important regulatory interests." Although *Anderson* and *Burdick* involved different types of burdens—the former a restriction on candidate's ballot access, and the latter a prohibition on write-in voting—Justice Stevens lead opinion concluded that the same sort of balancing test applies to voter identification laws.

Justice Stevens' opinion went on to uphold Indiana's law against a facial challenge, based on the state's interests in modernizing its election system, preventing voter fraud, and safeguarding voter confidence. While noting that the law may burden some voters, Justice Stevens found that burden "neither so serious nor so frequent as to raise any question about the constitutionality" of Indiana's law. Justice Stevens also emphasized that plaintiffs bore a "heavy burden of persuasion" because they were making a facial challenge to the law, seeking to have it declared invalid in all its applications. As the Court has done in other recent cases like *Washington State Grange v. Washington State Republican Party*, 552 U.S. 442 (2008) (Chapter 9.C), Justice Stevens noted that facial challenges are disfavored, seeming to leave the door open to future as-applied challenges against Indiana's law or others burdening the vote.

Justice Scalia's concurring opinion rejected the challenge to Indiana's voter identification law on more categorical grounds than Justice Stevens' lead opinion. While agreeing that the Court should apply the standard set forth in *Burdick*, he objected to a record-based "balancing" of the state's interests against the burdens imposed on individual voters. Instead, Justice Scalia urged a two-track approach, under which severe burdens on voting are subject to strict scrutiny while non-severe burdens are subject to deferential review. Justice Scalia argued that "individual impacts" of a law are irrelevant to measuring its severity. The proper question, instead, is whether the burdens "go beyond the merely inconvenient." Because Indiana's law did not impose a severe burden on voting but was "eminently reasonable," Justice Scalia agreed with Justice Stevens that it should be upheld. The difference is that Justice Stevens' lead opinion applied a context-specific balancing test, while Justice Scalia's concurring opinion applies a two-track test, which avoids detailed supervision of laws that merely impose an inconvenience on voters.

The dissenting opinions by Justice Souter and Justice Breyer both expressed the view that Indiana's law imposed an unconstitutional burden on certain voters. Like Justice Stevens' lead opinion, Justice Souter's dissenting opinion followed a balancing approach drawn from *Anderson* and *Burdick*. Justice Souter also agreed that the burden was not "severe" as defined in those cases. Where the two opinions diverged was in their weighing of the burdens on voters against the interests set forth by the state. Justice Souter found the burden imposed by Indiana's law to be serious, though not severe, given the financial and logistical challenge it presented to the roughly 43,000 voting-age residents lacking the required identification. Justice Souter also highlighted the state's failure to produce any evidence of a genuine problem with in-person voter impersonation fraud. Justice Breyer's dissent also applied a balancing test, finding that the burden imposed by Indiana's unusually restrictive law— particularly its burden on poor, elderly, and disabled voters—was not adequately justified by the state's asserted interests.

From a doctrinal perspective, the most significant aspect of *Crawford* is its application of *Anderson– Burdick* balancing to state laws that allegedly burden voting. A clear majority of justices thought that the Court should balance the asserted state interests against the burdens imposed on voters, even when those burdens are not severe. The characterization of the constitutional standard in Justice Stevens' lead opinion is very similar to that in Justice Souter's dissent, although they arrive at different conclusions in applying this standard. While Justice Breyer does not expressly rely on *Anderson* and *Burdick*, he too takes a balancing approach. By contrast, Justice Scalia's concurring opinion, while also citing *Burdick*, would eschew balancing in favor of a "two-track approach," under which severe burdens are presumptively unconstitutional and nonsevere burdens are subject to deferential review.

b. Other Burdens

Since *Crawford*, the lower courts have generally followed Justice Stevens' lead opinion, balancing the state's asserted interests against the burdens imposed by state election law. A noteworthy example is the Sixth Circuit's decision in *Northeast Ohio Coalition for the Homeless v. Husted*, 696 F.3d 580 (6th Cir. 2012) (*NEOCH*). That case challenged Ohio's rules for counting provisional ballots under the Fourteenth Amendment.*

Like other states, Ohio has many polling locations where voters from multiple precincts vote. Under Ohio law, ballots cast in the wrong precinct are not counted, even if the voter appears at the right polling location, but is directed to the wrong precinct due to a poll worker's error. In *NEOCH*, the Sixth Circuit relied on *Crawford* and applied the *Anderson–Burdick* balancing test. It concluded that there was a substantial burden on voters, over

---

* The author filed an amicus brief in support of plaintiffs on the issue of provisional ballots cast in the correct polling location but wrong precinct.

10,000 in recent federal election cycles, whose provisional ballots were rejected because they were cast in the wrong precinct. On the other side of the ledger, the state had scant interest in rejecting provisional ballots miscast due to poll worker error.

After balancing the interests on both sides, *NEOCH* found a likely equal protection violation for those voters who cast their ballots in the right polling location but wrong precinct due to poll worker error. For similar reasons, there was also a likely due process violation. On other hand, the court found no likely constitutional violation with respect to voters whose provisional ballot affirmations were lacking information required by state law, since those errors arose from voters' failure to follow simple instructions. *NEOCH* is therefore a good example of the application of the balancing test embraced by a majority of justices in *Crawford*, finding one aspect of Ohio provisional voting law likely unconstitutional and another likely constitutional.

3.   UNEQUAL TREATMENT

Another line of cases focuses on the unequal treatment of different groups of voters. The most noteworthy examples since 2000 are cases challenging the use of allegedly inferior voting technology in some parts of a state but not others. Other examples include challenges to the disparities in the handling of provisional ballots or in who may use early voting. In all of these cases, the core allegation is that the state is unconstitutionally discriminating in favor of some voters and against others, in violation of the Equal Protection Clause. In this sense, these cases are more similar to *Bush v. Gore* than *Crawford*, insofar as their focus is on differential treatment of certain groups of voters rather than the burdens imposed on individual voters. Yet the courts have generally applied the *Anderson–Burdick* framework, the same test used in *Crawford*, in assessing such claims.

a. Voting Equipment

The first wave of voting discrimination cases after *Bush v. Gore* challenged punch-card voting systems. Plaintiffs alleged that the use of these systems denied equal protection because voters using this type of system were significantly more likely to have their votes rejected than voters using other types of equipment. This phenomenon is generally attributed to problems that voters have in punching the chad completely, as in Florida's 2000 election, as well as the failure of these systems to notify voters when they mark their ballots improperly. Plaintiffs argued that these inter-jurisdictional disparities denied equal protection, effectively discriminating against voters using less reliable punch-card voting systems.

The Supreme Court did not decide any cases involving challenges to punch-card voting equipment, but several lower courts did.* The

---

* The author was co-counsel for plaintiffs in the *Common Cause v. Jones, Southwest Voter Registration Education Project v. Shelley*, and *Stewart v. Blackwell* cases, described in this section.

district courts in *Black v. McGuffage*, 209 F. Supp. 2d 889 (N.D. Ill. 2002) and *Common Cause v. Jones*, 213 F. Supp. 2d 1106 (C.D. Cal. 2001) both denied motions to dismiss constitutional claims challenging punch-card voting systems. Later, a panel of the Ninth Circuit ordered the postponement of California's 2003 recall election until punch-card systems could be replaced, on the ground that their continuing use likely denied equal protection, but that injunction was vacated by the *en banc* Ninth Circuit. The *en banc* court emphasized that enjoining an impending election is an extraordinary remedy, which was not justified in that case. *Southwest Voter Registration Education Project v. Shelley*, 344 F.3d 914 (9th Cir. 2003).

Perhaps the most significant punch-card voting system decision was *Stewart v. Blackwell*, 444 F.3d 843 (6th Cir. 2006). A divided panel of the Sixth Circuit found that Ohio's use of non-notice punch-card and optical-scan voting systems in some counties but not others likely violated the Equal Protection Clause. The panel relied on statistical evidence showing that voters in punch-card counties were about four times as likely not to have their votes counted as voters in counties using electronic equipment. Citing *Bush v. Gore*, the panel applied strict scrutiny and found that Ohio had failed to show that its continuing use of non-notice punch-card and optical-scan systems was narrowly tailored to a compelling state interest. A dissenting opinion by Judge Gilman, on the other hand, argued that *Bush v. Gore* should be given a narrow reading and that rational basis review should apply. The Sixth

Circuit later granted *en banc* review, vacating the panel decision. The *en banc* court ultimately concluded that the case was moot due to Ohio's planned replacement of the challenged voting equipment. This left no binding precedent from any circuit court on whether the use of punch-card voting machines violate equal protection.

After the Help America Vote Act of 2002 (HAVA) provided federal money for election improvements (Part B.3 below), many jurisdictions replaced their old voting equipment with electronic touchscreen systems. Some technology experts and advocates objected to paperless electronic voting technology, arguing that it is insufficiently secure. As a remedy, they demanded a voter-verifiable paper audit trail to be used in the event of a recount. Some states chose to adopt electronic systems with such a paper record. In other states, lawsuits were filed challenging the use of paperless electronic systems on constitutional grounds. Some of these cases alleged that the use of unreliable equipment denied equal protection, since voters were deprived of a paper record that could be used to verify the accuracy of election results.

Although the Supreme Court has not decided any cases challenging electronic voting systems on constitutional grounds, several lower courts have rejected such claims. The most noteworthy is *Wexler v. Anderson*, 452 F.3d 1226 (11th Cir. 2006), in which the Eleventh Circuit considered a constitutional challenge to Florida's deployment of paperless electronic systems. Plaintiffs, including

Democratic U.S. Congressman Robert Wexler of Florida, argued that voters using these systems were denied equal protection, because there was no paper ballot to review in the event of a manual recount. Citing *Anderson* and *Burdick*, as well as *Bush v. Gore*, the Eleventh Circuit rejected the claim. The court noted that plaintiffs "did not plead that voters in touchscreen counties were less likely to cast effective votes." It found the burden on these voters to be the product of a "reasonable, nondiscriminatory regulation," and thus declined to apply strict scrutiny, upholding Florida's use of paperless electronic systems based on the state's "important regulatory interests." The court also rejected a due process claim alleging that the use of paperless systems denied voters "fundamental fairness," finding any burden on voters justified by the same state interests. The Ninth Circuit had previously rejected a constitutional challenge to electronic voting technology on similar grounds in *Weber v. Shelley*, 347 F.3d 1101 (9th Cir. 2003).

b. Absentee Voting, Early Voting, and Provisional Voting

Other cases have alleged unequal treatment with respect to the counting of absentee and provisional ballots. The Minnesota Supreme Court considered federal constitutional claims of unequal treatment, in connection with the contested 2008 U.S. Senate election between the Republican candidate and then-incumbent Norm Coleman, and the Democratic candidate, author and comedian Al Franken. *In re Contest of General Election Held on November 4,*

2008, for Purpose of Electing a U.S. Senator from State of Minnesota (Sheehan v. Franken), 767 N.W.2d 453 (Minn. 2009). That court rejected Coleman's claim arising from local variations in the counting of absentee ballots. It was unpersuaded by Coleman's contention that the non-uniform treatment of absentee ballots denied equal protection. In contrast to *Bush v. Gore*, the court found that there were "clear statutory standards for acceptance or rejection of absentee ballots, about which all election officials received common training." The court also found it relevant that election officials did not know each absentee voter's choice of candidate when determining whether the ballot should count, also unlike Florida election officials in 2000. The court thus suggests that concern about election officials manipulating election results is at the root of *Bush v. Gore*. Finally, the Minnesota Supreme Court also rejected Coleman's claim that the trial court's requirement of "strict compliance" with absentee voting laws violated the Due Process Clause.

In addition to the Minnesota recount litigation, two Sixth Circuit cases arising from Ohio are noteworthy examples of litigation challenging unequal treatment of voters. The first, *Hunter v. Hamilton County Board of Elections*, 635 F.3d 219 (6th Cir. 2011) concerned disparities in the handling of provisional ballots cast in the wrong precinct. This case arose from an extremely close judicial election in southwestern Ohio. The issue was similar to that addressed in the subsequent *NEOCH* litigation, discussed above. Under Ohio law, provisional ballots cast in the wrong precinct are not counted. Contrary to state law, the county board of elections had counted some provisional ballots cast in the wrong precinct, but it refused to count other wrong-precinct provisional ballots. The Sixth Circuit upheld a preliminary injunction issued by the district court, on the ground that the unequal treatment of provisional ballots was likely unconstitutional. Citing *Crawford, Burdick* and *Anderson*, the Sixth Circuit concluded that the "discriminatory disenfranchisement" of some provisional voters likely denied them equal protection, given the state's failure to identify " 'precise interests' that justified the uneven treatment."

The other Sixth Circuit case concerned the unequal treatment of voters with respect to early voting. The Ohio state legislature amended its early voting laws in 2011. The amendments were ambiguous, but the Ohio Secretary of State interpreted them to eliminate in-person early voting for most voters during the last three days before Election Day, while allowing early voting for military voters and citizens who reside overseas. Military and overseas voters enjoy special protection for absentee ballots under the federal Uniformed and Overseas Citizens Absentee Voting Act (UOCAVA), but this does not include the right to in-person early voting.

In *Obama for America v. Husted*, 697 F.3d 423 (6th Cir. 2012), plaintiffs challenged the differential treatment of military and overseas voters, as compared to others, under the Equal Protection Clause. Applying the "flexible standard" set forth in *Anderson* and *Burdick*, the Sixth Circuit held this to be a likely equal protection violation. The court cited evidence that non-military voters would be precluded from voting if the last three days of early voting were eliminated, the court determined that Ohio had both "classified voters disparately and . . . burdened their right to vote." Finding insufficient evidence of administrative difficulties or a special need to accommodate military voters during this period, the Sixth Circuit concluded that the disparate treatment likely denied equal protection to those affected by the shortened early voting period.

The *Obama for America* decision combines *Bush v. Gore*'s focus on disparate treatment with *Crawford*'s focus on burdens to individual voters. Like the other cases discussed in this section, it applies the general *Anderson–Burdick* framework, which calls on courts to consider the "character and magnitude" of injuries resulting from a restriction on voting, as well as the state's asserted interests. In balancing the injuries imposed by a voting law against its benefits, courts will generally consider *both* unequal treatment of different groups of voters *and* the magnitude of the burden imposed on individual voters. The stronger the evidence of either type of injury, the heavier the state's burden of justification will be.

B.　FEDERAL STATUTES

So far, this chapter has concentrated on the federal constitutional law governing election administration. We now turn to federal statutory law. Although election administration is mostly a matter of state law and local practice, there are three especially important federal statutes germane to this area. The first is the Voting Rights Act of 1965 (VRA), as amended, discussed in Chapter 6 with reference to minority representation. This section will address the VRA's application to laws alleged to abridge *participation* by racial, ethnic, and language minorities. The second statute is the National Voter Registration Act of 1993 (NVRA), commonly known as the "Motor Voter" law, which expanded opportunities to register to vote in federal elections. The third statute is the Help America Vote Act of 2002 (HAVA). Enacted in the wake of the 2000 election, this statute represents the federal government's most comprehensive intervention in state and local election administration practices. There are other laws addressing the specific needs of specific populations, such as the Uniformed and Overseas Citizens Absentee Voting Act (UOCAVA) and the Americans with Disabilities Act of 1990 (ADA), but the VRA, NVRA, and HAVA are the most important federal statutes governing election administration.

1.　THE VOTING RIGHTS ACT

The VRA was originally designed to end the mass disenfranchisement of African Americans in the

South. As described in Chapter 2, black voters were prevented from registering and casting a meaningful vote through an array of devices, including literacy tests, poll taxes, all-white primaries, and threats of violence. State and local election administrators were largely responsible for maintaining this system of disenfranchisement. A key means through which the VRA dismantled this system was its elimination of literacy tests in Section 4. As enacted in 1965, the literacy test ban was applicable only to covered jurisdictions for a limited time, but it was later extended nationwide and made permanent. Section 5 was critical in stopping other restrictive election administration practices. Until the decision in *Shelby County v. Holder*, 133 S. Ct. 2612 (2013), Section 5 required covered jurisdiction to obtain preclearance for voting changes (see Chapter 6.A). In the early years of the VRA, Section 5 prevented state and local jurisdictions from adopting new exclusionary practices once old ones had been stopped.

The VRA remains important in election administration today. Three requirements of the VRA are especially noteworthy.

a. Section 2's "Results" Test

Section 2 of the VRA prohibits any voting practice that "results in" the denial or abridgement of the vote account of race. The 1982 amendments to the VRA added the "results in" language, displacing the requirement of discriminatory intent that existed under prior law (as described in Chapter 6.A). Since the 1982 amendments, most of the cases arising under Section 2 have concerned practices alleged to result in *vote dilution*, such as at-large election schemes or redistricting plans that allegedly weaken minority voting strength. The three-part test adopted in *Thornburg v. Gingles*, 478 U.S. 30 (1986), was designed to address claims of vote dilution. There have been fewer cases concerning the application of Section 2 to *vote denial*—that is, claims that an election administration law or practice disproportionately prevents racial minorities from voting. The Supreme Court has not decided any cases concerning Section 2's application to such laws or practices, and there is limited lower court precedent on the subject. See Daniel P. Tokaji, *The New Vote Denial: Where Election Reform Meets the Voting Rights Act*, 57 S. C. L. REV. 689 (2006).

The most significant Section 2 cases in the area of election administration concern state laws disenfranchising prisoners and felons. Thus far, federal circuit courts have upheld such laws against Section 2 challenges, relying in part on Supreme Court precedent holding that felony disenfranchisement laws are constitutional absent discriminatory intent. See *Simmons v. Galvin*, 575 F.3d 24 (1st Cir. 2009); *Hayden v. Paterson*, 594 F.3d 150 (2d Cir. 2010); *Farrakhan v. Gregoire*, 623 F.3d 990 (9th Cir. 2010). There have also been Section 2 challenges to punch-card voting equipment and restrictive voter identification laws, alleging that these practices have a discriminatory impact on minority voters. The panel in *Stewart v. Blackwell*, 444 F.3d 843 (6th Cir. 2006) (discussed in

Part A.3 of this chapter), allowed a Section 2 challenge to punch-card voting equipment to proceed, but the *en banc* court later vacated the opinion and found the case moot. There is little precedent on the application of Section 2 to voter identification and other election administration practices alleged to have a discriminatory impact on minority voters.

b. Section 5 Preclearance

Section 5 of the VRA requires covered jurisdictions to obtain preclearance of any new voting practices from either the U.S. Department of Justice or the federal district court in Washington, D.C. Congress reauthorized the preclearance requirement in 1970, 1975, 1982, and 2006, but the Supreme Court struck down the coverage formula in *Shelby County*, effectively ending Section 5 preclearance (see Chapter 6.A).

Before *Shelby County*, Section 5 applied to election administration rules, including those affecting voter registration, voter identification, and early voting. Although most preclearance denials involved practices affecting minority representation like redistricting plans, some election administration practices were stopped or modified due to Section 5. Examples include a Texas law requiring government-issued photo identification in order to vote, and a Florida law reducing the period for in-person early voting. See *Texas v. Holder*, 888 F. Supp.2d 113 (D.D.C. 2012) (three-judge court); *Florida v. United States*, 885 F. Supp.2d 299 (D.D.C.

2012) (three-judge court). These cases relied on statistical evidence that the changes to state law would have a retrogressive effect on minority voters.

c. Language Assistance

Through amendments to the VRA adopted in 1975, Congress required that some state and local jurisdictions provide language assistance to voters who are not proficient in English. These requirements are found in Section 4(f)(4) and Section 203 of the VRA. 42 U.S.C. §§ 1973b(f)(4), 1973aa–1a. Like Section 5, these provisions were temporary, but have been extended three times, in 1982, 1992, and 2006. The extension of the language assistance provisions was one of the most controversial aspects of the VRA reauthorization in 2006.

Section 4(f)(4)'s coverage formula is based upon low registration and participation rates in the 1972 election, in jurisdictions using English-only materials with a substantial (more than 5%) language-minority population. Section 203's formula covers jurisdictions in which more than 5% of the voting population or more than 10,000 voting-age citizens are of a particular language minority group and have limited English proficiency. Protected language minority groups include Native Americans, Asian Americans, Alaskan Natives, and people of Spanish heritage. 42 U.S.C. § 1973l(c)(3). Covered jurisdictions must provide election materials in the relevant languages, including registration forms and ballots, as well as oral assistance to voters who need it. Section 203, like Section 2, may be enforced through private actions.

2.   THE NATIONAL VOTER REGISTRATION ACT

The NVRA (42 U.S.C. § 1973gg) is commonly known as "Motor Voter" because of its best known provision, which requires that eligible citizens be given the opportunity to register for federal elections at state motor vehicle offices. This requirement, however, is just one of the means through which the NVRA sought to facilitate voter registration. The NVRA requires that eligible citizens be allowed to register at state public assistance offices and offices providing services to people with disabilities. The NVRA also imposes restrictions on states seeking to remove, or "purge," voters from the rolls. In addition, the statute mandates a uniform federal form for mail registration, which states are required to "accept and use." 42 U.S.C. § 1973gg–4(a)(1). States that had election day registration on the NVRA's effective date are exempt from the statute, so long as they retain election day registration.

There is evidence that the NVRA resulted in more people being registered, although the impact on turnout is more difficult to measure. Lower courts upheld the NVRA as a permissible exercise of Congress' power to regulate congressional elections under the Elections Clause in Article I, Section 4 of the Constitution. See *ACORN v. Edgar*, 56 F.3d 791 (7th Cir. 1995); *Voting Rights Coalition v. Wilson*,

60 F.3d 1411 (9th Cir. 1995). The NVRA's "accept and use" requirement was before the Supreme Court in *Arizona v. Inter Tribal Council of Arizona*, 133 S. Ct. 2247 (2013). By a 7–2 vote, the Court held that this language preempted an Arizona law requiring documentary proof of citizenship to register. As the Court explained, the federal mail registration form comes with state-specific instructions which, in the case of Arizona, do not require proof of citizenship. Justice Scalia's majority opinion concluded that the NVRA's "accept and use" requirement prohibited Arizona from rejecting federal voter registration applications that lack proof of citizenship. The majority cited Congress' broad power to preempt state laws under the Elections Clause. Justice Kennedy concurred in the judgment and in all of the majority opinion except its discussion of preemption. Justices Thomas and Alito dissented, both disagreeing with the majority's broad understanding of Congress' preemptive power under the Elections Clause.

3.   THE HELP AMERICA VOTE ACT

Congress' most comprehensive intervention in the realm of election administration was HAVA, 42 U.S.C. § 15301 et seq. This statute included both financial incentives and statutory requirements designed to improve state and local election administration. Broadly speaking, HAVA areas affected four areas of election administration:

- *Voting Equipment.* HAVA provided money for state to upgrade their voting technology and, in particular, to replace antiquated punch-card and lever voting machines. In addition, it imposed limited requirements on voting systems, including auditability, language access, and disability access.

- *Voter Identification.* HAVA did not impose a general voter identification requirement on all voters. Instead, HAVA imposed a limited identification requirements on voters who register by mail, requiring them to provide identifying information—including *but not limited* to photo identification—when they vote for the first time.

- *Provisional Ballots.* As the name suggests, provisional ballots are ballots that are cast provisionally, usually where there is some question about the voter's eligibility. This requirement was designed mainly to prevent eligible citizens from being denied the vote due to registration problems. HAVA requires states to provide provisional ballots to voters whose names do not appear on the registration list and to those who lack the requisite identification when they appear to vote.

- *Statewide Voter Registration Database.* Before HAVA, most voter registration lists were maintained at the local level. HAVA changed that, requiring that a database be maintained at the state level. It also requires that the information in statewide registration databases be "matched" against other records.

In addition to these substantive requirements, HAVA provided federal money to improve election administration and created a new federal agency, the Election Assistance Commission (EAC). The EAC was charged with distributing HAVA funds and serving as a clearinghouse for research, but was not given the authority to issue rules or regulations, except for the implementation of certain provisions of the NVRA. 42 U.S.C. § 1973gg–7(a). The EAC was thus given very limited power. Leonard Shambon, *Implementing the Help America Vote Act*, 3 ELECTION L.J. 424 (2004). As of 2013, the EAC had no commissioners, and legislation had been introduced to abolish the agency.

One of the most important questions regarding HAVA is whether it is enforceable by private litigants or only by the U.S. government. Unlike Section 2 of the VRA and the NVRA, there is no express private right of action in HAVA. The question is whether it may be enforced under 42 U.S.C. § 1983, which affords a private right of action to those whose rights under federal law have been violated by those acting under color of state law. Although Section 1983 is usually used to enforce federal *constitutional* rights, it may also be used to enforce federal *statutory* rights, where those rights are "unambiguously conferred." Daniel P. Tokaji, *Public Rights and Private Rights of Action: The Enforcement of Federal Election Laws*, 44 IND. L. REV. 113 (2010). The Sixth Circuit held that HAVA's provisional voting requirements are privately enforceable under Section 1983 in *Sandusky County Democratic Party v. Blackwell*, 387 F.3d 565 (2004), although it went on to conclude that Ohio's refusal to count wrong-precinct provisional ballots was consistent with HAVA. In *Brunner v. Ohio Republican Party*, 555 U.S. 5 (2008), however, the U.S. Supreme Court held that another provision of HAVA is not privately enforceable. *Brunner* concerned HAVA's registration matching requirement, which the Ohio Republican Party claimed was not being followed by Ohio's Democratic Secretary of State. In a one-paragraph *per curiam* opinion, the Court unanimously concluded that Congress had not authorized private enforcement of this requirement. Note that this does not necessarily mean that the Sixth Circuit was wrong in *Sandusky County Democratic Party*. It is possible that one part of HAVA contains an "unambiguously conferred right," enforceable under Section 1983, while a different part of the same statute does not.

C.   STATE LAWS

The laws governing election administration come mostly from state legislatures, subject to the federal constitutional and statutory restraints set forth above. Each state's election laws and institutions may be thought of as a sort of ecosystem, consisting of many mutually interdependent parts. While it is impossible to capture the variety and complexity of state laws governing election administration, an overview of the key features of state election ecosystems is provided below.* As this summary reveals, there are important differences in state laws governing the administration of elections.

1. INSTITUTIONAL ARRANGEMENTS

Every state has a chief election authority, as well as local officials charged with running elections. The predominant model is for the state's chief election official—usually the Secretary of State—to be selected through a partisan election. In a minority of states, the chief election authority is either an appointed official or a multi-member board. Only one state, Wisconsin, has a nonpartisan state election authority, the Government Accountability Board. At the local level, elections are administered at the county level in most states and at the municipal level in others. There is considerable variety in how local election authorities are chosen, but approximately two-thirds of local election officials are elected, and almost half of local jurisdictions have party-affiliated officials running elections. David C. Kimball & Martha Kropf, *The Street–Level Bureaucrats of Elections: Selection Methods for Local Election Officials*, 23 REV. POL'Y RES. 1257 (2006). Prominent models of local election administration include bipartisan boards of election, nonpartisan appointed officials, and partisan elected officials. The U.S. is an outlier with respect to its institutional arrangements. Independent

---

* The ecosystem metaphor and most of the material below is drawn primarily from Steven F. Huefner, Daniel P. Tokaji & Edward B. Foley, FROM REGISTRATION TO RECOUNTS: THE ELECTION ECOSYSTEMS OF FIVE MIDWESTERN STATES (2007).

election commissions are the norm in most democratic countries.

2.   VOTER REGISTRATION

Every state but one (North Dakota) requires voter registration. The primary reason for having voter registration is to ensure the integrity of elections by preventing people from voting multiple times or otherwise cheating. Most states require voters to register in advance of Election Day. Section 202 of the VRA (42 U.S.C. § 1973aa–1) prevents states from requiring that voters be registered more than 30 days before presidential elections. Many states require registration 30 days in advance for all elections. A minority of states have Election Day Registration (EDR), under which voters are not required to register before Election Day, but may instead simultaneously register and cast their ballots on Election Day. Studies of EDR find that it is associated with an increase in turnout in states where it has been implemented. States that have had EDR in place since the effective date of the NVRA are exempt from the requirements of that federal law. Under HAVA, all states with voter registration must have a statewide registration database.

3.   VOTER IDENTIFICATION

Voter identification is another area in which requirements vary dramatically from one state to another. Some states do not require that voters show identification. Among states that require identification, the most significant dividing line is whether government-issued photo identification is required. In some states, either photo or non-photo identification—such as a utility bill, bank statement, or other document with the voter's name—is accepted. In other states, photo identification is required. Of those states, some allow voters lacking the required identification to sign an affidavit at the polls verifying their identity. The strictest form of voter identification law requires voters to present a government-issued photo identification without such an affidavit exception. This type of law was upheld by the U.S. Supreme Court in *Crawford v. Marion County Election Board*, 553 U.S. 181 (2008) (Part A.2.a of this chapter). Many state constitutions explicitly protect the right to vote, however, and some state courts have found that their state constitutions prohibit strict photo identification requirements. See, e.g., *Weinschenk v. State of Missouri*, 203 S.W.3d 201 (Mo. 2006).

4. PROVISIONAL VOTING

Provisional ballots are used to accommodate voters as to whom there is some question of eligibility when they arrive at the polls. HAVA requires that states offer provisional ballots to those who find that their names are not on the registration list or who lack proper identification when they appear to vote. Some states use provisional ballots for other reasons as well, such as for voters who have moved prior to Election Day without notifying election officials. There are major differences between states in the number of provisional ballots cast and in the percentage of provisional ballots counted. Some state laws provide that provisional ballots are to be counted even if cast in the wrong precinct, while others reject such ballots. HAVA does not require that provisional ballots cast in the wrong precinct be counted, but the Sixth Circuit held that it likely violates the Constitution to reject provisional ballots cast in the wrong precinct due to poll worker error. *NEOCH v. Husted*, 696 F.3d 580 (6th Cir. 2012) (Part A.2 of this chapter). Very few provisional ballots are cast in states with EDR, since voters in those states can correct errors by re-registering on Election Day. In some other states, tens or even hundreds of thousands of provisional ballots are cast in each election.

5.   EARLY AND ABSENTEE VOTING

Traditionally, absentee voting was used by voters who were unable to vote at the polling place on Election Day—for example, because they were away from home or physically unable to travel to the polls due to serious illness or disability. Section 202 of the VRA requires that absentee voting be made available to voters in presidential elections, but states otherwise have considerable latitude when it comes to absentee voting. Nowadays, mail-in absentee ballots and in-person early voting are made available as a convenience to voters, allowing them to vote before Election Day. Most state laws now provide for "no excuse" absentee voting, under which voters may request and cast an absentee ballot without an excuse for not voting on Election Day. And many states now offer in-person early voting available for several days prior to Election Day, usually at central locations established by local election authorities. Nationally, around 30% of ballots in presidential elections are now cast prior to Election Day.

6.   VOTING EQUIPMENT

Prior to HAVA, various types of voting systems were used, including punch-card ballots, optical-scan ballots, lever machines, electronic voting machines, and hand-counted paper ballots. Today, most jurisdictions use either optical-scan ballots, electronic voting machines, or some combination of the two types of technology. Most states using optical-scan ballots have scanners at the polling place, allowing voters to check for overvotes before they officially cast their ballots. Some states have laws requiring that electronic voting machines generate a voter-verifiable paper audit trail, which the voter may check before leaving the polls and which may serve as the official ballot of record in the event of a recount. In addition, many states clarified their laws after *Bush v. Gore*, to delineate the circumstances in which an unambiguously marked paper ballot will be considered a valid vote.

7.   POLLING PLACE OPERATIONS

Although early and absentee voting has become increasingly common, most voters nationwide still vote at polling places on Election Day. States typically have detailed rules about how polling places are organized and staffed, as well as how voting is supposed to take place. Polling places are generally staffed by volunteer poll workers, who receive a modest stipend for their work. Poll workers perform the on-the-ground work of running elections. That includes setting up polling stations in the morning, checking voters' registration status when they come in to vote, instructing them on how to use voting equipment, closing down the polls at the end of the day, and transmitting preliminary results. They must also ensure that federal legal requirements are followed, including the language access requirements of the VRA (discussed in Part B.1.c of this chapter) and Title II of the Americans with Disabilities Act of 1990, which requires reasonable accommodations for voters with disabilities. In addition, HAVA requires that every polling place have at least one voting station that is accessible to people with physical disabilities, including those with visual impairments. State laws generally prohibit electioneering within the polling place but may allow observers at the polling place on Election Day. In addition, some states allow voters to be challenged, if there are reasons to question their eligibility to vote. The use of this procedure has sometimes given rise to litigation alleging that challenges are being exercised in a discriminatory or otherwise unconstitutional manner.

8.　CANVASSES, RECOUNTS, AND CONTESTS

The final stage of an election is to count the ballots and determine the winner, a process governed by state law. The initial tabulation of votes, usually completed on the night of the election, is preliminary and unofficial. After Election Day, state or local officials "canvass" the results to arrive at an official determination of the vote totals and certification of the winner. The canvassing process usually includes the counting of absentee and provisional ballots that were not part of the initial tabulation. The timetable for this process is prescribed by state law and can take weeks. State laws also provide procedures that may be used in the event of a close election. The first step is typically a recount of ballots. Some state laws mandate a recount if the margin is within a certain percentage, while others allow a recount only if a candidate or other interested party requests it. State laws also provide for judicial proceedings in cases where election results are disputed, sometimes referred to as "contests." Part D describes remedies that may be ordered in such proceedings.

D.　JUDICIAL REMEDIES

What should courts do when they conclude that an election practice violates federal or state law? The answer depends in part on whether the challenge takes place before or after Election Day. Before elections, the most common remedy against an illegal election practice is an injunction. When pre-election litigation is brought, it may be feasible to issue an injunction against the challenged practice before the election begins. Where that is not possible, a court may in rare circumstances issue an order that an election be postponed until the problem can be fixed.

In many instances, however, the problem is not discovered or challenged until after the election has already begun—and sometimes not until after the preliminary determination of the winner. As described above, the first step in disputing an election is usually a recount. Where post-election litigation such as a contest is brought, it is sometimes possible to remedy the error by correcting vote totals, either adding or subtracting votes. In extreme circumstances where an error places the result in doubt, a court may order that a new election be conducted. In addition, civil damages and criminal penalties are available for certain kinds of election misconduct.*

These remedial possibilities are described in greater detail below, with reference to representative cases. In thinking about remedies for election wrongs, it is important to keep in mind that all these remedies are subject to the constitutional limitations described in Part A of this chapter— including the requirements of equal protection set forth in the *Bush v. Gore* majority opinion and, possibly, the Article II limitations on presidential

---

* For a comprehensive discussion of remedial possibilities for election problems, see Steven H. Huefner, *Remedying Election Wrongs*, 44 HARV. J. LEGIS. 265 (2007).

elections referenced in *Bush v. Palm Beach Canvassing Board* and Chief Justice Rehnquist's *Bush v. Gore* concurrence.

1.   ENJOINING A PARTICULAR PRACTICE

When a pre-election challenge to an election practice succeeds, the conventional remedy is to enjoin that practice. For example, in *NEOCH v. Husted*, 696 F.3d 580 (6th Cir. 2012), after finding Ohio's practice of rejecting provisional ballots cast in the right polling location but wrong precinct due to poll worker error, the Sixth Circuit upheld a preliminary injunction requiring that these ballots be counted. So too, if a voter identification law is found to violate the federal or state constitution, the court would generally issue an injunction preventing its enforcement.

At the same time, the Supreme Court has cautioned that enjoining an electoral process very close to election may cause substantial disruption. *Purcell v. Gonzalez*, 549 U.S. 1 (2006). Partly for this reason, *Purcell* reversed a preliminary injunction that the Ninth Circuit had issued against Arizona's voter identification law, without ruling on the merits of plaintiffs' claims. Thus, on a preliminary injunction motion, the balance of equities may sometimes counsel in favor of allowing a challenged practice to remain in place. That is especially true where an injunction is sought on the eve of an election, or where plaintiffs have delayed in filing suit without good reason. In such cases, the equitable doctrine of laches may be asserted by the defendant.

2.   ENJOINING AN ELECTION

In rare instances, a court may enjoin an election entirely until the challenged practice is corrected. It bears emphasis, however, that postponing an election is an extraordinary remedy which a court will generally order only where there is no alternative. In *Reynolds v. Sims*, 377 U.S. 533 (1964), which held that state legislative elections are governed by the one person, one vote rule, the Court emphasized the importance of "avoid[ing] a disruption of the election process which might result from requiring precipitate changes that could make unreasonable or embarrassing demands on a State." Following *Reynolds*, the Fifth Circuit reversed a district court order enjoining an election for the Louisiana Supreme Court in *Chisom v. Roemer*, 853 F.2d 1186 (5th Cir. 1988), based on a violation of Section 2 of the VRA. The Fifth Circuit concluded that the state and local authorities, including the state legislature, should first be given a chance to correct the problem. Similarly, in *Southwest Voter Registration Education Project v. Shelley*, 344 F.3d 914 (9th Cir. 2003) (en banc), the Ninth Circuit refused to postpone the California recall election until punch-card voting equipment could be replaced. According to the Ninth Circuit: "The decision to enjoin an impending election is so serious that the Supreme Court has allowed elections to go forward even in the face of an undisputed constitutional violation." Noting that

California's recall election had already begun—with hundreds of thousands of absentee ballots already cast—the Ninth Circuit held that an injunction was improper, without deciding the plaintiffs' constitutional claims on the merits.

While enjoining an election is an exceptionally serious remedy, there are circumstances in which it may be necessary. The quintessential example is the decision by the New York Governor and courts to postpone primary elections on September 11, 2001, given the extraordinary disruption resulting from the terrorist attacks of that day. This horrific event, however, is the exception confirming the general rule that injunctions of elections already in progress should be avoided.

3.   ADJUSTING VOTE TOTALS

What happens when an election law violation is not challenged until after an election? This scenario most commonly arises in close elections, where a contest or comparable state judicial proceeding is brought to challenge the outcome. The trailing candidate typically argues that certain votes should be counted, or that certain some votes should be excluded from the vote total. An example of the former is the Florida 2000 litigation (Part A.1 above), in which then-Vice President Gore pursued manual recounts that would yield him additional votes.

An example of the latter type of case, one in which votes were excluded from the total, is *In re the Matter of the Protest of Election Returns and*

Absentee Ballots, 707 So. 2d 1170 (Fla. App. 3d Dist. 1998). In that case, the court found substantial evidence of widespread fraud involving absentee ballots in the 1997 Miami mayoral election. The trial court had vacated the election and ordered a new one conducted, but the appellate court determined that the appropriate remedy for this fraud was to void all absentee ballots and determine election results based solely on ballots cast at the polls. This was dubious remedy, however, given that it effectively denied the votes of many innocent citizens who cast legitimate absentee ballots. Nevertheless, a federal court subsequently rejected a federal constitutional challenge to the Florida court's remedy, finding "good reason" for voiding all absentee ballots and that "voters must be presumed to have known of Florida's procedure of voiding all absentee votes if there was evidence of fraud." *Scheer v. City of Miami*, 15 F. Supp. 2d 1338 (S.D. Fla. 1998).

On the other hand, in *Akizaki v. Fong*, 461 P.2d 221 (Haw. 1969), the Hawaii Supreme Court concluded that it was improper under state law to discard 174 absentee ballots, on the ground that 19 of them were invalid. The court found the discarding of valid votes because others were invalid to be "too harsh a result," instead invalidating the election so that the governor could call a new one.

What is the appropriate remedy where the order of candidates' names on the ballot does not conform to state law? Social scientists have long documented the "primacy effect," the advantage that the candidate at the top of the ballot enjoys, presumably because some voters will predictably settle for the first-listed candidate whom they find acceptable. California law requires that candidates' names be listed based upon a random draw but, in *Bradley v. Perrodin*, 2003 WL 22725661 (Cal. App. 2003), an unintentional error resulted in the wrong candidate's name being listed first. Relying on statistical evidence, the trial court had ordered 295 votes be shifted to the candidate who should have been listed first, but the state court of appeals reversed. Finding this shifting of votes effectively disenfranchised the affected voters, the court of appeals concluded that the proper remedy was to annul the election.

4.   VOIDING AN ELECTION

State and federal courts are generally reluctant to invalidate an election that has already been conducted, even when violations of federal or state law occurred. In general, they will only void an election and order a new one if the errors are of sufficient magnitude to place the result in doubt and there is no legal alternative.

That said, there are cases in which elections have been invalidated due to violations of state law, including *Akizaki v. Fong* and *Bradley v. Perrodin*, discussed in the preceding section. Another example is *Ippolito v. Power*, 30 A.D.2d 924 (N.Y. App. Div. 2d Dep't 1968), which invalidated an election in which the winning margin was just 17 votes, with 101 improper or suspect votes. Finding that the irregularities could have changed the result, the court ordered a new election.

Another example of a voided election is *Whitley v. Cranford*, 119 S.W.3d 28 (Ark. 2003). In that case, a justice of the peace race was erroneously left off some ballots. 183 of the ballots cast in that election did not include that contest, and the winning candidate prevailed by just 55 votes. The ballot error thus rendered the result uncertain. Accordingly, the court held that the election must be voided.

These cases are best regarded as exceptions to the general rule that elections will not be invalidated merely because there have been some irregularities. After all, there are irregularities in virtually every election. But the majority rule, as stated by the California Supreme Court, is that "it is the duty of the court to validate the election if possible; that is to say, the election must be held valid unless plainly illegal." *Rideout v. City of Los Angeles*, 197 P. 74 (Cal. 1921). An example of the application of this rule is the Florida Supreme Court's decision to reject the challenge to the so-called "butterfly ballot" used in Palm Beach County during the 2000 presidential election. There was evidence that many voters who intended to vote for Gore were confused by this ballot format, causing them to vote for Reform Party candidate Pat Buchanan instead. The Florida Supreme Court nevertheless declined to void the election, emphasizing the heavy burden on those seeking this remedy. *Fladell v. Palm Beach County Canvassing Board*, 772 So. 2d 1240 (Fla. 2000).

Special concerns may come into play where a federal court is asked to void a state election based on a violation of *federal* law. See Kenneth W. Starr, *Federal Judicial Invalidation as a Remedy for Irregularities in State Elections*, 49 N.Y.U. L. REV. 1092 (1974). It is very unusual for a federal court to set aside the results of a state election. The leading case is *Bell v. Southwell*, 376 F.2d 659 (5th Cir. 1967), which involved a Georgia election "conducted under procedures involving racial discrimination which was gross, state-imposed, and forcibly state-compelled." While recognizing that invalidation of a state election is a "[d]rastic, if not staggering" remedy, the Fifth Circuit found that remedy justified by the flagrant constitutional violations documented in the record. On the other hand, in *Hamer v. Ely*, 410 F.2d 152 (5th Cir. 1969), the court refused to set aside the results of a municipal election that was allegedly tainted with racial discrimination. The court rejected the claim of civil rights hero Fannie Lou Hamer that the election was fundamentally unfair. The court found that the conduct of the election "may have been shoddy," but quoting *Bell v. Southwell*, that "does not justify the 'drastic, if not staggering' procedure" of voiding an election.

5.　CIVIL DAMAGES

Although injunctive relief is the usual remedy sought in cases challenging defective election practices, damages are sometimes awarded where someone's right to vote is denied. In *Nixon v. Herndon*, 273 U.S. 536 (1927), the Supreme Court refused to dismiss a claim for $5,000 in damages, brought by a black voter who claimed that he had been unconstitutionally prevented from voting due to a Texas law prohibiting blacks from participating in Democratic Party primaries. In *Wayne v. Venable*, 260 F. 64 (8th Cir. 1919), the Eighth Circuit affirmed an award of $2,000 damages to each of two voters denied the right to vote in Arkansas congressional elections. A more recent example is *Taylor v. Howe*, 225 F.3d 993 (8th Cir. 2000), in which the court held that an award of damages was an appropriate remedy in a case brought under 42 U.S.C. § 1983, for harassment and the intentional denial of the right to vote on account of race.

6.   CRIMINAL PENALTIES

Some violations of election law are punishable through criminal sanctions. Although criminal prosecutions cannot cure a violation that has already occurred, they may punish wrongdoers and deter similar violations in the future. Federal law criminalizes conspiracies to deprive people of their constitutional rights, as well as deprivation of constitutional rights under color of state law. 18 U.S.C. §§ 241, 242. The application of federal criminal law to state election officials was upheld in *United States v. Classic*, 313 U.S. 299 (1941). Federal criminal laws prohibit various forms of election-related misconduct, including paying people to vote, voter impersonation fraud, voting more than once, voter intimidation, submitting false registration forms, voting by noncitizens or ineligible felons, and registering or voting under a false name or address. States have comparable laws allowing for the prosecution of fraud and other election-related misconduct by election officials, voters, and others.

CHAPTER 8
DIRECT DEMOCRACY

To this point, this nutshell has focused mainly on the law governing representative democracy, which involves the election of candidates to public office. This chapter turns to direct democracy, which allows the people to vote directly on proposed laws and the retention of public officials. Part A addresses the history and principal mechanisms of direct democracy—the initiative, referendum and recall—as well as its pros and cons. Part B describes state substantive and procedural requirements. Part C discusses federal constitutional restraints on direct democracy in the states.

A. BACKGROUND

Direct democracy has a venerable history, stretching from the plebiscites of Ancient Greece and Rome, to New England town meetings, to state and local ballot initiatives of today. Madison famously contrasted a "pure democracy" in which citizens govern directly from a "republic" in which the people delegate power to representatives who govern. In *Federalist #10* (Chapter 1.A), he argued that pure democracy was more vulnerable to the mischief caused by faction, which he argued would inevitably lead to "turbulence and contention." The Constitution instead established a republican form of democracy at the federal level, in which the people act not directly but through their chosen representatives.

To this day, there is no direct democracy at the federal level, but most states have some form of direct democracy that supplements representative democracy. Every state but Delaware requires a public vote to amend the state constitution. Starting in the late Nineteenth Century, Populists and then Progressives urged the expansion of direct democracy. Direct democracy was viewed as a means by which to return power to the people and check the influence of wealthy special interests such as railroads. Many states adopted the three chief mechanisms of direct democracy: initiatives, referendums, or recalls.

The *initiative* is the mechanism of direct democracy that usually receives the most attention. Initiatives allow voters to adopt changes to state law directly, rather than going through the state legislature. If an initiative petition receives the requisite number of signatures, as set forth in state law, then the measure will appear on the ballot and become law if voters approve it. States may allow for the enactment of statutes, constitutional amendment, or both through initiatives.

The *referendum*, by contrast, allows voters to repeal a statute that has already been enacted by the legislature. As with initiatives, referendums qualify for the ballot through the collection of petition signatures. Usually, that will stop the challenged statute from going into effect until the election. If voters disapprove of the statute enacted by the state legislature, then it will never take effect.

Today, most states' laws provide for an initiative, referendum, or both. The terms "ballot measures" and "ballot propositions" are generally used, and will be used here, to include both initiatives and referendums. Ballot propositions were widely used in the early decades of the Twentieth Century. Their use declined significantly in the 1940s through 1960s, but increased again in the ensuing decades. Richard J. Ellis, DEMOCRATIC DELUSIONS: THE INITIATIVE PROCESS IN AMERICA (2002). Most initiative activity has been concentrated in a handful of states, with over 60% originating in six states (Arizona, California, Colorado, North Dakota, Oregon, and Washington). M. Dane Waters, INITIATIVE AND REFERENDUM ALMANAC (2003).

The third form of direct democracy is the *recall*, which allows citizens to remove an elected official before the expiration of his or her term. Like the initiative and referendum, a recall is placed on the ballot by collecting petition signatures. Recalls are less common than initiatives and referendums. The most prominent example in recent years is the 2003 recall of California Governor Gray Davis, the first state governor to be recalled in more than eight decades, who was replaced by actor-turned-politician (and now actor again) Arnold Schwarzenegger.

The chief rationale for direct democracy is to provide a check on elected politicians. Though sometimes referred to as a "gun behind the door," ballot measures are used frequently in some states. Between 1990 and 2000, there were 458 initiatives on the ballot nationwide. In California, for example, more initiatives were approved in the last two decades of the Twentieth Century than in the preceding 68 years, dating back to the initiative's adoption in the state.

There is a vigorous public and scholarly debate over direct democracy, with sharply differing perspectives on its pros and cons. The arguments commonly made in favor of direct democracy include the following:*

- It enables the people to hold elected officials and government generally *accountable.*

- It provides a *safety valve* against government being dominated by special interests, especially those with considerable resources to devote to lobbying.

- It promotes *democratic self-government* by giving the people a direct voice in the lawmaking process and spurring public debate over important issues.

- It allows *less powerful groups* to propose ideas to the public.

- It may help increase *voter turnout.*

The arguments commonly made against direct democracy include the following:

- It *undermines representative democracy.*

---

* These are mostly drawn from Thomas E. Cronin, DIRECT DEMOCRACY: THE POLITICS OF INITIATIVE, REFERENDUM, AND RECALL (1989).

- It *creates voter confusion* due to the large number and complexity of ballot measures, which many voters lack the competency to understand or assess.

- It leads to *unsound legislation*, given the absence of a review process (comparable to legislative committees) by which to fix problems.

- It *does nothing to reduce the influence of special interests*, and may actually exacerbate the disproportionate influence of wealthy interests, due to the high cost of qualifying a ballot measure and running a campaign.

- It *distorts the lawmaking agenda*, especially when it comes to funding, and leads to undesirable "ballot-box budgeting."

- It enables the *tyranny of the majority*, endangering the rights of unpopular individuals and groups who constitute a numerical minority of voters.

While there are varying opinions on the desirability of direct democracy, there is little question that the process for qualifying initiatives, referendums, and recalls today are quite different from what was envisioned by their original Populist and Progressive advocates. Getting something on the ballot is an expensive endeavor, in which professional consultants and paid signature gatherers play an important role. In a large state, it costs millions to get a ballot proposition or recall on the ballot. Campaigns are also expensive. Although the literature on the effect of money is mixed, there is evidence that large expenditures can be effective when used in opposition to a ballot measure, but are less effective when used in support of a ballot measure.

The remainder of this chapter focuses on laws and procedures governing the process of direct democracy. Part B discusses state substantive and procedural requirements, including the process for judicial review. Part C addresses federal constitutional requirements applicable to the process and products of direct democracy.

B.   STATE REQUIREMENTS AND JUDICIAL REVIEW

State laws impose both substantive and procedural constraints on direct democracy. We start with the single subject rule and other state rules limiting the substance of initiatives. Next, we consider the state procedural rules governing ballot propositions, including the qualification process. Finally, we turn to state rules regarding judicial review, including the availability of pre-election review of ballot measures.

1.   SINGLE SUBJECT RULES

Most initiative and referendum states have some form of a "single subject" rule. As the name suggests, this rule requires that a ballot measure address only one subject. There are also single subject rules applicable to laws enacted by legislative bodies. Most states purport to use the same rule for ballot measures and legislative enactments—although some courts apply the rule more strictly to ballot measures.

There are two main justifications for the application of the single subject rule to initiatives. One is that it prevents the *voter confusion* that might arise from an initiative encompassing multiple subjects. The other is that it prevents *logrolling*, the practice of packaging multiple items together in a single initiative, one or more of which would lack majority support if proposed on its own. Florida, Colorado, and Washington are among the states to have applied a strict version of the single subject requirement to initiatives. In addition, some states have "separate vote" requirements, which perform a similar function by requiring separate votes on items that are not sufficiently related. Oregon and Montana are notable for their application of a strong version of the separate vote requirement.

Single subject requirements have engendered a great deal of litigation, largely because there are multiple ways of characterizing the "subject" addressed by almost any ballot measure. The more broadly an initiative's subject matter is characterized, the more likely it will be found to satisfy the single subject rule. Conversely, the more narrowly an initiative's subject is described, the more likely it will be found in violation of this rule.

Florida has been the most stringent in the application of the single subject rule to ballot initiatives. Although Florida used to apply the same degree of deference to legislative enactments and initiatives, the Florida Supreme Court expressly adopted a more stringent standard for initiatives in *Fine v. Firestone*, 448 So. 2d 984 (Fla. 1984). The court based its less deferential approach to initiatives on the ground that initiatives do not go through the same process of legislative debate and public hearing as legislative enactments. *Fine* disallowed an amendment affecting governmental authority to tax, government user-fee operations, and the funding of capital improvements through revenue bonds. In so doing, the court rejected the argument that the initiative addressed the single subject of "revenue."

The Florida Supreme Court applied its strict standard again in *In re Advisory Opinion to the Attorney General*, 632 So.2d 1018 (Fla. 1994). That decision invalidated an initiative prohibiting the state, municipalities, or other government entities from establishing "any right, privilege, or protection for any person based upon any characteristic, trait, status, or condition, other than race, color, religion, sex, national origin, age, handicap, ethnic background, marital status, or familial status." The term "sex" was defined so as to exclude sexual orientation discrimination from protection. The court found that this initiative violated the single subject requirement in the Florida constitution. While its proponents argued that discrimination was the sole subject of the proposed amendment, the court found fault with the initiative for addressing both civil rights and the powers of a variety governmental entities, including municipalities, executive agencies, and the judiciary. The court also objected to the inclusion of ten different classifications that would be entitled to protection from discrimination, noting that some voters might favor anti-discrimination protection on some of these grounds while opposing others.

At the other end of the spectrum is the relatively deferential approach historically applied by the California Supreme Court. *Fair Political Practices Commission v. Superior Court*, 599 P.2d 46 (Cal. 1979), exemplifies the deferential approach. In that case, the California Supreme Court upheld the state's Political Reform Act, adopted by initiative in 1974. This initiative included provisions establishing the Fair Political Practices Commission, imposing disclosure requirements, limiting campaign spending, regulating lobbyists, establishing conflict-of-interest rules, regulating ballot pamphlet summaries of ballot measures, and establishing auditing procedures. The California Supreme Court applied a deferential standard, asking whether the provisions of the initiative are "reasonably germane" to one other. It concluded that the provisions of the Political Reform Act were all "reasonably germane to the subject of political practices." Thus, in contrast to the Florida Supreme Court, the California Supreme Court defined the subject of the initiative at a high level of generality.

The California Supreme Court has not been altogether consistent in its deferential application of the single subject rule. In *Senate of the State of*

California v. Jones, 988 P.2d 1089 (Cal. 1999), the California Supreme Court struck down a proposed initiative on single subject grounds. The initiative in that case would have changed the method for setting state legislators' salaries, restricted reimbursement of legislators for travel and living expenses, penalized legislators for not approving a budget by the deadline, and reassigned responsibility for redistricting from the legislature to the state supreme court. The court found that the redistricting change was not "reasonably germane" to the rest of the initiative, rejecting the argument that "voter involvement" was the single subject on the ground that it was too broad. In *Manduley v. Superior Court*, 41 P.3d 3 (Cal. 2002), however, the California Supreme Court returned to a more deferential posture, upholding an initiative that addressed the sentencing of repeat offenders, gang-related criminal activity, and the juvenile justice system. The common purpose of these provisions, *Manduley* found, was to address juvenile and gang-related crime.

While some commentators support the robust enforcement of single subject rules, others have criticized state courts for applying their single subject rules aggressively. The leading complaint is that judges tend to be influenced by their own policy views when considering single subject challenges, given the elasticity in the definition of the subject addressed by an initiative. See Daniel H. Lowenstein, *Initiatives and the New Single Subject Rule*, 1 ELECTION L.J. 35 (2002). There is some empirical support for this proposition, with one study finding a strong correlation between judges' partisan affiliations and their votes in single subject cases. John G. Matsusaka & Richard L. Hasen, *Aggressive Enforcement of the Single Subject Rule*, 9 ELECTION L.J. 399 (2010).

2. AMENDMENTS AND REVISIONS

In addition to the single subject rule, state laws impose various other substantive limitations on initiatives. Some states allow initiatives that "amend" the state constitution, but not ones that "revise it." Oregon and California are among the states with this type of limitation on making constitutional changes through the initiative process.

The California Supreme Court considers both quantitative and qualitative factors in determining whether a proposed change is an impermissible revision, rather than a permissible amendment. In *Raven v. Deukmejian*, 801 P.2d 1077 (Cal. 1990), it struck down an initiative providing that the state constitution shall not be construed to give greater rights to criminal defendants than the U.S. Constitution. The California Supreme Court thought the effect of this initiative to be "devastating," because it would deprive state courts of their authority to interpret the state constitution more broadly than the federal constitution. On the other hand, it upheld an initiative that imposed term limits on state elected officials, reduced the legislature's budget, and eliminated pensions for future state legislators, on the ground that it imposed no "change in [the] fundamental structure [of state government] or the foundational powers of its branches." *Legislature v. Eu*, 816 P.2d 1309 (Cal. 1991).

Most recently, California's distinction between constitutional amendments and revisions has arisen in relation to gay marriage. After the California Supreme Court held that a statutory ban on gay marriage violated the California Constitution, *In re Marriage Cases*, 183 P.3d 384 (Cal. 2008), voters enacted an initiative (Proposition 8) changing the state constitution to forbid recognition of same-sex marriages. In *Strauss v. Horton*, 207 P.3d 48 (Cal. 2009), the California Supreme Court held that Proposition 8 was a permissible amendment to the state constitution, rather than an impermissible revision. From a quantitative perspective, the court thought it "obvious" that Proposition 8 was just an amendment and not a revision, because it added only one fourteen-word section to the state constitution. The more difficult question was whether Proposition 8 amounted to a revision from a qualitative perspective, given the importance of the right taken away by the initiative. *Strauss* held that a qualitative revision is one that "makes[s] a fundamental change in the nature of the governmental plan or framework established by the Constitution." Thus, the fact that an initiative involves an important constitutional right is not enough to make it a revision. While Proposition 8 may have taken away an important right, the court concluded that it did not work a fundamental change; therefore, it was a permissible amendment rather than an impermissible revision.

3. OTHER CONTENT LIMITATIONS

People's Advocate v. Superior Court, 226 Cal. Rptr. 640 (Cal. App. 3d. Dist. 1986) exemplifies two other limitations on the initiative power. *People's Advocate* involved a challenge to a statutory initiative in California, entitled the "Legislative Reform Act of 1983." The initiative altered the internal operations of the state legislature and limited future appropriations. Because it was a *statutory* initiative, it had to comply with the requirements of the California Constitution.

The court in *People's Advocate* concluded that the initiative statute violated the state constitution on two grounds. First, the initiative impermissibly infringed on the legislature's power to make rules governing its operations. Specifically, the court found that the initiative invaded the state assembly and state senate's powers over their committees, staff, and internal proceedings under Article IV, Sections 7 and 11 of the California Constitution. Second, the court concluded that the initiative improperly restricted *future* state legislatures, through its limits on appropriations in support of the legislature. This limitation violated Article IV, section 12 of the California Constitution, which governs the appropriations process and gives the state legislature power to control the enforcement of budgets. The initiative impermissibly sought to tie the hands of future legislatures. The court proceeded to hold that other provisions of the initiative relating to public meetings and the public reporting of expenditures, not challenged in their own right, were severable from the unconstitutional portions and could therefore be given effect.

Note that California is one of many states which allow initiatives to amend the state constitution, as well as initiatives to amend statutes. As in some other states, the only difference is that an initiative constitutional amendment requires more signatures to get on the ballot than does an initiative statute. If the proponents of the Legislative Reform Act had proceeded by initiative constitutional amendment rather than initiative statute, the changes would presumably have been upheld (assuming they could be considered amendments rather than revisions to the state constitution).

In contrast to the California Constitution, as interpreted in *People's Advocate*, the Illinois Constitution *only* allows initiatives that alter legislative structures and procedures. The rationale is that the legislature itself is unlikely to propose changes to its own processes, even though they may be necessary. Illinois courts have strictly interpreted the state constitution's narrow scope for the initiative. For example, in *Coalition for Political Honesty v. State Board of Elections*, 359 N.E.2d 138 (Ill. 1976), the state supreme court held that initiatives must make *both* structural *and* procedural amendments to the legislative process to be constitutional. And in *Chicago Bar Association v. State Board of Elections*, 561 N.E.2d 50 (Ill. 1990), it struck down an initiative on the ground that it was not *limited* to structural and procedural changes, but also addressed the subject of increasing taxes or other revenues.

States have various other restrictions on the use of the initiative. They include bars against initiatives that:

- *Levy taxes or make appropriations.* The rationale is that, without such a restriction, a large percentage of the state's budget is controlled by past initiatives—as is the case in California. Philip L. Dubois & Floyd Feeney, LAWMAKING BY INITIATIVE (1998).

- *Resolve administrative questions,* as opposed to legislative questions. See *Foster v. Clark,* 790 P.2d 1 (Or. 1990) (rejecting an initiative to change a street name because it was an administrative issue).

- *Reverse decisions made by the legislature,* although such changes may be permitted by referendum.

- *Declare an opinion* on a public policy question, without legislating on the subject. See *AFL–CIO v. Eu,* 686 P.2d 609 (Cal. 1984).

4. PROCEDURAL REQUIREMENTS

States vary dramatically in the number and frequency with which the mechanisms of direct democracy are used. This variation is attributable in no small part to variations in states' procedural requirements for getting on the ballot. Here are the typical requirements:*

- *Number of signatures.* All direct democracy states require that petitioners gather a prescribed number of signatures to qualify for the ballot. This is often set as a proportion of votes cast for governor in the most recent gubernatorial election. Those signing must be registered voters, except in North Dakota which does not have voter registration.

- *Geographic distribution.* Some states require that petitioners show support throughout the state, not just in larger counties, by requiring that signatures be obtained from a prescribed number of counties.

- *Time period for collection.* States vary in their limitations on how long petitions may be circulated for signatures, ranging from 50 days to 360 days.

- *Title and Summary.* Because initiatives and referendum can be lengthy, all states provide for a brief summary of the proposal and most provide for an even shorter title, usually written by a state official.

- *Voting Requirements.* Some states require a majority of those voting on the measure to enact it, while others require a majority of all people

---

* These are drawn from David B. Magleby, *Direct Legislation in the American States*, in REFERENDUMS AROUND THE WORLD (1994).

voting in that election (including those who abstain from the measure). Some states require a supermajority.

An issue that sometimes arises with regard to the qualification of initiatives is whether strict compliance or only substantial compliance with procedural requirements is required. An example is *Costa v. Superior Court*, 128 P.3d 675 (Cal. 2006), which involved minor discrepancies between the text of the initiative filed with the Attorney General and the version circulated for signatures. The court rejected an attempt to remove the initiative from the ballot, holding that an "unreasonably literal or inflexible application" of the rules would be inconsistent with the purpose of the initiative process.

5.   JUDICIAL REVIEW

Litigation surrounding direct democracy is common. A frequent subject of litigation is compliance with procedural requirements. For example, a ballot measure's proponents may challenge a state official's decision that an initiative petition has not obtained the requisite number of valid signatures, or opponents may challenge the decision that it has. Proponents or opponents of ballot measures may also challenge the title and summary written by a state official, such as the Attorney General or Secretary of State. There are often lawsuits over a ballot measure's consistency with substantive requirements of state law, such as the single subject rule or the prohibition against constitutional revisions. Statutory initiative may be challenged over whether they comply with substantive requirements of the state constitution, as in *People's Advocate*. Both statutory and constitutional initiatives may also be challenged on the grounds that they violate the U.S. Constitution. (Some common federal constitutional challenges to state initiatives are discussed in Part C below.)

Under what circumstances is pre-election judicial review appropriate? In general, courts will consider challenges to compliance with *procedural* requirements in advance of an election. The reviewability of substantive challenges is a different matter. Some courts take the position that substantive challenges should not be considered until after the election. See, e.g., *Tilson v. Mofford*, 737 P.2d 1367 (Ariz. 1987). Others will consider challenges to ballot measures that allegedly violate state or federal constitutional law, on the ground that there is no point in having a vote on a measure that is "clearly unconstitutional." *Wyoming National Abortion Rights League v. Karpan*, 881 P.2d 281 (Wyo. 1994). Another approach is to distinguish two different types of substantive challenges: (1) those arguing that the ballot measure fails to comply with state substantive requirements for initiatives or referendums (e.g., the single subject rule), and (2) those arguing that the ballot measure's substantive requirements violate the federal or state constitution. The California Supreme Court differentiates between these two categories, holding that the former type of claim is "susceptible to resolution either before or after the election,"

Independent Energy Producers Association v. McPherson, 136 P.3d 178 (Cal. 2006), while the latter may presumptively be brought only after the election.

C.   FEDERAL CONSTITUTIONAL LIMITS

As a formal matter, state laws adopted through the initiative process are subject to the same constitutional restraints as state laws adopted through the legislative process. That said, there are some federal constitutional requirements that play an especially prominent role when it comes to the process and products of direct democracy. Although the Court has held challenges based on the Republican Guarantee Clause to be nonjusticiable, the First Amendment imposes restraints on state procedures for direct democracy, including the process of collecting petition signatures. In addition, certain types of ballot measures are susceptible to challenges under particular provisions of the U.S. Constitution, most notably the Equal Protection Clause and Qualifications Clause.

1.   THE REPUBLICAN GUARANTEE CLAUSE

Article IV, Section 4 of the U.S. Constitution provides in pertinent part that: "The United States shall guarantee to every state in this union a republican form of government. . ." Some have argued that direct democracy, at least in some of its forms, violates the Republican Guarantee Clause. This rests in part on the distinction that Madison drew in *Federalist #10* (Chapter 1.A), between a "republic" (by which he meant representative democracy) on the one hand, and a "democracy" (by which he meant direct democracy).

The Supreme Court has long held that claims under the Republican Guarantee Clause are nonjusticiable political questions. See *Luther v. Borden*, 48 U.S. 1 (1849) (Chapter 4.A). In *Pacific States Telephone & Telegraph Co. v. Oregon*, 223 U.S. 118 (1912), the Court relied on *Luther v. Borden* to reject a challenge to an Oregon initiative taxing certain corporations. *Pacific States Telephone & Telegraph* thus reaffirmed that constitutional claims based on the Republican Guarantee Clause, including challenges to state initiatives, are nonjusticiable political questions that a federal court may not decide. State courts have followed the Supreme Court in declining to rule on whether direct democracy violates the Republican Guarantee Clause. See, e.g., *Lowe v. Keisling*, 882 P.2d 91 (Or. Ct. App. 1994).

2. SPEECH AND PETITION RIGHTS UNDER THE FIRST AMENDMENT

While claims under the Republican Guarantee Clause are nonjusticiable, the First Amendment may be used to challenge state procedures for qualifying initiatives. Two Supreme Court decisions, both arising from Colorado, are especially significant with respect to state regulation of initiative petition circulation.

The first is *Meyer v. Grant*, 486 U.S. 414 (1988), in which the Court struck down a Colorado law making it a felony to pay petition circulators. The Court first concluded that the circulation of initiative petitions is protected political expression under the First Amendment, and that restrictions on petition circulation are subject to "exacting scrutiny" under *Buckley v. Valeo*, 424 U.S. 1 (1976) (Chapter 9.A). This level of constitutional scrutiny requires a "substantial relation" between the regulation and a "sufficiently important" government interest. *Meyer* reasoned that petition circulation is protected speech under the First Amendment, because it involves "interactive communication" between the circulator and the potential signatory. The Court rejected the argument that the state's greater power to eliminate ballot measures entirely encompasses the lesser power to restrict speech involving proposed initiatives. The Court went on to conclude that Colorado's ban on professional circulators did not satisfy exacting scrutiny. Specifically, *Meyer* concluded that the ban was not justified by the asserted interests in ensuring grassroots support for initiatives and preventing false signatures. The state had failed to demonstrate that the speech restriction was necessary to meet these concerns. In particular, the Court found the argument that paid petition circulation leads to greater fraud speculative.

Since *Meyer*, some lower courts have considered the related question whether the state may regulate the *manner* in which petition circulators are paid. The Eighth Circuit upheld a North Dakota law prohibiting circulators from being paid on a per-signature basis, citing the increased risk of fraud that this incentive would create. *Initiative and Referendum Institute v. Jaeger*, 241 F.3d 614 (8th Cir. 2001). On the other hand, the Sixth Circuit struck down an Ohio law prohibiting payment of petition circulators on any basis other than time worked. *Citizens for Tax Reform v. Deters*, 518 F.3d 375 (6th Cir. 2008). As the Sixth Circuit explained, the Ohio law was more onerous than those in other states, in that it banned not only per-signature payments, but also such practices as paying bonuses based on productivity, requiring circulators to collect a minimum number of signatures, and perhaps even the firing of a circulator for failing to collect sufficient signatures. The Sixth Circuit declined to reach the question whether a less onerous law, like North Dakota's, would violate the First Amendment.

The other Supreme Court case of special importance to petition circulation is *Buckley v. American Constitutional Law Foundation*, 525 U.S. 182 (1999) (*ACLF*). In that case, the Supreme Court struck down a Colorado law which mandated that petition circulators be registered voters. The Court found that the decision whether to register "implicates political thought and expression," and is thus protected by the First Amendment. Without specifying the level of scrutiny, the *ACLF* Court concluded that the registration requirement was not justified by the state's asserted interest in making sure that circulators who violate the law are subject to subpoena, as there were other means to serve this interest. The *ACLF* Court also struck down

Colorado's requirement that petition circulators wear name badges, finding that it would discourage people from circulating, but declined to rule on the requirement that circulators wear a badge indicating whether they are paid or volunteer. On similar grounds, the *ACLF* Court struck down Colorado's requirement that petition circulators' names and addresses, as well as the amounts paid to each, be disclosed. (The related subject of campaign finance disclosure is addressed in Chapter 10.E.)

ACLF's decision to strike down some provisions of Colorado's law rested on the interest in protecting the anonymity of petition *circulators*. In *Doe v. Reed*, 130 S. Ct. 2811 (2010), the Court considered a related issue: the anonymity of petition *signatories*. The Court rejected a broad challenge to a provision of Washington's Public Records Act making referendum petitions—including the names and addresses of signatories—subject to public disclosure. The case arose from a referendum petition seeking to stop a state statute expanding domestic partnership rights, including rights for same-sex couples. The petition's sponsor and some signatories alleged that the state law requiring disclosure of petitions violated the First Amendment. The majority opinion, written by Chief Justice Roberts and joined by five other justices, resolved the case on narrow grounds. It applied the test drawn from campaign finance disclosure cases (Chapter 10.E), requiring a substantial relation between the disclosure requirement and a sufficiently important governmental interest. The majority went on to find the state's asserted interest in election integrity sufficient to sustain the disclosure statute against a facial challenge. It left open the possibility, however, that plaintiffs might prevail in a narrower challenge to disclosure of the specific petitions in this case, if they were able to produce evidence of threats, harassment, or reprisals against those signing the petition in question.

Although eight of nine justices in *Doe v. Reed* agreed that the Court should reject the First Amendment challenge to disclosure of referendum petitions generally, there were six additional opinions. These opinions expressed divergent views not only on future as-applied challenges to disclosure laws, but also on whether petition signatories are best thought of as private citizens or legislators.

The lone dissenter in *Doe v. Reed* was Justice Thomas, who thought compelled disclosure of signatories unconstitutional, because it "severely burdened [First Amendment] rights and chills citizen participation in the referendum process." Justice Thomas would have applied strict scrutiny, and found wanting the state's claimed interests in ensuring integrity and informing voters. Justice Alito, though joining the majority opinion, suggested a similarly skeptical posture toward compelled disclosure. While believing that there was an interest in preserving electoral integrity, he suggested that there are better means of serving this end. Justice Alito asserted that the state's "asserted informational interest will not in any case be sufficient to trump the First Amendment rights of signers and circulators who face a threat of harassment."

At the other end of the spectrum in *Doe v. Reed* was Justice Scalia, who did not join the majority opinion. Justice Scalia argued that people signing petitions act as legislators. Thus, they are not entitled to assert First Amendment protection from public disclosure. In contrast to the majority, Justice Scalia did not think that states should be required to demonstrate a "sufficiently important government interest" to justify a disclosure requirement. He argued that making people "stand up in public for their political acts fosters civic courage, without which democracy is doomed" and that a society that shields direct democracy from public disclosure "does not resemble the Home of the Brave." The remaining justices who wrote or joined concurring opinions (Justices Breyer, Sotomayor, Stevens, and Ginsburg) likewise thought that as-applied challenges to disclosure laws should rarely if ever be allowed.

After the Supreme Court's decision remanding *Doe v. Reed*, the district court rejected the as-applied claim, finding insufficient evidence of threats and harassment.

3.   POLITICAL RESTRUCTURING AND THE EQUAL PROTECTION CLAUSE

Some scholars have argued that direct democracy is especially likely to lead to the tyranny of the majority, because ballot initiatives lack the checks on majoritarianism—and therefore the protection for minorities—that exist with representative democracy. See, e.g., Derrick A. Bell, Jr., *The Referendum: Democracy's Barrier to Racial Equality*, 54 WASH. L. REV. 1 (1978). While this critique of direct democracy has partly focused on racial minorities, it has also included other groups constituting a numerical minority such as gays and lesbians, who are arguably less able to protect their interests through direct democracy than through representative democracy. See Hans A. Linde, *When Initiative Lawmaking Is Not "Republican Government": The Campaign Against Homosexuality*, 72 OR. L. REV. 19 (1993). For this reason, some have argued that initiatives affecting minorities should receive more searching judicial review, or "hard looks." Julian N. Eule, *Judicial Review of Direct Democracy*, 99 YALE L.J. 1503 (1990). This argument is related to the process-based theory growing out of *Carolene Products* footnote 4 (Chapter 1.D), which suggests that courts should be especially attentive to defects in the political process that disadvantage discrete and insular minorities. On the other hand, not all scholars agree that minorities fare worse under direct democracy than representative democracy, pointing out that some of the most repressive laws were enacted by state legislatures. Richard Briffault, *Distrust of Democracy*, 63 TEX. L. REV. 1347 (1985).

There have been several important cases challenging ballot initiatives under the Equal

Protection Clause of the Fourteenth Amendment, on the ground that they unduly infringe on the political rights of a numerical minority. As a formal matter, the same equal protection standard applies to laws enacted through direct democracy and those enacted by legislative bodies. Thus, proving unconstitutional discrimination generally requires a showing of a discriminatory purpose, not just disproportionate impact. See *Washington v. Davis*, 426 U.S. 229 (1976). As a practical matter, however, courts— including the Supreme Court—have sometimes looked more skeptically at laws that are the products of direct democracy.

The most prominent examples of judicial skepticism toward initiatives disadvantaging racial minorities are cases involving the restructuring of the political process. In *Hunter v. Erickson*, 393 U.S. 385 (1969), the Supreme Court struck down an initiative amending the City Charter of Akron, Ohio, in reaction to a fair housing ordinance that the Akron City Council had adopted. The initiative required that any ordinances regulating race discrimination in housing be approved by a majority of voters before they could become law. *Hunter* found this initiative to be an explicit racial classification, because it treated racial housing matters differently from other housing matters, placing "special burdens on racial minorities within the governmental process." Those seeking protection from racial discrimination were required to surmount an obstacle—securing approval of a majority of voters—to which other participants in the political process were not subject. Because the

Akron initiative placed special political burdens on racial minorities, the *Hunter* majority concluded that it must satisfy "the most rigid scrutiny." The Court rejected the city's claimed interests in "mov[ing] slowly" in the realm of race relations and distributing legislative power as it desired, as insufficient to justify the political burden on racial minorities. Comparing the initiative to vote dilution (Chapters 4.B and 6.A), the Court concluded that "the State may no more disadvantage any particular group by making it more difficult to enact legislation in its behalf than it may dilute any person's vote or give any group smaller representation than another of comparable size."

Another case involving the restructuring of the political process to disadvantage racial minorities is *Washington v. Seattle School District No. 1*, 458 U.S. 457 (1982) (*Seattle School District*). At issue in *Seattle School District* was a statewide ballot initiative whose practical effect was to prohibit local school boards from adopting busing to achieve racial integration. Although the initiative did not specifically mention race, the Court found that it was "effectively drawn for racial purposes." It went on to conclude that the initiative impermissibly restructured the political process to the disadvantage of racial minorities. By removing local school boards' authority to adopt integrative busing programs and shifting that authority to the state level, the initiative imposed a special political burden on racial minorities.

On the same day the Court decided *Seattle School District*, it also decided *Crawford v. Board of Education*, 458 U.S. 527 (1982). In *Crawford*, the Court upheld a California initiative forbidding state courts from ordering busing to achieve desegregation unless a federal court would do so to remedy an equal protection violation. The distinction between the initiatives in these two cases is that the one in *Seattle School District* imposed burdens on minorities' participation in the political process (specifically, local school boards), while the one in *Crawford* affected judicial remedies, but not the political process.

In recent years, lower courts have considered the applicability of the political restructuring doctrine, articulated in *Hunter* and *Seattle School District*, to statewide bans on public affirmative action. Among the states to have adopted such bans are California and Michigan, both of which enacted initiatives prohibiting "preferential treatment" based on race. In *Coalition for Economic Equity v. Wilson*, 122 F.3d 692 (9th Cir. 1997), the Ninth Circuit upheld California's Proposition 209. The Sixth Circuit reached the opposite conclusion in *Coalition to Defend Affirmative Action v. Regents of the University of Michigan*, 701 F.3d 466 (6th Cir. 2012) (en banc). The Supreme Court has granted certiorari and will hear the case in its October 2013 Term.

Initiatives disadvantaging gays and lesbians have also been challenged under the Equal Protection Clause. The most important case to date is *Romer v.*

Evans, 517 U.S. 620 (1996), which struck down a Colorado initiative prohibiting localities from adopting or enforcing anti-discrimination protections for gays and lesbians. The Colorado Supreme Court found the initiative unconstitutional because it impeded the "fundamental right to participate equally in the political process." *Evans v. Romer*, 882 P. 2d 1335 (Colo. 1994); *Evans v. Romer*, 854 P.2d 1270 (Colo. 1993). Citing *Hunter* and *Seattle School District*, the state court concluded that the Colorado initiative imposed a comparable burden on gays' and lesbians' participation in the political process and applied strict scrutiny.

The U.S. Supreme Court affirmed in *Romer v. Evans*, though on different grounds than the state court. Justice Kennedy's opinion focused on two aspects of the initiative. First, the Court noted the initiative's imposition of a "broad and undifferentiated disability on a single named group." According to the Court, making it more difficult for gays and lesbians to seek aid from the government than other groups was "a denial of equal protection of the laws in the most literal sense." Although the Court declined to rely on *Hunter* and *Seattle School District*, this line of reasoning—focusing on the political burden placed upon a minority group—bears a strong similarity to the political restricting doctrine articulated in those cases. Second, *Romer* concluded that the Colorado initiative could only be understood as the product of discriminatory animus, given the discontinuity between its breadth and the reasons offered for it. Because Colorado's initiative lacked a rational relationship to legitimate government interests, it violated the Equal Protection Clause.

Most recently, supporters of same-sex marriage challenged California's Proposition 8, an initiative constitutional amendment limiting marriage to opposite-sex couples. This initiative was enacted in response to the California Supreme Court decision, holding that it violates the California Constitution to preclude gays and lesbians from marrying. *In re Marriage Cases* (Part B.2 above). A federal district court concluded that Proposition 8's gay marriage ban violates equal protection, and the Ninth Circuit affirmed, relying heavily on *Romer. Perry v. Brown*, 671 F.3d 1052 (9th Cir. 2012). The Supreme Court vacated the Ninth Circuit's ruling on the ground that Proposition 8's proponents lacked standing to appeal. *Hollingsworth v. Perry*, 133 S. Ct. 2652 (2013). Because California officials had declined to appeal the district court's ruling and proponents lacked standing to appeal, the immediate effect of the Court's ruling was to leave in place the district court's ruling that Proposition 8 is unconstitutional—and thus to reinstate gay marriage in California. The long-term effect *Hollingsworth* may be to leave some initiatives without a constitutional defense, when they are opposed by state officials.

4. TERM LIMITS AND THE QUALIFICATIONS CLAUSES

Initiatives imposing limits on congressional terms have also triggered searching judicial review. Held out as a means of removing entrenched incumbents, term limits are arguably the very sort of lawmaking that direct democracy was designed to promote. Between 1990 and 1994, virtually all the states with direct democracy adopted term limits for legislative office. While there are strong process-based arguments for searching review of initiatives disadvantaging minorities, one might argue that term limits deserve special deference from courts given their objective of preventing entrenched incumbency. That has not, however, been the case. The U.S. Supreme Court has held that congressional term limits violate the U.S. Constitution. Term limits for state legislative office do not violate the U.S. Constitution, although some have been struck down on state constitutional grounds.

In *U.S. Term Limits v. Thornton*, 514 U.S. 779 (1995), the Court considered an Arkansas initiative that would have imposed term limits on the state's congressional delegation. Specifically, Arkansas' initiative amended the state constitution to provide that congressional candidates were not eligible to have their names placed on the ballot, once they had been elected to three two-year terms in the House or two six-year terms in the Senate.

Writing for the majority, Justice Stevens concluded that Arkansas' congressional term limits violated the Qualifications Clauses of the U.S. Constitution (contained in Article I, Sections 2 and 3). These clauses set forth the qualifications for members of the U.S. House and Senate (minimum age, length of citizenship, and residency in the state). The Court relied on *Powell v. McCormack*, 395 U.S. 485 (1969), which had held the Constitution's list of qualifications to be exclusive. This meant that states lack the power to add qualifications for members of Congress.

U.S. Term Limits quoted *Powell* for the "fundamental principle of our representative democracy . . . 'that the people should choose whom they please to govern them.' " It did not matter that incumbents who had served the prescribed number of terms were only prevented from having their names placed on the ballot and could still be elected as write-in candidates. Because the initiative's goal was to prevent the reelection of termed-out candidates, it was unconstitutional. In a footnote, the Court found "little significance" in the fact that term limits were adopted by initiative rather than by the state legislature. Neither the state legislature nor the people of Arkansas had the power to impose new qualifications on members of Congress. Term limits could only be imposed through an amendment to the U.S. Constitution.

Justice Thomas dissented in *U.S. Term Limits*, joined by Chief Justice Rehnquist, Justice Scalia, and Justice O'Connor. The dissenters thought it ironic that the Court relied on the right of the people to choose who should govern them, when the people of Arkansas themselves had voted to impose term limits on their elected representatives in Congress. According to the dissent, the Constitution was simply silent on the question whether states may impose term limits or other qualifications for congressional office. Justice Thomas also thought it significant that the initiative only prevented incumbents from having their names placed on the ballots. Because incumbents could still be elected as write-in candidates, they were not actually disqualified. Noting the "enormous advantages" of incumbency, Justice Thomas asserted that the people of Arkansas had merely attempted to "level the playing field on which challengers compete with [incumbents]."

After *U.S. Term Limits*, those supporting congressional term limits pursued creative means of promoting their adoption. Missouri adopted an initiative the following year, designed to induce support for a "Congressional Term Limits Amendment" to the U.S. Constitution. The initiative "instruct[ed]" the state's congressional delegation to use their power to support this amendment. It also provided that those who refused to take prescribed actions to support the amendment were to have the statement "DISREGARDED VOTERS' INSTRUCTION ON TERM LIMITS" placed next to their names on subsequent ballots. In addition, nonincumbent congressional candidates who refused to take a "Term Limit" pledge would have the statement "DECLINED TO PLEDGE TO SUPPORT TERM LIMITS" placed next to their names.

In *Cook v. Gralike*, 531 U.S. 510 (2001), the Supreme Court struck down Missouri's initiative. This time, the Court was unanimous although there was disagreement on the rationale. Justice Stevens again wrote the majority opinion, which concluded that Missouri lacked power under the Elections Clause (Article I, Section 4) to disadvantage candidates in this way for failing to support term limits. Such directives could not, in the Court's view, be deemed a regulation of the time, place, or manner of conducting congressional elections. Missouri's initiative was an impermissible attempt to "dictate electoral outcomes." The four justices who had dissented in *U.S. Term Limits* all concurred in the judgment, although Chief Justice Rehnquist (joined by Justice O'Connor) would have relied on the First Amendment instead of the Elections Clause.

If states are prohibited from imposing term limits on members of Congress, are they also barred from recalling them? No member of Congress has ever been recalled. One court has ruled that congressional recalls violated the U.S. Constitution.

Under Article I, Section 5, each house of Congress has the power to judge the qualifications of its members, and may expel its members by a two-thirds vote. Through an initiative adopted in 1993, New Jersey amended its state constitution to allow members of Congress to be recalled. The plaintiff in *Committee to Recall Robert Menendez from the Office of U.S. Senator v. Wells*, 7 A.3d 720 (N.J. 2010), sought to recall one of the state's U.S. senators, but the New Jersey Supreme Court concluded that such a recall violated the Constitution by a 4–2 vote. Quoting *U.S. Term Limits*, the court relied on " 'basic principles of our

democratic system' established in the Constitution."
The two dissenters disagreed with the majority's
constitutional analysis. They accused the majority of
seeing the U.S. Senate as "an institution immune
from criticism" and "an elitist institution the
members of which should not have to be troubled by
what the people they represent believe." Other
states have express provisions for recalls that either
expressly allow for members of Congress to be
recalled or could be so interpreted, but there are no
other published decisions addressing the
constitutional question.

CHAPTER 9
POLITICAL PARTIES

A. PARTIES IN THE U.S. POLITICAL SYSTEM

Political parties play in essential role in democracy. They provide a means by which citizens may organize themselves politically and select leaders who will represent their interests. The structure of election laws plays a significant role in determining the kinds of political parties that develop and their role in the political system.

Almost from the beginning, the U.S. has had a two-party system. Shortly after the Constitution became law in the late Eighteenth Century, the Federalist Party and Republican (or Democratic–Republican) Party were established. After the demise of the Federalist Party, the Democratic–Republican Party split into the Jacksonian group which became the Democratic Party, and the Whig Party. As the Whig Party disintegrated in the mid-Nineteenth Century, the Republican Party formed. Since then, the Democratic Party and Republican Party have remained the two major parties in the U.S., although their ideological views, policy positions, and regional bases of support have shifted significantly over time.

The U.S. thus not only has had a strong two-party system almost since its formation, but has had the *same two major parties* since before the Civil War. There have occasionally been important third party

and independent candidates, but none of them have
been elected President and relatively few have been
elected to lower office. While other democracies also
have political parties, the strength and longevity of
the two-party system in the U.S. is distinctive.
Many democratic countries have multiple parties,
with two, three, or even sometimes sharing power in
the legislature.

What accounts for the exceptionally strong two-
party system in the U.S.? This phenomenon is
generally attributed to the combination of plurality
elections for single-member districts and national
presidential elections. Single-member districts,
where the candidate with the most votes wins, tend
to push democratic countries toward a two-party
system. The second party is able to maintain a
"monopoly of the opposition," because it has the best
chance of defeating the party in power. E.E.
Schattschneider, PARTY GOVERNMENT (1942). Thus,
with plurality elections for single-member districts,
those who might be inclined to vote for third parties
tend to avoid doing so for fear of wasting their votes.
By contrast, in proportional representation systems,
political parties may win seats in the legislature
and share power, even when they garner much less
than half the vote. The tendency toward two-party
systems in countries with single-member districts
elected on a plurality basis is known as *Duverger's
Law*. See Maurice Duverger, POLITICAL PARTIES (2d
English ed. 1959). Third parties may sometimes
prosper regionally, but this is more likely to happen
in a *parliamentary system*—in which the head of
government is the leader of the party with majority

support in the legislature—than in a presidential system. Because a regional party cannot expect to win a national election, it eventually tends to lose its regional support to major parties that have a realistic chance of obtaining the presidency.

The fact that the U.S. is a durable two-party state does not necessarily mean that the parties themselves are unified. There have been great variations over time in the strength of the two major parties' leadership, in terms of choosing candidates and enjoying the loyalty of voters and candidates. Although we nowadays tend to focus on the *national* parties, state and local parties played a greater role in political organizing for most of American history. National parties did not assume the prominence they have today until the Twentieth Century.

Some political scientists have argued that American political parties are not as strong as they should be. In 1980, for example, Morris Fiorina argued that strong and cohesive parties were essential to ensure "collective responsibility" within a democracy, allowing people to think and act collectively. Morris P. Fiorina, *The Decline of Collective Responsibility in American Politics*, 109 DAEDALUS 25 (1980). He argued that parties had unfortunately declined in strength, permitting interest groups to exert greater influence and making it more difficult to govern effectively. In the intervening decades, we have arguably seen an increase in the strength of the parties. Relatedly, political scientists have documented an increase in political polarization among citizens as well as those elected to office, which also tends to make it more difficult to govern. See Richard H. Pildes, *Why the Center Does Not Hold: The Causes of Hyperpolarized Democracy in America,* 99 CAL. L. REV. 273 (2011). That is especially true where there is divided government—that is, where one major party controls the legislative branch and the other controls the executive branch, or the two chambers of a bicameral legislature are split between the major parties.

Another distinction between the U.S. and other democracies is the relatively limited legal regulation of political parties. The Constitution does not mention political parties. Some of the Framers would have viewed them as "factions" detrimental to good governance. There was an increase in laws affecting political parties at the state level starting in the Nineteenth Century. Most significant was the creation of direct primary elections, in which a party's candidates for office are chosen by eligible voters.

Today, state and local government entities administer the primary elections as well as general elections, in which the parties' chosen candidates run against each other. Single-member districts and presidential elections are largely responsible for our two-party system, as described above. But federal law has played a limited role in regulating political parties, with the conspicuous exceptions of the White Primary Cases (Part B below) and campaign finance laws (Chapter 10).

One line of precedent views the parties as private organizations, independent of the state and protected from interference like other non-governmental actors. Thus, the First Amendment limits government's authority to regulate expressive and associational activities of political parties. On the other hand, the essential role that party primaries play in our system of government makes them public, or at least quasi-public actors, in some respects. For this reason, the Supreme Court has held that racial discrimination in party primaries violates the Constitution.

Parties thus occupy a distinctive position in the U.S. system of government. They are neither completely private nor completely public entities, and they have constitutional obligations as well as constitutional rights. Part B discusses the obligations of major political parties, including the prohibition on racial discrimination in primary elections. Part C discusses the associational rights of parties under the First Amendment. Part D addresses access to the ballot, an issue of particular importance to independent and minor party candidates. Part E addresses the constitutional limits on the state allocating or withholding other benefits based on party status.

B.   CONSTITUTIONAL OBLIGATIONS OF PARTIES: THE WHITE PRIMARY CASES

For most of U.S. history, political parties were considered private associations. As such, they were subject to the limited constraints applicable to private groups but not to the constitutional constraints applicable to government actors. The U.S. Constitution imposes obligations on federal, state, and local government actors, but not generally on private individuals or groups acting independently of the government. (An exception is the Thirteenth Amendment, which prohibits slavery generally and thus imposes obligations on private as well as public actors.)

State regulation of parties increased in the early Twentieth Century. In 1903, Wisconsin became the first state to require political parties to choose their nominees through a direct primary. Other states followed. This raised the question whether federal law governed political party primaries. At first, the Supreme Court said that it did not. In *Newberry v. United States*, 256 U.S. 232 (1921), the Court considered whether a federal statute limiting campaign contributions and expenditures applied to a U.S. Senate primary. The Court concluded that the statute did not apply, because the regulation of primaries fell outside the scope of federal power. Justice MacReynolds' opinion for the Court reasoned that primaries "are in no sense elections for an office but merely methods by which party adherents agree upon candidates whom they intend to offer and support for ultimate choice by all qualified electors." As such, the regulation of primaries fell outside the scope of the Elections Clause in Article I, Section 4, which allows Congress to make or alter regulations governing congressional elections.

Under the rationale of *Newberry*, party primaries were treated as private affairs, not public elections. The implication was that they were not subject to the constitutional constraints that govern state actors. In a series of subsequent cases, however, the Court concluded that the Constitution *does* apply to political party primaries, at least insofar as people are excluded from participating on the basis of race.

The White Primary Cases arose from the state of Texas. At the time, Texas—like the rest of the South—was solidly Democratic. As a practical matter, the Democratic Party primary was the only game in town, so exclusion from that primary was tantamount to disenfranchisement.

The first of the White Primary Cases was *Nixon v. Herndon*, 273 U.S. 536 (1927), in which the Court struck down a Texas law prohibiting blacks from voting in the Democratic Party primary. The Court relied on the right to equal protection under the Fourteenth Amendment. This was the most straightforward of the White Primary Cases, because the enactment of a state law left no real doubt that there was state action sufficient to violate the Constitution. Justice Holmes' opinion for the Court declined to reach the question whether the Fifteenth Amendment was also violated, because the Fourteenth Amendment violation was so obvious. The implications of *Nixon v. Herndon* were limited, because in most other southern states African Americans were prevented from participating in Democratic primaries by party rules rather than state law. See Michael Klarman, *The*

White Primary Rulings: A Case Study in the Consequences of Supreme Court Decisionmaking, 29 FLA. ST. U. L. REV. 55 (2001).

After *Nixon v. Herndon,* Texas repealed the statue and enacted a new one, giving the Democratic Party's executive committee the power to determine who could vote in party primaries. The executive committee then adopted a resolution barring blacks from voting in the primary. The next case, *Nixon v. Condon,* 286 U.S. 73 (1932), struck down the resolution, reasoning that the Texas statute had given the party a power it did not previously possess. Accordingly, the party was effectively acting as an agent of the state. By discriminating on the basis of race, the party had violated the Fourteenth Amendment's Equal Protection Clause. *Nixon v. Condon* thus rested on the party being a state actor, but only because the state had enacted a law giving the party power to determine who could vote in its primaries.

Three weeks after *Nixon v. Herndon,* the Texas Democratic Party adopted a new resolution at its convention limiting membership in the party to white citizens. The rationale upon which *Nixon v. Herndon* rested thus disappeared, because the party had acted on its own rather than pursuant to a power granted by the state legislature. On this ground, the Court unanimously declined to strike down the party's exclusion of blacks in *Grovey v. Townsend,* 295 U.S. 45 (1935). Justice Roberts' opinion for the Court reasoned that parties were private associations, not state actors, and thus that their primaries were not subject to the Fourteenth and Fifteenth Amendments. Although Texas law required primaries to be conducted, the *Grovey* Court found it significant that the state did not pay the expenses for party primaries, furnish the ballots used in primaries, or count votes. It also relied on Texas state court decisions holding that political parties were associations of private individuals that have the power to define their membership.

Grovey turned out to be a temporary setback for civil rights advocates seeking to end the White Primary. They were aided by an intervening decision that did not directly concern racial discrimination. In *United States v. Classic*, 313 U.S. 299 (1941), the Court considered an indictment charging Louisiana officials with fraud in connection with a congressional primary election. The district court had dismissed the indictment, based on *Newberry*'s rationale that party primaries are not elections subject to Congress's power under the Elections Clause of Article I, Section 4. But the Supreme Court expressly overruled *Newberry* in *Classic*. Although *Classic* did not overrule (or even mention) *Grovey*, it signaled a greater willingness to consider primaries public elections rather than simply a private association's means of choosing its candidates.

The Court explicitly overruled *Grovey* by an 8–1 vote in *Smith v. Allwright*, 321 U.S. 649 (1944), this time relying on the Fifteenth Amendment. Justice Reed's opinion for the majority found the party to be a state actor in its conduct of primary elections, given the responsibilities imposed upon it under state law. The Court emphasized the pervasive state regulation of and involvement in party primaries, which effectively made them state functions. In addition, the Court noted that primaries had become an integral part of the mechanism for choosing elected officials. In less than a decade between *Grovey* and *Smith v. Allwright*, the Court had shifted from unanimously viewing party primaries as essentially private affairs, to almost unanimously viewing them as state action.

The final nail in the coffin was *Terry v. Adams*, 345 U.S. 461 (1953), the last of the White Primary Cases. *Terry* involved the Jaybird Democratic Association of Fort Bend County, Texas, a political club that held a straw vote prior to the Democratic Party primary. Voting in the Jaybird pre-primary was open to whites only. Although the Jaybird winner had no official status, that candidate invariably went on to win both the Democratic primary and the general election. The Court held that the Jaybirds' exclusion of blacks violated the Fifteenth Amendment by an 8–1 vote, although the majority justices divided into three groups. Writing for three justices, Justice Black expressed the view that the state was using the primary to "ratify the result of the prohibited [Jaybird] election," in an impermissible attempt to circumvent the Fifteenth Amendment. Justice Frankfurter concurred, finding the Jaybird vote to be "the action of the entire white voting community" and thus "as a practical matter the instrument of . . . the officials of the local Democratic party and, we may assume, the elected officials of the county." Justice Clark, writing for four justices, concluded that the Jaybird Democratic Association was an "auxiliary" of the local Democratic Party, thus subject to the Fifteenth Amendment under *Smith v. Allwright*.

The White Primary Cases establish that party primaries are constrained by the Constitution, at least when citizens are excluded on the basis of race. They do not, however, stand for the principle that political parties are state actors in all their activities.

Outside the context of race-based exclusion, it is uncommon for political parties' actions to be successfully challenged on the ground that they are violating the Constitution. A rare exception is *Ammond v. McGahn*, 390 F. Supp. 655 (D.N.J. 1975). In that case, the federal district court concluded that the New Jersey State Democratic Caucus had violated the First and Fourteenth Amendments, by excluding one of its members in retaliation for her exercise of free speech rights. According to the district court, the Caucus "functions as an arm of the State Legislature and is an essential part of the legislative process," relying in part on *Terry v. Adams*. After the Caucus voted to readmit her, the district court's ruling was reversed on the ground that there was no irreparable injury to the plaintiff state legislator. *Ammond v. McGahn*, 532 F.2d 325 (3d Cir. 1976). Other courts have been less receptive to legislators' constitutional claims against party leadership. See, e.g., *Davids v. Akers*, 549 F.2d 120 (9th Cir. 1977).

That parties are considered state actors for some purposes does not, moreover, mean that they are without constitutional rights. In this sense, labeling political parties as either "public" or "private" actors is overly simplistic. Fixation on this distinction tends to obscure the more important question: What is the proper relationship between the government and political parties? See Daniel Hays Lowenstein, *Associational Rights of Major Political Parties: A Skeptical Inquiry*, 71 TEX. L. REV. 1741 (1993). As the White Primary Cases establish, parties may act unconstitutionally when they exclude people from participating on certain grounds. At the same time, parties also have some constitutional rights—most notably, the First Amendment right to associate and, in some circumstances, to avoid association.

C.   ASSOCIATIONAL RIGHTS OF PARTIES

Questions regarding the associational rights of parties have arisen in three lines of cases. The first involves presidential nominations, where conflicts have occasionally arisen between national parties and state parties with regard to the seating of delegates to party conventions. The second line of cases concerns state primary elections, centering on the state's authority to regulate participation by people who are not party members. The third involves the regulation of political parties' internal processes.

1.   PRESIDENTIAL NOMINATIONS

Major party nominees for U.S. President are chosen through a vote of delegates to the parties' national conventions. Both major parties have rules for delegate selection—including the number of delegates, the allocation to each state, the method by which they are selected, and the timing of delegate selection. States select their delegates to the national convention through either a primary election or a caucus, at which party members meet, deliberate, and vote in person.

The most significant legal issues to have arisen from the selection of presidential delegates involve disputes between the national party organization and state parties. Because state parties have power in the state legislature, their position on presidential delegate selection may be written into state law. There are three significant Supreme Court cases on the subject.

The first is *O'Brien v. Brown*, 409 U.S. 1 (1972), which involved disputes over the California and Illinois delegations to the 1972 Democratic National Convention. The Credentials Committee had upheld challenges to both delegations, but the D.C. Circuit concluded that the committee's ruling as to California denied due process because those delegates had been chosen in conformity with state law. The Supreme Court stayed that aspect of the D.C. Circuit's ruling. The *per curiam* opinion in *O'Brien* noted that the case raised difficult questions regarding justiciability and state action. But the Court focused on the fact that the

Credential Committee's decision on the seating of delegates was subject to review at the Convention itself. According to *O'Brien*, the Convention was the proper forum for resolving disputes between the national party and state parties.

Ultimately, the 1972 Democratic Convention reversed the Credential Committee's decision to disqualify the California delegation, but upheld the decision to disqualify the elected Illinois delegation because it did not comply with national party guidelines. But the elected delegation obtained a state court injunction against an alternative delegation, which complied with national party rules, participating in the Democratic Convention. The U.S. Supreme Court eventually held that the state court was without power to interfere with the Convention in this way in *Cousins v. Wigoda*, 419 U.S. 477 (1975). According to *Cousins*, the state court was wrong to give primacy to state law instead of national party rules governing the selection and seating of delegates. The Court held that the national party had a protected right of association under the First Amendment, and that the state court injunction was not justified by compelling interests. Following *O'Brien*, the *Cousins* Court said that the Convention was the proper forum for resolving the intraparty dispute. While neither case is precise regarding the scope of parties' associational rights, they suggest that courts should be very hesitant to interfere in disputes regarding presidential delegates.

The third significant case involving presidential nominations is *Democratic Party of the United States v. Wisconsin ex rel. La Follette*, 450 U.S. 107 (1981) (*La Follette*), which concerned Wisconsin's delegates to the 1980 Democratic National Convention. National party rules limited participation in delegate selection to Democratic Party members, but Wisconsin had long used "open" primaries in which eligible voters—regardless of party affiliation—may vote in whatever party primary they choose. A state court ordered the national party to seat the state's delegates, elected through an open primary in contravention of national party rules. The U.S. Supreme Court reversed in *La Follette*, holding that the national party had no obligation to seat the elected slate of delegates. While Wisconsin was free to conduct elections using an open primary, the national party was not obliged to seat delegates chosen in contravention of party rules. Thus, national parties are not required to seat delegates chosen in compliance with state law but in violation of party rules.

2.　STATE PRIMARIES

Political parties have also asserted the First Amendment to challenge state laws regulating their association with voters in primary elections. In some cases, parties have challenged laws *preventing* them from associating with voters who are not party members. In other cases, parties have challenged state laws *requiring* them to associate with non-party members.

Tashjian v. Republican Party of Connecticut, 479 U.S. 208 (1986), was a successful challenge of the first type. *Tashjian* struck down a state "closed primary" law, mandating that voters be registered members of a party in order to vote in that party's primary. The Connecticut Republican Party had adopted a party rule allowing independent voters (those not registered with any party) to vote in Republican primary elections. But the state legislature, then controlled by Democrats, refused to change state law to allow independents to vote in the Republican primary. The Connecticut Republican Party challenged the rule under the First Amendment, as an impermissible burden on its right to associate with non-members.

Justice Marshall's opinion for the *Tashjian* majority applied strict scrutiny to the restriction and found that it was not narrowly tailored to a compelling interest. The Court rejected as "insubstantial" the state's asserted interests in administrability, the prevention of party raiding, avoiding voter confusion, and the integrity of the two-party system. Justice Scalia dissented, joined by Chief Justice Rehnquist and Justice O'Connor. The dissent asserted that the majority exaggerated the importance of the party's interest in associating with independent voters while minimizing the interests of Republican Party members whose votes were diluted by outsiders' participation.

On the other hand, the Court rejected a minor party's challenge to a "semi-closed" primary in *Clingman v. Beaver*, 544 U.S. 581 (2005). Oklahoma law allowed both party members and independents to vote in a party's primary. Members of one party, however, could not vote in another party's primary. The Libertarian Party objected to this restriction, because it wanted members of other parties to be able to vote in its primary. In a portion of the opinion that spoke only for a four-justice plurality, Justice Thomas rejected the argument that Oklahoma's system denied anyone's associational rights, since voters affiliated with other parties were free to disaffiliate, thus enabling them to vote in the Libertarian primary. In another portion of the opinion which spoke for a majority, Justice Thomas rejected the argument that strict scrutiny applied. The Court concluded that there was no "severe" burden on associational rights. It distinguished *Tashjian* on the grounds that Oklahoma voters were not required to register as Libertarians in order to vote in that party's primary. *Clingman* found the state's interests in preserving the identifiability of parties, facilitating party-building, and preventing "strategic voting" by outsiders sufficient.

Under *Tashjian* and *Clingman*, then, states must allow independent voters to vote in a party primary if the party so desires. But states need not allow members of one party to vote in another party's primary.

A related line of cases considers when a political party may be compelled to associate with voters or candidates *against the party's wishes*. The Court struck down one form of open primary in *California Democratic Party v. Jones,* 530 U.S. 567 (2000), based on the political parties' right not to associate with nonmembers. Through an initiative constitutional amendment, California replaced its closed primary system with a type of open primary called the "blanket primary." In a prototypical open primary system, voters may go to the polls on primary election day and obtain whatever party's ballot they choose—but they must vote for *that party's* candidates in all contests on the primary ballot. With California's blanket primary, by contrast, *all parties' candidates* in all contests appeared on all primary ballots. A voter could vote for a Democratic candidate for U.S. Senate contest, a Republican candidate for U.S. House contest, and a Libertarian candidate for state senate. For each contest on the primary ballot, the candidate from each party with the most votes would advance to the general election. The Democratic and Republican parties both challenged California's blanket primary, on the ground that they were unconstitutionally forced to associate with non-party members.

Writing for the majority in *California Democratic Party*, Justice Scalia held that California's blanket primary violated the First Amendment. The majority reasoned that the blanket primary placed a heavy burden on the parties' associational freedom and therefore must satisfy strict scrutiny. It proceeded to reject seven claimed state interests, including the argument that the blanket primary was necessary to avoid "disenfranchising" nonmembers who would otherwise be denied an effective vote. Justice Stevens, joined by Justice

Ginsburg, dissented. The dissent argued that the blanket primary actually expanded participation rather than limiting it and that the majority had given short shrift to the state's asserted interests.

In a later decision, the Court upheld a different form of blanket primary. The State of Washington had been using a blanket primary like California's until *California Democratic Party*. It then adopted a variant on the "nonpartisan blanket primary" (also known as the "top-two" or Louisiana system). The nonpartisan blanket primary effectively eliminates party primaries altogether. For each contest, the two candidates with the most votes proceed to the general election, regardless of their party affiliation. Usually, this results in a Democrat and Republican facing each other. If, however, two Republicans (or two Democrats) are the top vote-getters, then candidates of the same party face each other in the general election.

A purely *nonpartisan* blanket primary would presumably be constitutional, since the parties are not compelled to associate with nonmembers—they are effectively taken out of the business of nominating candidates through primary elections. In the variant adopted by the state of Washington, however, each candidate was allowed to indicate his or her "party preference" on the ballot. The parties argued that this violated their associational rights.

In *Washington State Grange v. Washington Republican Party*, 552 U.S. 442 (2008), the Supreme Court upheld Washington's blanket primary against a facial challenge. The Court applied the *Anderson–*

Burdick standard (Part D below), under which
"severe" burdens on voting are subject to strict
scrutiny, while nonsevere burdens are subject to
less searching review. It went on to find that the
burden on associational rights was not severe.
Justice Thomas' opinion for the majority
distinguished *California Democratic Party v. Jones*
on the ground that Washington's system was not
used to select the parties' nominees. Instead, the top
two candidates in the primary proceeded to the
general election, regardless of party affiliation. The
Court rejected the argument that the parties had a
constitutional right to designate their nominees on
the ballot. Finally, it considered whether party-
preference designations represented a form of
compelled association that would confuse voters.
While recognizing the possibility that some voters
might misinterpret the ballot designations as party
endorsements, the Court found this argument
insufficient to sustain a facial challenge to
Washington's system. Strict scrutiny did not apply
because there was no severe burden on the parties'
associational rights. Justice Scalia, joined by Justice
Kennedy, dissented.

Taken together, the decisions in *California
Democratic Party* and *Washington State Grange*
establish that (1) states may not compel parties to
associate with nonmembers by requiring that
nonmembers be allowed to vote in party primaries,
but (2) if states choose to eliminate party primaries
altogether by going to a top-two system, they may
allow candidates to indicate their party preference
on the ballot. But *Washington State Grange* leaves

the door open to an as-applied challenge, where voters are misled into believing that a candidate is endorsed by a party.

3.   PARTY GOVERNANCE

Another category of party association cases involves state efforts to regulate parties' internal affairs. In *Eu v. San Francisco County Democratic Central Committee,* 489 U.S. 214 (1989), the Court struck down various California laws regulating parties, including a ban on their endorsing candidates in primaries. The case grew out of a dispute within the Democratic Party, with a local party organization challenging rules supported by the state party and written into state law. Nevertheless, Justice Marshall's opinion for the Court concluded that the state laws were subject to strict scrutiny because of the burden they imposed on the party's speech and associational rights. The Court went on to find that the endorsement ban served no compelling interest. *Eu* also struck down a state law regulating the parties' internal governance, which included term limits on state party chairs. This restriction was also subjected to strict scrutiny because of its burden on the associational rights of parties and their members. While recognizing that the state has an interest in fair and orderly elections, the Court concluded that these regulations were not necessary to serve that interest.

More recently, the Court rejected a constitutional challenge in another intra-party dispute. Plaintiffs in *New York State Board of Elections v. Lopez Torres*, 552 U.S. 196 (2008), challenged a complex system for choosing state judges in the State of New York, which allegedly gave too much control over nominations to party leaders. Plaintiffs argued that, under this system, party bosses effectively determined the nominees, denying insurgent candidates a "fair shot" of getting the party nomination. The Democratic and Republican state parties, on the other hand, both intervened to defend the law. This case was thus different from others described above, in that party members were effectively seeking to assert their own associational rights against the leaders of political parties.

In an opinion by Justice Scalia, the Court in *Lopez Torres* unanimously rejected the argument that New York's system violated the Constitution, holding that there was no constitutional right to a "fair shot" of winning the party's nomination. The Court dismissed the idea that party members could assert associational rights against party leaders, at least in this context. For a critical perspective on the Court's unwillingness to examine the barriers to competition in the system for selecting judges, see Ellen D. Katz, *Barack Obama, Margarita Lopez Torres, and the Path to Nomination*, 8 ELECTION L.J. 369 (2009).

D. BALLOT ACCESS

Getting on the ballot is an issue of particular interest to independent and minor party candidates. As discussed in Part A, the United States has had a strong two-party system almost from its inception. But independent and third-party candidates do occasionally win elections. While they have not enjoyed much success in presidential elections, third-party and independent candidates have sometimes garnered a significant number of votes. The most recent example is H. Ross Perot, who received 18.9% of the presidential vote in 1992. Even when they have no realistic chance of winning, third-party and independent candidates can affect the outcome of the race. In Florida's disputed 2000 presidential election, for example, the number of votes going to Green Party candidate Ralph Nader (97,488) was much greater than the final margin separating major party candidates George W. Bush and Al Gore (537). Some believe that Gore would have won the election had Nader not been on the ballot.

There are rarely legal questions about major-party candidates' access to the general election ballot, although these issues do occasionally surface in the major parties' primaries. Most legal issues arise from third-party and independent candidates' efforts to get on the general election ballot. Largely out of concern these candidates will play the role of spoiler, major parties sometimes fight these efforts vigorously. In 2004, for example, supporters of John Kerry aggressively opposed Nader's efforts to get on the ballots in key swing states.

Although the requirements for getting on the ballot are the subject of state law, third parties and independent candidates often argue that state ballot access requirements violate the U.S. Constitution because they are too onerous. Access to the ballot is not the main factor that limits the success of minor parties in the U.S., as noted in Part A. That phenomenon is best explained by the combination of single-member districts with plurality elections and a presidential system. But high barriers to ballot access can prevent third-party and independent candidates from injecting issues they care about into political discourse.

In a number of cases, the Supreme Court has considered whether barriers to ballot access violate the Constitution. Some of these cases have been decided under the Equal Protection Clause, others under the First Amendment. In *Williams v. Rhodes*, 393 U.S. 23 (1968), the Supreme Court struck down Ohio's very early deadline (February 7) for third-party candidates to get on the general election ballot. The Court relied both on the First Amendment right of political association and the Fourteenth Amendment right to cast an effective vote. In *Jenness v. Fortson*, 403 U.S. 431 (1971), however, the Court upheld a Georgia law requiring that independent candidates obtain signatures from 5% of registered voters in the jurisdiction to get on the ballot. And in *Storer v. Brown*, 415 U.S. 724 (1974), the Court upheld a California law preventing independent candidates from appearing on the general election ballot if they had been registered with a political party in the previous year. While some previous decisions had applied heightened scrutiny, *Storer* observed that some degree of regulation is necessary to ensure fair, honest, and organized elections. The fact that the law placed a burden on potential candidates seeking to run for office was not enough to show a violation the Equal Protection Clause. But *Storer* was imprecise about what burdens are acceptable, saying there is "no litmus-paper" test for separating constitutional and unconstitutional burdens on ballot access.

While the Court has still not drawn a bright line between acceptable and unacceptable burdens on access to the ballot, it has provided more guidance in subsequent cases. In *Anderson v. Celebrezze*, 460 U.S. 780 (1983) and *Burdick v. Takushi,* 504 U.S. 428 (1992), the Court articulated the constitutional standard that is generally used to challenge regulations limiting ballot access. In fact, the *Anderson–Burdick* test is now used in cases challenging a variety of election rules, including the blanket primary (in *Washington State Grange,* Part C) and voter ID laws (in *Crawford v. Marion County Election Board*, Chapter 7.A).

In *Anderson*, the Court considered—and struck down—an early filing deadline in Ohio. Independent presidential candidate John Anderson challenged the state's requirement that independent candidates collect petition signatures by March to get on the November ballot. Quoting *Storer*, the Court in *Anderson* reiterated that there is no "litmus-paper test" separating acceptable and unacceptable burdens on voting and association, given that substantial regulation of the electoral process is necessary. The Court said that "the State's important regulatory interests are generally sufficient to justify reasonable, nondiscriminatory restrictions." It went on to say, however, that courts should balance the "character and magnitude" of the burden imposed by the law against the "the precise interests put forward by the State" to justify that burden. In addition to determining the strength of those interests, courts should consider "the extent to which those interests make it necessary to burden the plaintiff's rights." *Anderson* thus prescribed a *balancing test*, weighing the state's regulatory interests against the burden imposed by the law. Applying this test, the Court found that the burden on "independent-minded" voters' freedom of choice and freedom of association was not justified by the state's asserted interests in voter education, equal treatment for all candidates, and political stability.

Burdick provides further guidance on the constitutional standard. In *Burdick,* the Court rejected a First and Fourteenth Amendment challenge to Hawaii's ban on write-in voting, alleged to infringe on rights of association and voting choice. Citing *Anderson*, the Court in *Burdick* emphasized that election laws necessarily impose some burdens on individual voters, so strict scrutiny cannot apply to them all. According to *Burdick*, the "rigorousness of our inquiry into the propriety of a state election law depends upon the extent to which a challenged regulation burdens First and Fourteenth Amendment rights." When a regulation imposes a "severe" burden, strict scrutiny applies and the law may only be upheld if narrowly tailored to a compelling state interest. On the other hand, laws that impose only "reasonable, nondiscriminatory restrictions" may generally be justified based on "the State's important regulatory interests."

Under the *Anderson–Burdick* test, then, severe burdens on voting and association are subject to strict scrutiny, while less searching review applies to nonsevere burdens. Courts are to consider the "character and magnitude" of the burden imposed by an election law, weighing it against the "precise interests put forward by the State."

Applying this standard, *Burdick* found that the write-in voting ban imposed only a slight burden on voters, which was justified by the interests in preventing "sore loser" candidacies in general elections and "party raiding" in primary elections (switching to another party in order to manipulate the outcome of that party's primary). Although *Burdick* itself involved write-in voting rather than a candidate's ability to get on the ballot, the *Anderson–Burdick* standard has been applied to ballot access restrictions and various other state rules alleged to burden voting and association.

In between *Anderson* and *Burdick*, the Court decided an important case having to do with minor-party candidates' access to the ballot. In *Munro v. Socialist Workers Party*, 479 U.S. 189 (1986), the Court upheld the state of Washington's rules for access to the general election ballot. At the time, Washington still had a blanket primary, like the one later struck down in *California Democratic Party v. Jones* (Part C.2 of this chapter). Under this system, all candidates of all parties appeared on every voter's primary election ballot, and voters could select their candidate of choice regardless of party affiliation. The top vote-getter from each party would advance to the general election, but *only* if that candidate received at least 1% of the votes cast for that office. The Socialist Workers Party candidate in a primary election for U.S. senator received just 0.09% of the total vote in that primary, far less than what was required to qualify for the general election. The party challenged Washington's restriction under the First and Fourteenth Amendments.

In an opinion by Justice White, *Munro* reaffirmed that states are entitled to require that candidates have substantial support to qualify for the general election ballot. The state was not required to make a "particularized showing" of the interests alleged to support its rule—in that case, voter confusion, overcrowded ballots, or frivolous candidacies. Requiring such proof, the Court worried, would lead to endless litigation over the sufficiency of the state's evidence. It was enough that the state legislature *perceived* that the ballot in Washington was becoming "cluttered" by candidates without much voter support. It did not matter that minor party candidates might be excluded from the general election ballot, even though turnout in primaries tends to be much lower.

Justice Marshall, joined by Justice Brennan, dissented in *Munro*. The dissent focused on the distinctive value that minor-party candidates add to political discourse: "The minor party's often unconventional positions broaden political debate, expand the range of issues with which the electorate is concerned, and influence the positions of the majority, in some instances ultimately becoming majority positions." Thus, even if a third-party candidate has no realistic chance of winning, his or her participation in the general election has great value—both to voters who share the candidate's views and to the broader political discourse. According to Justice Marshall, the majority failed comprehend the important role that third parties play in our system. The *Munro* dissent argued that strict scrutiny applied. Because the 1% rule effectively served as a near total bar on minority party candidates' access to the ballot and the state had failed to satisfy strict scrutiny, Justice Marshall would have held this rule unconstitutional

In *Timmons v. Twin Cities Area New Party*, 520 U.S. 351 (1997), the Court considered a question closely related to ballot access and, as in *Munro*, took a deferential approach. *Timmons* involved a state ban on "fusion candidacies," in which a candidate's name may appear on the ballot as candidate for more than one party—usually a major party and a minor party. Fusion candidacies can be a way of building the strength of third parties, while allowing major party candidates to avoid losing support. Most states, however, prohibit fusion candidacies. The plaintiff in *Timmons* was a local third party, which wanted to support the Democratic candidate for the state legislature. Neither the candidate nor the state Democratic Party organization objected. Nevertheless, the Court rejected the minor party's First and Fourteenth Amendment challenge to the ban on fusion candidacies.

Chief Justice Rehnquist's opinion for the *Timmons* majority applied the *Anderson–Burdick* test, weighing the "character and magnitude" of the burden imposed by the state against its asserted interests. It upheld the ban on fusion candidacies, finding that its impact on the minor party's associational rights was not severe, given that the party and its members were still free to endorse, support, or vote for any candidate they liked. Following *Munro*, the Court declined to require "empirical verification" of the state's asserted interests in protecting the integrity, fairness, and efficiency of the electoral process. Allowing fusion candidacies, the majority suggested, would threaten to turn the ballot into "a billboard for political advertising." The Court also credited the state interest in promoting "political stability" and avoiding "excessive factionalism." While the state may not completely insulate the two major parties from competition, it is entitled to adopt rules that will have the practical effect of favoring the two-party system in order to promote stability.

Justice Stevens, joined by Justice Ginsburg and Souter, dissented. The dissent argued that the majority had given too much credence to the state's claimed interest in political stability. In a portion of the dissent joined only by Justice Ginsburg, Justice Stevens argued that the law had both the effect and intent of disadvantaging third parties. This fact, the dissent argued, weighed against the law's constitutionality—not in favor of it, as the majority opinion might be read to suggest.

Although the Court has generally been deferential to ballot access rules, there is an important exception. The Court has looked skeptically at high filing fees to get on the ballot. In *Bullock v. Carter*, 405 U.S. 134 (1972), the Court struck down a Texas law requiring that candidates pay a filing fee to get on the primary ballot for local office. The Court found that the size of the fees gave it a "patently exclusionary character," having a negative impact on voter choice which tended to "fall more heavily on the less affluent segment of the community." In other words, candidates supported by less affluent voters were more likely to be negatively affected. In *Lubin v. Panish*, 415 U.S. 709 (1974), the Court struck down a $701.60 filing fee for candidates seeking to run for the Los Angeles County Board of Supervisors. Although the fee was fairly modest when judged in light of the size of the district for which candidates were running—each of which had almost two million people—the Court in *Lubin* held it unconstitutional on the ground that it was "exclusionary as to some aspirants." *Lubin* left open, however, the state's option to require that candidate show a modicum of support by obtaining a prescribed number of petition signatures. As the above cases demonstrate, the Court has viewed such signature requirements more deferentially than filing fees.

CHAPTER 10

CAMPAIGN FINANCE REGULATION

Election campaigns cost money, and lots of it. Much of that money is spent on advertising and other communications designed to influence votes on particular candidates or ballot measures. Election-related communications are protected by the First Amendment, as are the contributions and expenditures that fund them. Yet there are serious concerns about the influence that campaign money may have, both on election results and on the decisions that public officials make once elected. For over a century, Congress and other legislative bodies have tried to limit the influence of campaign money on elections and politics. In the past four decades, there have been many Supreme Court decisions considering the constitutionality of campaign finance laws, a number of them striking down federal or state statutes under the First Amendment. Among the most prominent of these decisions is *Citizens United v. Federal Election Commission*, 558 U.S. 310 (2010) (discussed below, Part B), which struck down a ban on corporations funding campaign ads from their treasuries.

This chapter summarizes campaign finance law, including the constitutional restraints on regulation as well as the statutes governing federal elections. It also discusses some state laws, including those providing public financing for election campaigns. Part A provides *background* on campaign finance regulation, including the modes of regulation, the values underlying the debate, and the constitutional framework. Part B discusses limits on *expenditures* by individuals, corporations, unions, and other groups. Part C turns to limits on *contributions*, including individual contributions to candidates and political parties. Parts D and E address *public financing* and *disclosure* rules respectively.

A. BACKGROUND

Before delving into the details of campaign finance law, it is important to have a basic understanding of the different *modes of regulation* and the *underlying values* animating the political and legal debate. An understanding of these modes of regulation and competing values will help inform discussion of the court decisions discussed in the remainder of this chapter. After summarizing the modes of regulation and competing values, we turn to the *constitutional framework* for analyzing campaign finance regulation, established in *Buckley v. Valeo*, 424 U.S. 1 (1976). This framework remains in effect to this day.

1.   MODES OF REGULATION

There are four basic modes of regulating the financing of electoral campaigns:

- *Expenditure limits* regulate the direct spending of money to influence election campaigns. This mode of regulation includes laws imposing a specific dollar limit on the amount that may be spent in support of or against candidates, as well as outright bans on certain entities (such as corporations or unions) spending money to influence elections. As we shall see, the Court has looked with skepticism on expenditure limits.

- *Contribution limits* regulate the giving of money to another person or entity to support an election campaign. The most prominent example is the limit on how much each person may give to a candidate. There are also limits on how much may be given to party organizations.

- *Public financing* is the provision of public funds to candidates or parties, to reduce their reliance on private donors. Rather than imposing a ceiling on expenditures or contributions, public financing attempts to raise the floor. Candidates typically obtain public financing by making a threshold showing of viability—for example, by raising a certain number of small-dollar contributions.

- *Disclosure* requires that information be made available to the public about contributions or expenditures. Candidates, political parties, and other entities may be required to disclose their donors, the amounts they receive, and how much they spend on campaign-related activities. Another form of disclosure is to require a disclaimer in advertisements, indicating the person or entity responsible.

As a general matter, expenditure limits are considered the most intrusive form of regulation and disclosure the least, with contribution limits and public financing in between. The constitutional standards applied to these different forms of regulation are discussed in greater detail below.

2.   COMPETING VALUES

There are important values at stake on both sides of the debate over campaign finance regulation. These values come into play in political debates over whether to regulate, as well as legal debates over the constitutionality of laws that have been adopted.

The most prominent argument made in support of campaign finance regulation is the *prevention of corruption and the appearance of corruption.* This is the only argument that the Court has accepted as a justification for contribution limits. At the core of the anti-corruption rationale is the worry that campaign contributions may be exchanged for political favors, which is known as *quid pro quo* corruption. In addition, supporters of campaign finance laws often argue that they are needed to prevent the appearance of corruption. Even if there is no *quid pro quo* exchange of campaign money for a political favor, large contributions may create the appearance of improper influence. An alternative way of viewing this rationale is the *avoidance of conflicts of interest,* between legislators' self-interest in reelection and their obligation to their constituents. Daniel Hays Lowenstein, *On Campaign Finance Reform: The Root of All Evil Is Deeply Rooted,* 18 HOFSTRA L. REV. 301 (1989). Relatedly, supporters of regulation argue that it is important for voters to have *public confidence* in the political process, and that large contributions or expenditures undermine that confidence.

Another important value asserted in support of regulation is the *promotion of equality* or a "level playing field." See Edward B. Foley, *Equal–Dollars–Per–Voter: A Constitutional Principle of Campaign Finance*, 94 COLUM. L. REV. 1204 (1994). The concern is that people and entities with large amounts of wealth will have disproportionate influence on either election results or policymaking. This is closely related to the "anti-distortion" rationale, the concern that it distorts democratic politics if wealthy entities—especially large corporations—have a stronger voice than ordinary people, and are thus able to drown out their voices. Inequality in the realm of campaign finance may bear particularly heavily on racial minorities, thus denying them equal participation in the political process. See Spencer Overton, *The Donor Class: Campaign Finance, Democracy, and Participation*, 153 U. PA. L. REV. 73 (2004). The Supreme Court has emphatically rejected equality as a rationale for limits on campaign spending, as set forth below.

Other values cited in support of campaign finance regulation include the *promotion of competitive elections*, *protecting candidates' time*, and *informing the electorate*. Some forms of campaign finance regulation may promote competition by making it easier for candidates without personal wealth or wealthy friends to run for office. Regulation may also help prevent entrenchment by allowing challengers to compete more successfully against incumbents. Another asserted rationale for regulation is to ensure that candidates—including current officeholders—are not forced to spend too much of their time raising money. The reality of contemporary politics is that candidates for office must raise considerable sums to fund their campaigns. For those who are current officeholders, this necessarily limits the time they can spend performing their official duties. Finally, disclosure rules are justified as a means to inform the electorate. Disclosure may help voters make better decisions by letting them know candidates' sources of financial support. It may also help inform citizens of the interest groups seeking to influence public officials, thus allowing those officials to be held accountable.

On the other side of the debate, regulatory skeptics cite First Amendment values in support of their arguments. They argue that contribution and expenditure limits are a *threat to liberty and autonomy*, because they limit the ability of individuals to express their political views. Money may not literally be speech, but it is difficult to engage in effective political communication without financial resources. Moreover, regulatory skeptics argue, campaign-related expression is core political speech that should enjoy a high level of First Amendment protection. See Bradley A. Smith, UNFREE SPEECH: THE FOLLY OF CAMPAIGN FINANCE REFORM (2001).

In addition, campaign finance regulation may be seen as an *infringement on political association*. One of the ways that individuals organize politically is by pooling their resources for campaign-related activities. This may be done by donating to a candidate's campaign, political party, or other group seeking to influence an election. Rights of political association enjoy constitutional protection. Opponents of regulation believe that some campaign finance regulations interfere with protected associational activity.

Some also oppose disclosure rules—generally considered the least intrusive form of regulation—on the ground that they constitute an *invasion of privacy*. They cite a long tradition of anonymous speech in the U.S., which disclosure requirements threaten to chill.

Regulatory skeptics also deny that campaign finance regulation meaningfully advances the values its supporters tout. In fact, regulation may actually have unintended consequences that compromise those values. Limits on campaign finance regulation are enacted by legislative bodies, which have a strong incentive to protect their own interests and those of their parties. Far from promoting competition, skeptics argue, some regulations have *anti-competitive effects*—tending to advance the interests of the party in power or incumbents generally. Challengers may find it more difficult to wage a viable campaign with regulations than without them.

In addition, skeptics argue that some campaign finance regulations *increase the time spent fundraising* by candidates. In particular, contribution limits force candidates to spend considerable time raising small-dollar contributions from a large number of donors, rather than obtaining big donations from just a few people, which would take less time.

Finally, skeptics argue that some forms of regulation cause a *weakening of political parties* and *degradation of political discourse.* An unintended consequence of our current regime is that more money tends to flow to outside groups. As we shall see, candidates and parties may be subject to contribution limits, but groups engaged solely in independent expenditures may not. This tends to push more money to outside groups, weakening parties. Samuel Issacharoff & Pamela S. Karlan, *The Hydraulics of Campaign Finance Reform*, 77 TEX. L. REV. 1705 (1999). It may also result in a less civil political discourse, since outside groups are not accountable to the people in the same way that candidates are. Accordingly, outside groups may be more willing to run negative ads. Even if those ads are effective, they may have a negative effect on political discourse.

3. THE CONSTITUTIONAL FRAMEWORK: *BUCKLEY V. VALEO*

The Supreme Court established the basic framework for judicial review of campaign finance laws in *Buckley v. Valeo*, 424 U.S. 1 (1976). Although it has been refined over the years, the *Buckley* framework remains in place with respect to the four modes of regulation discussed above:

expenditure limits, contribution limits, public financing, and disclosure requirements.

At issue in *Buckley* were the 1974 amendments to the Federal Election Campaign Act of 1971 (FECA), codified at 2 U.S.C. § 431 *et seq.* These amendments established a comprehensive scheme of campaign finance regulation for federal elections, including both congressional and presidential elections. *Buckley* upheld some provisions of this scheme while striking down others under the First Amendment. The Court's unsigned *per curiam* opinion was very long, consuming 138 pages, with another 83 pages of concurring and dissenting opinions. As explained below, the *Buckley* Court struck down FECA's expenditure limits, upheld its contribution limits, upheld presidential public financing, and upheld its disclosure requirements (with some limitations) against facial constitutional challenges.

The most important part of *Buckley* is the portion concerning expenditure and contribution limits. The Court observed that these limits "operate in an area of the most fundamental First Amendment activities," given that they affect political expression and association. It rejected the argument that campaign contributions and expenditures should be viewed as regulating conduct rather than speech, saying that the fact that money is involved does not reduce the "exacting scrutiny required by the First Amendment."

The Court in *Buckley* proceeded to draw a sharp line between expenditure limits and contribution limits, holding that the former enjoy a greater degree of constitutional protection than the latter. *Buckley* provided two reasons for its distinction between expenditures and contributions.

First, the Court explained, expenditure limits impose a more substantial limitation on speech than do contribution limits. As an example, the Court noted that FECA's $1,000 limit on expenditures relative to a clearly identified candidate would directly prevent people from speaking. Contribution limits do not have the same direct impact on speech. A contribution to a candidate's campaign serves as a general expression of support but does not convey a specific message. A contribution is thus more like a "symbolic act." While contributing money is protected association under the First Amendment, it has less expressive value than an expenditure.

The second distinction between expenditures and contributions involves the risk of corruption. *Buckley* said that contributions pose a greater risk of "real or apparent corruption" than do expenditures. When one makes a contribution to a candidate's campaign, there may be reasons for concern about *quid pro quo* corruption—i.e., the exchange of money for political favors. That same concern does not exist, the Court thought, when someone makes an *independent expenditure* in support of a candidate. If an expenditure is made independently of the candidate's campaign, without any coordination, then by definition there has been no exchange of money for political favors. By contrast, a *coordinated expenditure*—made in cooperation or with the consent of the candidate—does present a risk of corruption, and may therefore be treated as a contribution.

Buckley was imprecise about the level of scrutiny that should be accorded to expenditure and contribution limits. Subsequent cases, however, have understood *Buckley* to require *strict scrutiny* for expenditure limits, meaning that they must be narrowly tailored to a compelling government interest. Less searching scrutiny applies to contribution limits. As *Buckley* put it, contribution limits need to be "closely drawn" to a "sufficiently important interest," and the dollar amount need not be "fine tun[ed]." See *Nixon v. Shrink Missouri Government PAC*, 528 U.S. 377 (2000) (discussed in Part C.2 below).

In addition to drawing a distinction between contribution and expenditure limits, *Buckley* addressed the government interests that may justify regulation. The Court held that the prevention of corruption and the appearance of corruption are permissible interests. On this basis, it upheld FECA's contribution limits. Specifically, the Court upheld the $1,000 limit on individual contributions to candidates and campaign committees, $5,000 limit on contributions by political committees (including political action committees or PACs), and a $25,000 aggregate limit on an individual's total contributions to all candidates and committees in a calendar year.

On the other hand, *Buckley* rejected the promotion of equality or equalization of resources as an acceptable rationale for limiting campaign money. In what is surely the most quoted (and criticized) line from *Buckley*, the Court said "the concept that government may restrict the speech of some elements of society in order to enhance the relative voice of others is wholly foreign to the First Amendment. . . ." Because equality was not acceptable justification for FECA's expenditure limits, the government was left to rely on the anti-corruption interest. But the Court held the anti-corruption interest insufficient to support expenditure limits, because independent expenditures do not pose the same risk of *quid pro quo* corruption as do contributions. Accordingly, the Court struck down the $1,000 limitation on independent expenditures relative to a clearly identified candidate. It also struck down FECA's limits on candidates' expenditure of personal or family resources in support of their campaigns, as well as limits on total expenditures by federal candidates.

The Court in *Buckley* upheld FECA's public financing scheme and, with some modification, its disclosure requirements. FECA provided for public financing for presidential elections, but not for congressional elections. The idea was to eliminate publicly financed candidates' reliance on private money in presidential general elections. While expenditure limits are impermissible, *Buckley*'s footnote 65 said that Congress may condition acceptance of public financing on a candidate's agreement to abide by expenditure limits.

The principal argument against FECA's public financing scheme was that it unfairly discriminated against third party and independent candidates. FECA's public financing scheme distinguished between "major" parties (those whose candidate received more than 25% of the vote in the last presidential election), "minor" parties (those whose candidate received 5–25% of the vote), and "new" parties (those whose candidate received less than 5%). Major-party candidates received more public financing than minor parties. New party candidates received no money before the general election but were eligible for post-election payments if they wound up getting more than 5% of the popular vote. Citing the ballot access cases (discussed in Chapter 9.D), the Court rejected the argument that FECA's scheme unconstitutionally discriminated against third parties. Congress had an interest, *Buckley* held, in not funding "hopeless" candidacies and in avoiding "splintered parties and unrestrained factionalism" (quoting *Storer v. Brown*). Moreover, the *Buckley* Court ruled that public financing was, if anything, less burdensome on third parties than restrictions on ballot access. No candidate was prevented from appearing on the ballot, and no voter was prevented from voting for his or her preferred candidate.

Buckley also upheld FECA's disclosure requirements, which were challenged as overly broad because of their applicability to minor-party and independent candidates as well as small-dollar contributors. FECA imposed disclosure obligations on candidates and political committees, which it defined to include groups making contributions or expenditures exceeding $1,000 in a calendar year. FECA required these groups to register and file quarterly reports with the Federal Election Commission (FEC), the federal agency created to enforce the statute. Individuals and other groups were also required to report contributions and expenditures, other than contributions to a candidate or political committee.

While recognizing that disclosure has the potential to infringe on the exercise of First Amendment rights, *Buckley* found that there were sufficiently important interests to uphold FECA's disclosure requirement against a facial challenge. *Buckley* applied "exacting scrutiny" to the disclosure requirement, requiring that there be a "substantial relation" to a "sufficiently important" government interest. The Court identified three specific interests supporting disclosure: (1) *informing the electorate* of where campaign money comes from and how it is spent, (2) *deterring corruption and avoiding the appearance of corruption*, by exposing large contributors who may be seeking special treatment, and (3) *gathering information needed to detect violations of contribution limits*. It rejected the argument that minor parties were entitled to a blanket exemption from the disclosure requirements, while leaving the door open to as-applied challenges if a group could show a "reasonable probability" that disclosure would subject contributors to "threats, harassment, or reprisals from either Government officials or private parties."

The *Buckley* Court also considered the argument that the disclosure requirements were unconstitutionally vague. While finding no vagueness with FECA's requirement that *contributions* be disclosed, it did see a problem with the requirement that *expenditures* be disclosed. FECA defined expenditures as monies used "for the purpose of ... influencing" an election or nomination. The Court upheld the disclosure requirement as to candidates as well as political committees, which it understood to include only groups (1) that are affiliated with a candidate or (2) whose "major purpose" is the nomination or election of candidates. As for other individuals and groups, *Buckley* narrowed the statute in order to save it. Specifically, it interpreted "expenditure" as limited to "funds used for communications that *expressly advocate* the election or defeat of a clearly identified candidate." *Buckley*'s footnote 52 defined "express advocacy" as communications using words "such as 'vote for,' 'elect,' 'support,' 'cast your ballot for,' 'Smith for Congress,' 'vote against,' 'defeat,' 'reject.'" These are known as the "magic words." Under *Buckley*'s narrowing construction of FECA, only funds used for such express advocacy—the so-called "magic words"—were considered expenditures subject to the disclosure requirement. As so narrowed, the Court upheld the disclosure requirement as sufficiently related to the interest in informing voters.

Finally, *Buckley* upheld small-dollar disclosure and recordkeeping requirements. FECA required disclosure of contributions to a candidate or political committee over $100 (later raised to $200). The Court reasoned that the appropriate threshold for disclosure was best left to Congress. It also upheld a requirement that political committees keep records of contributions over $10.

While the Court has refined the standards for reviewing campaign finance regulations in the intervening decades, the basic constitutional framework established in *Buckley* remains in place. Expenditure limits are subject to strict scrutiny. With narrow exceptions that have now been overruled, restrictions on independent expenditures are unconstitutional. Contribution limits, on the other hand, are constitutional if closely related the important interest of preventing corruption or the appearance of corruption. Public financing is generally permissible so long as candidates are not compelled to accept it, although the Court has held that strict scrutiny applies to schemes that penalize speech in support of privately financed candidates (Part D below). Disclosure requirements must be substantially related to a sufficiently important government interest, but are generally acceptable unless there is a reasonable probability of threats, harassment or reprisals

B.   EXPENDITURE LIMITS

Recall that *Buckley* held that limits on independent expenditures in candidate elections are subject to heightened scrutiny. *Buckley* struck down FECA's limits on individual expenditures, as well as those applicable to candidates and their campaigns, on the grounds that (1) they were not tailored to the interest in preventing corruption or its appearance, and (2) equality is not a sufficient basis on which to restrict campaign spending. Later cases clarify that expenditure restrictions are subject to strict scrutiny, so may only be upheld if narrowly tailored to a compelling government interest.

Because *Buckley* settled the question of individual expenditure limits, the major issues that have arisen since then surround expenditures by political parties, corporations, labor unions, and other groups. The Court first addressed expenditure restrictions in the context of ballot measure campaigns, and later in the context of candidate campaigns. As explained below, the current constitutional rule is that *independent expenditures* by corporations, labor unions, and other entities cannot be restricted with respect to either type of campaign. However, the government may regulate *coordinated expenditures* as contributions. It appears that the same constitutional rule applies to spending in connection with judicial elections, although the Court has recognized that large independent expenditures require judges to recuse themselves, at least in extreme circumstances.

1.　BALLOT MEASURE CAMPAIGNS

Limits on expenditures in connection with ballot measure campaigns violate the First Amendment. In *First National Bank of Boston v. Bellotti*, 435 U.S. 765 (1978), the Court struck down a Massachusetts statute prohibiting banks and business corporations from making contributions or expenditures in connection with ballot measures.

Justice Powell's opinion for the *Bellotti* Court held that speech does not lose its First Amendment protection merely because its source is a corporation. According to *Bellotti*, the First Amendment does more than simply protect individuals' self-expression; it also "afford[s] the public access to discussion, debate, and the dissemination of information and ideas." Drawing an analogy to discrimination based on the subject or the speaker, the Court concluded that a ban on corporate campaign speech threatens to "give one side of a debatable public question an advantage." Turning to the state's justifications, the Court concluded that—in contrast to candidate elections— there is no genuine risk of corruption with ballot measures. It is not possible to corrupt an initiative in the same way that a person can be corrupted. The Court also rejected equality as a rationale for limiting corporate campaign speech, quoting *Buckley*'s admonition that "restrict[ing] the speech of some elements of our society in order to enhance the relative voice of others is wholly foreign to the First Amendment." Finally, *Bellotti* rejected the state's asserted interest in protecting shareholders. Even assuming shareholder protection is a compelling interest, the Court found that the state law was not sufficiently tailored to this interest.

Justice White dissented in *Bellotti*, joined by Justices Brennan and Marshall. Justice White thought that restrictions on corporate speech raised issues quite different from restrictions on individual speech. Unlike individuals, for-profit corporations have no interest in self-expression, nor do corporate expenditures meaningfully serve their shareholders' interest in self-expression. Justice White also thought the state interest in regulation to be much stronger with respect to corporate spending, given the amount of wealth they control. The state had an interest, he argued, in preventing wealthy entities from gaining an unfair advantage in the political process. Justice White further argued that the state had an interest in protecting shareholders from being compelled to support speech with which they disagreed. Justice Rehnquist wrote a separate dissent, arguing that business corporations had no constitutionally protected right to be free from state restrictions on their political expression.

2. POLITICAL PARTY EXPENDITURES

Buckley prohibited restrictions on independent expenditures by individuals in candidate campaigns, while allowing coordinated expenditures to be treated as contributions and subject to reasonable limits. In *Colorado Republican Federal Campaign Committee v. Federal Election Commission*, 518 U.S. 604 (1996) (*Colorado Republican I*) and *Federal Election Commission v. Colorado Republican Federal Campaign Committee*, 533 U.S. 431 (2001) (*Colorado Republican II*), the Court drew a comparable line for independent expenditures by political parties.

In *Colorado Republican I,* the Court considered whether the state party could be restricted from making independent expenditures in a U.S. Senate race. The Court struck down FECA's limitation on independent expenditures by political parties without a majority opinion. Writing for three members of the Court, Justice Breyer followed *Buckley* in holding that the anti-corruption interest could not justify a restriction on the party's independent expenditures, without ruling on whether coordinated expenditures could be restricted. Writing for three other members of the Court, Justice Kennedy thought the restriction impermissible as to both independent and coordinated expenditures by the party.

In *Colorado Republican II,* however, the Court held that a party's coordinated expenditures may be treated as the functional equivalent of contributions, and therefore subjected to limits. Justice Souter's majority opinion concluded that FECA's limitations on coordinated expenditures by parties was closely drawn to the sufficiently important interest in preventing corruption— including the circumvention of contribution limits.

Taken together, *Colorado Republican I* and *Colorado Republican II* establish that the government may not restrict independent expenditures by political parties, but it may restrict coordinated expenditures. Specifically, coordinated expenditures may be treated as contributions and subjected to the same restrictions. The constitutionality of different forms of contribution limits are described in Part C below.

3.   CORPORATIONS AND UNIONS

a. Federal Law

Federal statutes have long restricted corporate and union funds from being used to influence candidate elections. Since 1907, Congress has prohibited corporations from making contributions in connection with federal elections. That prohibition was later extended to labor unions and applied to expenditures by both corporations and unions. FECA incorporated these prohibitions, while permitting corporations and unions to pay administrative expenses for "separate segregated funds," commonly referred to as corporate and union PACs. Corporations and unions could not fund these PACs from their treasuries. But the PACs could accept contributions from stockholders, executives, and individuals affiliated with the organization. Corporate or union PACs were, in turn, free to make contributions to federal candidates as well as expenditures. As described below, the Court struck down the federal ban on corporate-funded independent expenditures in *Citizens United v. Federal Election Commission*, 558 U.S. 310 (2010). Under *Citizens United*, bans on corporate independent expenditures (and presumably those of unions) violate the First Amendment.

The federal ban on corporate and union expenditures had been in effect for decades before the Court directly confronted its constitutionality. *Buckley* did not address the constitutionality of this ban, though a footnote in *Bellotti* suggested restrictions on corporate expenditures in candidate elections (unlike those in ballot measure elections) could be justified by the anti-corruption interest. In *Federal Election Commission v. National Right to Work Committee,* 459 U.S. 197 (1982), the Court upheld the requirement that those contributing to corporate PACs be attached to it in some way by the corporation's structure. And in *Federal Election Commission v. National Conservative Political Action Committee,* 470 U.S. 480 (1985), the Court struck down a limit on political committees' expenditures in support of publicly financed presidential candidates. But these cases did not directly address the constitutionality of the federal ban on corporate and union expenditures.

b. Nonprofit Corporations

In *Federal Election Commission v. Massachusetts Citizens for Life, Inc.,* 479 U.S. 238 (1986) (*MCFL*), the Court considered the constitutionality of the federal ban, as applied to *nonprofit* corporations formed for ideological purposes. An anti-abortion group sent out a newsletter expressly urging readers to vote for pro-life congressional candidates. After determining that the organization's newsletter was express advocacy, prohibited under FECA, the Court concluded that the statute could not constitutionally be applied to groups like MCFL. It specifically pointed to three characteristics of the group: (1) it was formed for the express purpose of promoting political ideas, (2) it had no shareholders or others with a claim to its assets or earnings, and (3) it was not established by a business corporation or labor union. Thus, under *MCFL*, the government could not ban independent expenditures by nonprofit corporations formed for ideological purposes.

c. For–Profit Corporations and Unions

(1) Austin v. Michigan Chamber of Commerce

In *Austin v. Michigan Chamber of Commerce*, 494 U.S. 652 (1990), the Court finally considered whether business corporations could be prohibited from making independent expenditures from their treasuries to influence candidate elections. *Austin* involved a Michigan law prohibiting corporations from using treasury funds to support or oppose candidates for state office. Like FECA, Michigan law allowed corporations to establish separate segregated funds, which were permitted to make expenditures in support of state candidates. The Michigan Chamber of Commerce was a nonprofit corporation, but it received funding from for-profit business corporations. Hence, it was barred from making independent expenditures.

The Court upheld Michigan's ban on corporate expenditures on a 6–3 vote. Justice Marshall's opinion for the Court applied strict scrutiny under the First Amendment, but found that the law was narrowly tailored to a compelling interest. In particular, the Court held that the state had a compelling interest in preventing "the corrosive and distorting effects of immense aggregations of wealth that are accumulated with the help of the corporate form and that have little or no correlation to the public's support for the corporation's political ideas." Although the Court described this as an anti-corruption interest, it was quite different from the interest in preventing *quid pro quo* corruption, upon which *Buckley* had relied. Rather, *Austin*'s anti-distortion rationale was a variant of the equality rationale. The scheme did not require equalization of resources, but it did seek to prevent inequalities of resources from distorting the political system. *Austin* proceeded to hold that the Chamber was not exempt from the ban under *MCFL*, because it was formed for nonpolitical as well as political purposes, had members who were comparable to shareholders, and was not really independent of business corporations. If the Chamber were exempt under *MCFL*, it would be too easy to circumvent the ban on corporate expenditures. The Court also rejected a challenge based on the Equal Protection Clause. Justice Scalia and Justice Kennedy (joined by Justices O'Connor and Scalia) wrote separate dissenting opinions.

(2) McConnell v. FEC

Under *Austin*, the government could prohibit business corporations from making independent expenditures from their treasuries. In *McConnell v. Federal Election Commission*, 540 U.S. 93 (2003), the Court reaffirmed *Austin* and extended its holding to labor unions. Recall that federal law had long prohibited corporations *and* unions from making contributions and expenditures from their treasuries, requiring them to form a separate segregated fund (or PAC) instead. Under *Buckley*'s interpretation of FECA, the expenditure ban was limited to express advocacy—that is, to ads using so-called magic words like "vote for" or "vote against." This construction of FECA made it very easy for corporations and unions to get around the ban, by running ads purporting to address policy issues that were really campaign ads. Proponents of campaign finance reform often referred to these as "sham issue ads."

The Bipartisan Campaign Reform Act of 2002 (BCRA, also known as McCain–Feingold) amended FECA. One of the major changes made by BCRA was to close the perceived issue ad loophole. (The other major change made by BCRA, its prohibition on "soft money," is discussed in Part C.3 below.) Specifically, BCRA broadened covered expenditures to include "electioneering communications," defined as broadcast, cable, and satellite communications referring to a specific candidate for federal office within 30 days of a primary election or 60 days of a general election.

McConnell interpreted BCRA to incorporate the *MCFL* exemption—meaning that nonprofit ideological corporations were exempt. As so interpreted, *McConnell* upheld BCRA's ban on corporate- and union-funded electioneering communications against a facial challenge, by a 5–4 vote. The relevant portion of the majority opinion was co-authored by Justice Stevens and Justice O'Connor, who switched her position from *Austin*. Chief Justice Rehnquist (who switched his position in the opposite direction) and Justices Kennedy, Scalia, and Thomas dissented from this portion of *McConnell*.

(3) Citizens United v. FEC

The Roberts Court has taken a less deferential approach to campaign finance regulation than did the late Rehnquist Court. The key change on the Court was the replacement of Justice O'Connor with Justice Alito who, along with Chief Justice Roberts, has voted with the *McConnell* dissenters.

In *Federal Election Commission v. Wisconsin Right to Life*, 551 U.S. 449 (2007) (*WRTL*), the Court held that BCRA's ban on corporate-funded electioneering communications could not constitutionally be applied to certain ads. The controlling opinion by Chief Justice Roberts concluded that the ban was unconstitutional as applied to ads that are not the "functional equivalent of express advocacy." An ad could only meet this definition if it were "susceptible of no reasonable interpretation other than as an appeal to vote for or against a specific candidate." Three other justices (Scalia, Kennedy, and Thomas) would have gone further, holding the electioneering ban unconstitutional as to all corporate-funded ads. The decision in *WRTL* opened up a major hole in the regime created by BCRA. Ads were exempt from the ban, if they could reasonably be understood as something other than an appeal to vote a certain way.

In *Citizens United v. Federal Election Commission*, 558 U.S. 310 (2010), the Court struck down BCRA's prohibition on corporate electioneering communications, overruling *Austin* and the portion of *McConnell* discussed above. *Citizens United* arose from a film entitled *Hillary: The Movie*, a 90–minute documentary harshly critical of then-Senator Hillary Clinton. The nonprofit organization that released the film, Citizens United, wanted to show the documentary through video-on-demand and to run ads supporting it in 2008, at which time Clinton was a candidate for the Democratic nomination for President.

Justice Kennedy's opinion for the five-justice majority first concluded that the *Hillary* documentary and ads for it fell within BCRA's definition of electioneering communication. The Court also concluded that Citizens United was subject to the ban on corporate- and union-funded electioneering, and not within the *MCFL* exemption, because it received some of its funding from for-profit corporations.

Turning to the First Amendment issue, the Court in *Citizens United* applied strict scrutiny, requiring the government to show that the law was narrowly tailored to serve a compelling interest. The fact that corporations could form a PAC did not solve the First Amendment problem, because the ban on corporate-funded electioneering burdened speech based on the identity of the speaker. The Court proceeded to reject the government's three asserted interests: anti-distortion, anti-corruption, and shareholder protection.

In rejecting the anti-distortion interest, *Citizens United* expressly overruled *Austin* and the portion of *McConnell* that had relied on *Austin*. The Court found these precedents inconsistent with *Buckley*'s premise that government has a cognizable interest in promoting equality by limiting the speech of some elements of society. The Court also rejected the government's argument that the anti-corruption interest could support the ban on corporate-funded electioneering communications. It viewed this rationale as limited to the reality or appearance of *quid pro quo* corruption, and found no evidence of such corruption to support a ban on independent expenditures by corporations.

Finally, *Citizens United* rejected the argument that the ban on corporate-funded electioneering was justified by the interest in protecting dissenting shareholders. Any such interest, the Court suggested, could be corrected by changing the procedures of corporate governance. The ban on electioneering communications was also overinclusive, insofar as it applied to corporations with only one shareholder.

Citizens United thus held the ban on corporate independent expenditures violated the First Amendment. The majority opinion concluded by emphasizing that BCRA's this ban effectively suppressed speech in the realm of politics, where free expression is most essential.

Justice Stevens dissented, joined by Justices Ginsburg, Breyer, and Sotomayor. The dissent observed that there is a significant difference between corporate and human speakers, in particular that corporations are not members of "We the People." Noting that Congress had prohibited corporate contributions to federal election campaigns since 1907, Justice Stevens accused the majority of rejecting a century of history in treating this distinction as insignificant. He would have upheld the ban on corporate expenditures based on the anti-corruption rationale, taking a broader view of this interest than the majority. According to Justice Stevens, the problem of "undue influence" was a form of corruption that Congress was entitled to address, and had addressed through the prohibition on corporate- and union-funded expenditures. The dissent understood *Austin*'s anti-distortion rationale as "simply a variant on the classic government interest in protecting against improper influences on officeholders that debilitate the democratic process." Justice Stevens also thought the ban on corporate independent expenditures was justified by the interest in protecting shareholders from corporate electioneering communications with which they disagree. He concluded by asserting that: "While American democracy is imperfect, few outside the majority of this Court would have thought its flaws included a dearth of corporate money in politics."

Under *Citizens United*, the federal government may not prohibit corporations from funding independent expenditures in candidate campaigns from their treasuries. Accordingly, they are no longer required to set up separate PACs in order to make such expenditures. The same constitutional rule applies to state expenditure limits, as the Court made clear in *American Tradition Partnership v. Bullock,* 132 S. Ct. 2490 (2012). The one-paragraph *per curiam* opinion in that case holds that states may not ban corporate expenditures any more than the federal government.

Although the Court did not specifically address the federal ban on union-funded expenditures in *Citizens United*, its rationale applies with equal force expenditures by labor unions. Thus, the law after *Citizens United* is that restrictions on independent expenditures by any individual, corporation, union, or other group violate the First Amendment.

4.   JUDICIAL ELECTIONS

While federal judges are appointed and enjoy life tenure, most states have some form of judicial elections. Regulations on judicial election campaigns are subject to the same constitutional constraints as those that apply to other candidate elections. Judicial candidates and their supporters enjoy rights of free speech, just as in other elections. Thus, in *Republican Party v. White*, 536 U.S. 765 (2002), the Court struck down a state rule prohibiting judicial candidates from announcing their views on a disputed legal or political questions.

There are, however, circumstances in which elected judges are required to recuse themselves due to large campaign spending by those with an interest in a case before them. In *Caperton v. A.T. Massey Coal Co.*, 556 U.S. 868 (2009), the Court held that the Due Process Clause obliged an elected state supreme court judge to recuse himself. The case involved a multi-million judgment against the A.T. Massey Coal Company. Knowing that the state supreme court would be hearing the appeal, the company's CEO of spent over $3 million in support of the supreme court candidate who ultimately won. Almost all of that money took the form of independent expenditures. The CEO's contributions and expenditures exceeded the total amount spent by all other supporters of that judicial candidate combined. His expenditures were more than triple that of the judicial candidate's own campaign.

Justice Kennedy's opinion for the Court in *Caperton* held that the Due Process Clause required the judge to recuse himself. Given the CEO's "significant and disproportionate influence," along with the temporal proximity of his campaign spending and the appeal, there was a constitutionally unacceptable probability of bias. Chief Justice Roberts dissented, joined by Justices Scalia, Thomas, and Alito.

C.   CONTRIBUTION LIMITS

As discussed in Part A, the Court has generally been more deferential to the regulation of campaign contributions than to the regulation of independent expenditures. *Buckley* upheld FECA's individual limit on contributions to candidates for office, as well as its limits on contributions by political committees and its aggregate limits. While strict scrutiny applies to expenditure limits, contribution limits may be upheld if closely drawn to a sufficiently important interest. See *Nixon v. Shrink Missouri Government PAC*, 528 U.S. 377 (2000). Coordinated expenditures may constitutionally be treated as contributions, and are so treated by federal law. Complications arise, however, with respect to contributions made to entities other than candidates' campaigns, such as political parties, political committees, and nonprofits. This Part discusses contribution limits in various contexts: (1) contributions to ballot measure campaigns, (2) contributions to candidates, (3) contributions to political parties (4) contributions to PACs, Super PACs, and other outside groups, and (5) aggregate contribution limits.

1. BALLOT MEASURE ELECTIONS

As discussed above (Part B.1), states may not restrict expenditures in connection with ballot measure campaigns. But may states or municipalities limit *contributions* to ballot measure campaigns? In *Citizens Against Rent Control v. City of Berkeley*, 454 U.S. 290 (1981) (*CARC*), the Court held that they may not. *CARC* struck down a municipal ordinance setting a $250 limit on contributions to committees formed to support or oppose ballot measures. The Court applied "exacting judicial scrutiny," finding that the contribution limit infringed on both freedom of association and freedom of expression. It rejected the city's argument that the ordinance was needed to promote voter confidence or protect the integrity of the political system. Following *Bellotti*, the Court reasoned that ballot measures, unlike candidates for office, are not susceptible to *quid pro quo* corruption.

2.   CONTRIBUTIONS TO CANDIDATES

The Court has been more hospitable to limits on contributions to candidates. The constitutional standard applicable to limits on individual contributions to candidates is that they be "closely drawn" to a "sufficiently important interest," and need not be "fine tune[d]." This language derives from *Buckley*. In *Nixon v. Shrink Missouri Government PAC*, 528 U.S. 377 (2000), the Court clarified that it is a form of "heightened scrutiny" but is less stringent than strict scrutiny.

Shrink Missouri upheld contribution limits applicable to candidates for state office, which ranged from $275 for some candidates for state representative to $1,075 for candidates for statewide office. In upholding these limits, the Court suggested that large campaign contributions tend to create a "perception of corruption." Although there was little evidence of actual *quid pro quo* corruption, the majority cited evidence that some elected officials may have been overly compliant to large contributors. The *Shrink Missouri* Court thought this evidence comparable to that which had been found sufficient to uphold the federal contribution limits in *Buckley*. It took a broad view of the anti-corruption rationale, placing more emphasis on public perceptions of impropriety than on hard evidence of *quid pro quo* corruption. It also took a deferential posture with respect to the dollar limit, declining to second-guess the state's judgment. Justice Kennedy and Justice Thomas (joined by Justice Scalia) dissented.

The Roberts Court has taken a less deferential approach to contribution limits. In *Randall v. Sorrell*, 548 U.S. 230 (2006), a splintered Court struck down Vermont's contribution limits. Vermont law set individual contribution limits of $200 for state representative candidates, $300 for state senate candidates, and $400 for candidates for statewide office. The limits were not indexed for inflation. It also limited individuals to $2,000 in contributions to a political party during a two-year election cycle.

Randall struck down Vermont's contribution limits by a 6–3 vote. There was no majority opinion, but Justice Breyer's lead opinion (joined by Chief Justice Roberts and, in pertinent part, Justice Alito) was controlling. While applying the "closely drawn" to a "sufficiently important interest" standard, drawn from *Buckley* and *Shrink Missouri*, Justice Breyer's opinion cautioned that low limits may allow "incumbents to insulate themselves from effective electoral challenges." The lead opinion found "danger signs" of unfairness, including the difficulty that challengers were likely to face in mounting a viable campaign with such low contribution limits. Judging Vermont's limits the "lowest in the Nation," Justice Breyer found that they would substantially restrict challengers' ability to compete against incumbents. He also found fault with the fact that Vermont's contribution limits muted the voice of parties, hampered volunteer participation, were not indexed for inflation, and were not buttressed by any special evidence of need. Justice Kennedy and Justice Scalia (joined by Justice Thomas) concurred, asserting broader grounds for striking down Vermont's contribution limits. Justices Stevens and Souter (joined by Justices Ginsburg and Stevens) dissented.

Randall did not disturb *Buckley*'s upholding of the contribution limits for federal candidates. Recall that FECA set individual contributions limits of $1,000. This is sometimes referred to as the "hard money" limit, in contrast with "soft money" described in Section 3 below. BCRA raised the hard money contribution limit to $2,000, indexed for inflation. For the 2013–14 election cycle, the limits were set at $2,600–meaning that an individual could contribute $2,600 to a federal candidate's primary campaign, and another $2,600 to the same candidate's general election campaign.

In *McConnell v. Federal Election Commission*, 540 U.S. 93 (2003), the Court turned away a constitutional challenge to BCRA's increased contribution limits for lack of standing. It also rejected a challenge to the "Millionaire's Amendment" for lack of standing. The millionaire's amendment increased the contribution limit for candidates facing a wealthy, self-financed opponent.

Specifically, the amendment tripled the contribution limit for candidates whose opponents spent more than $350,000 of their personal funds in support of their campaigns. The Millionaire's Amendment was designed to level the playing field for those facing a wealthy, self-financed opponent.

While BCRA's hard money contribution limits remain in place, the Roberts Court struck down the Millionaire's Amendment in *Davis v. Federal Election Commission*, 554 U.S. 724 (2008). Justice Alito's opinion for the five-justice majority applied strict scrutiny, finding that the Millionaire's Amendment imposed a penalty on candidates' expenditures of their own resources in support of their campaigns. The Court deemed this a "substantial burden" on free expression, which had to be justified by a compelling interest. It rejected both anti-corruption and equality as rationales that could support the Millionaire's Amendment. Justice Stevens dissented, joined in part by Justices Souter, Ginsburg, and Breyer.

Federal law still prohibits corporations and unions from making contributions to candidates. Recall that *Citizens United* (Part B.3.c of this chapter) struck down the prohibition on corporate *independent expenditures* in support of federal candidates. Does that mean that the ban on corporate contributions is unconstitutional? So far, the answer is no. In *Federal Election Commission v. Beaumont*, 539 U.S. 146 (2003), decided before *Citizens United*, the Court upheld the ban on corporate contributions, based in part on the interest in avoiding circumvention of the individual contribution limits. Since *Citizens United*, circuit courts have rejected constitutional challenges to bans on corporate contributions. *United States v. Danielczyk*, 683 F.3d 611 (4th Cir. 2012), *cert. denied*, 133 S. Ct. 1459 (2013); *Ognibene v. Parkes*, 671 F.3d 174 (2d Cir. 2012), *cert. denied*, 133 S. Ct. 28 (2012).

Some jurisdictions have attempted to regulate campaign contributions in other ways. One circuit court upheld a local law restricting the *timing* of contributions, prohibiting them more than one year before an election. *Thalheimer v. City of San Diego*, 645 F.3d 1109 (9th Cir. 2011). But the same court struck down a ban on large contributions in the three weeks immediately preceding an election. *Family PAC v. McKenna*, 685 F.3d 800 (9th Cir. 2012). That court had previously struck down a state law restricting the percentage of funding that could come from out-of-district contributors. *VanNatta v. Keisling*, 151 F.3d 1215 (9th Cir. 1998).

3. CONTRIBUTIONS TO POLITICAL PARTIES

In addition to restricting electioneering communications (Part B.3) and raising the individual contribution limits (Part C.2), BCRA sought to plug the so-called "soft money" loophole. Before BCRA, contributors who had reached FECA's $1,000 "hard money" limit often gave money to political party committees. These funds, which were not subject to limits, came to be known as "soft money." Candidates for office and their campaigns would sometimes encourage donors who had "maxed out" on the hard money limit to make soft money contributions instead. In theory, these funds were supposed to be used for activities influencing state elections. But the FEC ruled that parties could fund mixed-purpose activities—designed to influence federal elections as well as state and local elections—with soft money. As a result, the amount of soft money raised by the political parties increased significantly.

In response to these developments, Title I of BCRA banned soft money. It prohibited national political party committees from soliciting, receiving, or spending these previously unregulated monies. BCRA also enacted restrictions on state and local parties, to prevent soft money from finding new channels. Finally, BCRA prohibited federal candidates and officeholders from receiving, spending, or soliciting soft money.

The Supreme Court upheld BCRA's soft money restrictions by a 5–4 vote in *McConnell v. Federal Election Commission*, 540 U.S. 93 (2003). The relevant portion of the majority opinion was jointly authored by Justices Stevens and O'Connor. They treated the soft money ban as a contribution limit, requiring only that it be closely drawn to a sufficiently important interest, as *Buckley* and *Shrink Missouri* prescribe. The Court upheld the soft money ban based on the government's interest in curbing corruption and the appearance of corruption. Key to this ruling was the majority's broad conception of the anti-corruption interest.

This interest was not limited to *quid pro quo* corruption, but also included the unequal access—and possible influence—that big soft-money donors enjoyed.

In cases decided after *McConnell*, most notably *Citizens United*, the Roberts Court has adopted a narrower conception of the anti-corruption rationale than that embraced in *McConnell*. It is therefore possible that the Court will revisit and overrule *McConnell*'s holding on the soft money ban, just as it overruled *McConnell*'s holding on corporate electioneering communications in *Citizens United*.

4.   OUTSIDE GROUPS

In addition to candidates' campaigns and political parties, there are a variety of other organizations that engage in campaign-related activities. These include PACs, other 527 organizations, Super PACs, and some nonprofit organizations.

a. PACs

FECA defines "political committee" to include a broad range of groups engaged in electoral activities. The term includes: (1) groups that receive contributions exceeding $1,000 or make expenditures exceeding $1,000 in a calendar year, (2) separate segregated funds established by corporations and labor unions (see Part B.3 above), and (3) certain local party committees. 2 U.S.C. § 431(4). *Buckley* narrowed the definition of "political committee" in order to rescue the disclosure requirement from constitutional challenge, interpreting this term to include only those groups with a "major purpose" of nominating or electing candidates. Political committees are subject to regulation under FECA, including contribution limits and disclosure.

The term "political action committee" or "PAC" is not used in FECA. It is generally used to refer to "multicandidate political committees," defined as political committees with more than 50 contributors that have been registered for at least six months and, except for state party committees, have made contributions to at least five federal candidates. 2 U.S.C. § 441a(a)(4). Entities that meet this definition are allowed to make contributions to federal election campaigns of up to $5,000, as opposed to the lower limit (originally $1,000, up to $2,600 in 2013–14) applicable to other political committees. An individual may contribute no more than $5,000 per calendar year to each PAC. As discussed in Part A.3 of this chapter, *Buckley* upheld the contribution limits for PACs.

There are thousands of PACs of various types. Many PACs were established by corporations and labor unions as "separate segregated funds" (see Part B.3 above), allowing them to engage in electoral activity on behalf of the entities that created them. The Court upheld the requirement that those contributing to a corporate PAC be connected to it as a shareholder, executive, administrator, or member, in *Federal Election Commission v. National Right to Work Committee,* 459 U.S. 197 (1982). There are also PACs established by members of Congress and other political leaders, referred to as Leadership PACs. Other PACs are unconnected to any corporation, labor union, or political party.

b. 527s

Some groups engaged in campaign-related activities fall outside FECA's definition of "political committee." They include some "527" organizations, named after the section of the Internal Revenue Code setting forth the tax rules applicable to political organizations. Section 527 defines a "political organization" as "a party, committee, association, fund, or other organization . . . organized and operated primarily for the purpose of directly or indirectly accepting contributions, or both, for an exempt function." 26 U.S.C. § 527(e)(1). An "exempt function" is, in turn, defined to include "influencing or attempting to influence the selection, nomination, election, or appointment of any individual to any Federal, State, or local public office." 26 U.S.C. § 527(e)(2).

Section 527 political organizations are required either to disclose contributions and expenditures or to pay a tax at the top corporate income tax rate (currently 35%) on their exempt function income. Some but not all 527s are also "political committees" subject to FECA. Not all political organizations are political committees because the definition of political organization under § 527 is different from the definition of political committee in FECA. Organizations that are regulated as political committees are not subject to disclosure under Section 527.

In the 2004 election cycle, a number of Section 527 political organizations were formed and began accepting large contributions from wealthy individuals, but claimed that they were not subject to contribution limits or disclosure requirements, because they neither made contributions nor engaged in express advocacy. The FEC issued fines against some of these 527s, concluding that they should have registered because their major purpose was to influence federal elections.

c. Super PACs and Nonprofits

After the decision in *Citizens United*, a new kind of organization began to proliferate. The technical term is "independent-expenditure only committees," but they are commonly referred to as Super PACs. These entities make independent expenditures, but do not make contributions to candidates. Super PACs may receive unlimited contributions. The creation of Super PACs is a result of the D.C. Circuit's decision in *Speechnow.org v. Federal Election Commission*, 599 F.3d 686 (D.C. Cir. 2010) (en banc). SpeechNow was a nonprofit political organization under Section 527 and was formed only to make independent expenditures.

At issue in *Speechnow.org* was the constitutionality of applying FECA's contribution limits and reporting requirements to independent-expediture only committees. While SpeechNow fell within FECA's definition of a "political committee," the D.C. Circuit concluded that it violates the First Amendment to limit contributions to an organization that only makes independent expenditures. The court relied on *Citizens United*'s holding that there is no valid constitutional interest in limiting independent expenditures. For this reason, *Speechnow.org* unanimously concluded that limiting contributions to independent-expenditure only committees likewise serves no cognizable interest. The D.C. Circuit went on to uphold the constitutionality of applying FECA's *disclosure* requirements to independent-expenditure only committees. After *Speechnow.org*, the FEC issued advisory opinions concluding that corporations and labor unions, as well as individuals, may make unlimited contributions to independent-expenditure only committees, now known as Super PACs.

In addition to Super PACs and other 527 political organizations, a number of groups organized under Section 501(c) of the Internal Revenue Code now routinely engage in independent spending to influence election results. These include social welfare organizations created under Section 501(c)(4), as well as labor organizations created under Section 501(c)(5) and trade associations created under Section 501(c)(6). These groups are not treated as PACs, so long as their primary purpose is not to influence elections. Under current law, contributions to these entities only need to be disclosed if made "for the purpose of" election-related activity. These groups are, however, required to disclose their expenditures for express advocacy and electioneering communications.

5.   AGGREGATE LIMITS

Recall that *Buckley* (Part A.3) upheld the individual limit in contributions to a particular candidate (then $1,000) as well as the *aggregate limit*—that is, the limit on the total contributions an individual could make (then $25,000). The Court concluded that this aggregate limit was a "modest restraint" on protected association, justified by the interest in preventing evasion of the individual contribution limits. Aggregate limits for federal elections remain in place, now indexed for inflation. For the 2013–14 cycle, the aggregate contribution limit—the most that a person may contribute to all federal candidates, party committees and other political committees—was set at $123,200. There also are aggregate limits of $48,600 in contributions to all federal candidates and $74,600 to all PACs and parties. The constitutionality of these limits is before the Supreme Court in *McCutcheon v. Federal Election Commission*.

D.   PUBLIC FINANCING

Given the unconstitutionality of restrictions on independent expenditures and the questions surrounding contribution limits, public financing has long seemed like an attractive alternative to some advocates of campaign finance reform. Rather than imposing a ceiling on how much can be raised or spent, public financing systems provide public funds to qualifying candidates. In exchange, candidates agree to limits on how much they raise, how much they spend or, in "clean money" systems, forego private financing altogether. Advocates of public financing argue that it reduces corruption and the appearance of corruption, by decreasing candidates' reliance on private money. They have also argued that it helps promote equality or a level playing field, by giving candidates with less wealth—or less wealthy supporters—an opportunity to compete. The federal public financing scheme for presidential elections, state public financing schemes, and the constitutional limits on public financing are discussed in turn.

1.   PRESIDENTIAL ELECTIONS

Federal law provides public financing for presidential elections, but not for congressional elections. Like all public financing schemes, it is voluntary; candidates cannot constitutionally be required to accept it.

The basic framework established by FECA and upheld in *Buckley* (Part A.3) remains in place today. Public funding is available both for primaries and for general elections. It is funded through a "check off" by taxpayers. To qualify for public financing, primary candidates are required to raise at least $5,000 in each of twenty states, counting only the first $250 given by each contributor. FECA provided qualifying candidates with matching federal funds for contributions up to $250. Candidates who accept public financing for the primaries agree to accept expenditure limits, including both a nationwide limit and a limit for spending in each state. FECA also provides public financing for general election campaigns, on the condition that participating candidates agree to an expenditure limit in the same amount. The idea is that general election candidates who accept public financing will not raise or spend any private money for that phase of the campaign. In practice, however, the amount provided has not kept up with the increasing costs of running campaigns. Accordingly, the presidential public financing system has become a virtual dead letter, not likely to be used by serious candidates in future presidential elections.

2.   STATE PUBLIC FINANCING

A handful of states and some local jurisdictions have implemented public financing systems. The details of these public financing schemes vary significantly. Arizona and Maine adopted full public financing (or "clean money") schemes in 2000, offering participating candidates public monies to pay the full cost of state legislative campaigns. Candidates qualify for public financing by raising a prescribed amount in small-dollar contributions. Minnesota and Wisconsin are among the states that have adopted partial public financing schemes. One of the local jurisdictions to have adopted public financing is New York City, which in 2004 started matching contributions up to $175 at a six-to-one ratio. In other words, a $100 contribution to a candidate is matched with $600 in public funds, giving the candidate's campaign a total of $700. There is some evidence that public financing schemes can increase the pool of candidates available to run and increase the likelihood of a competitive race, but only if the amount provided is commensurate with the resources that candidates require to mount an effective campaign. Kenneth Mayer, Timothy Werner & Amanda Williams, *Do Public Funding Programs Enhance Electoral Competition?*, in THE MARKETPLACE OF DEMOCRACY 245 (2006).

3. CONSTITUTIONAL LIMITS

The Court upheld the presidential public financing scheme in *Buckley*, saying that public money may be conditioned on a candidate's agreement to abide by expenditure limits. The Court also rejected the argument that the presidential public financing scheme unfairly discriminated against minor parties (Part A.3). Other public financing schemes have been challenged on the grounds that they are coercive, giving candidates no real choice but to accept public money and the limits that come with it.

The Supreme Court has not addressed the question of when public financing schemes are unconstitutionally coercive, but it has struck down a public financing scheme on the ground that it placed substantial burdens on *privately financed* candidates and their supporters. In *Arizona Free Enterprise Club's Freedom Club PAC v. Bennett*, 131 S. Ct. 2806 (2011) (*Arizona Free Enterprise*), the Court considered a challenge to Arizona's Citizens Clean Elections Act, which was enacted by initiative. As with other public financing systems, candidates for state office could choose whether to accept public financing. Those candidates who opted in agreed to expenditure limits. Publicly financed candidates would receive an initial allotment of funds, the amount depending on the office. The distinctive feature of Arizona's system was that the additional amounts to a publicly financed candidate depended on how much was raised and spent *on the other side.* Privately financed candidates were free to spend as much as they wished. But once the amount raised by or spent in support of a privately financed candidate exceeded the initial allotment to the publicly financed candidate, the state would "match" each additional dollar spent to support the privately financed candidate. Matching funds were triggered by independent expenditures in support of a privately financed candidate, as well as by monies raised or spent by the candidate himself. The idea was to allow publicly financed candidates to compete with well-financed opponents, effectively equalizing the resources available to each side.

Chief Justice Roberts' opinion for the five-justice majority struck down Arizona's scheme under the First Amendment. The Court concluded that Arizona's matching funds scheme effectively penalized privately financed candidates and their supporters. In this respect, Arizona's scheme was deemed comparable to BCRA's "Millionaire's Amendment," struck down in *Davis v. Federal Election Commission* (Part C.2). Both schemes gave a benefit to a candidate's opponent, in response to activities that are protected by the First Amendment. Because the state's public financing scheme imposed a "substantial burden" on speech, the Court applied strict scrutiny. It proceeded to hold that Arizona's scheme was not narrowly tailored to a compelling interest. Following *Buckley* and *Citizens United*, the Court rejected the equality rationale—or "leveling the playing field"—as an impermissible justification for burdening protected expression. It also rejected Arizona's reliance on the anti-corruption rationale, finding the burden on speech too great to be sustained based on this justification.

Justice Kagan dissented in *Arizona Free Enterprise*, joined by Justices Ginsburg, Breyer, and Sotomayor. Justice Kagan's dissent emphasized that Arizona's scheme did not limit anyone's speech. It was a subsidy, not a penalty, designed to ensure that candidates receive the appropriate level of funding. She thus disagreed that the scheme imposed a substantial burden on speech. Even if strict scrutiny applied, Justice Kagan thought the state had a compelling interest in preventing corruption and its appearance, arising from candidates' dependence on large private contributions.

Arizona Free Enterprise does not render all public financing schemes unconstitutional, nor does it mean that all are subject to strict scrutiny. The majority opinion was careful to emphasize this point, noting that it did not "call into question the wisdom of public financing as a means of funding political candidacy." The decision does, however, make it more difficult for states to develop public financing schemes that are at once viable and affordable. A scheme that allocates public financing based on the amount raised or spent on the other side will likely be judged a "penalty" on speech, subject to strict scrutiny. The argument that the scheme is designed to make candidates less reliant on private donors is insufficient to uphold it.

E.   DISCLOSURE

Disclosure requirements have generally been viewed with less suspicion than limits on expenditures and contributions. That is because requiring disclosure of campaign-related money does not necessarily impede it from being given or spent. On the other hand, compelled disclosure may have a chilling effect on would-be donors and spenders. People may fear negative consequences if the government or someone else (such as an employer) find out they have financially supported a candidate, party, or other group that is regarded with disfavor.

The Supreme Court accords heightened scrutiny to disclosure requirements, in recognition of their potential chilling effects and impact on privacy. The Court has subjected mandatory disclosure rules to "exacting scrutiny" under the First Amendment, requiring a substantial relation between the disclosure requirement and a sufficiently important government interest. Although this may sound stringent, it is less so than the strict scrutiny applied to expenditure limits. As a practical matter, it is also less stringent than the scrutiny accorded to contribution limits. That is largely because the

Court has been relatively generous in the government interests it recognizes as justifications for disclosure.

Starting with *Buckley*, the Court has recognized three interests that may justify disclosure requirements: (1) *informing the electorate* of where campaign money comes from and how it is spent, (2) *deterring corruption and avoiding the appearance of corruption*, by exposing large contributors who may be seeking special treatment, and (3) *gathering information needed to detect violations of contribution limits.* Based on these interests, *Buckley* upheld FECA's disclosure requirements, including the requirement that political committees register and report and that those making contributions over $100 be disclosed. The Court rejected arguments that these requirements were unconstitutionally overbroad, although it left open the possibility that specific groups might bring an as-applied challenge. In order to save expenditure disclosure from a vagueness challenge, the Court narrowed FECA's scope. It interpreted "political committees" to include only those under the control of a candidate or having the major purpose of influencing elections. For other groups, the Court held that disclosure is only required for expenditures in support of "express advocacy"—i.e., communications using so-called "magic words" like "vote for" or "vote against" (see Part A.3).

Relying on *Buckley*, the Supreme Court upheld BCRA's expansion of FECA's disclosure requirements in both *McConnell* and *Citizens*

United. Under BCRA, anyone expending more than $10,000 on electioneering communications must file a disclosure statement identifying the person making the expenditure, the amount spent, the election to which it was directed, and the names of certain contributors. BCRA also required that electioneering communications include a disclaimer, indicating that "___ is responsible for the content of this advertising." *McConnell* upheld these requirements against a facial challenge, reasoning that they would help voters make informed choices. For the same reasons, *Citizens United* upheld these requirements as applied to *Hillary: The Movie* and ads for that documentary. Only Justice Thomas dissented from this aspect of *Citizens United*, believing BCRA's disclosure requirements unconstitutional because of their tendency to chill speech.

Although the other eight justices in *Citizens United* disagreed with Justice Thomas' position regarding the chilling effect of disclosure, the Court has allowed as-applied exceptions to disclosure in limited circumstances. A disclosure requirement may not constitutionally be applied where there is a reasonable probability of threats, harassment, or reprisals from either government officials or private parties. This exception was stated in *Buckley* and applied in *Brown v. Socialist Workers '74 Campaign Committee*, 459 U.S. 87 (1982), to exempt a minor party from disclosure under FECA. The Socialist Workers Party was able to produce evidence that party members had been harassed by the FBI and that party leaders had been victims of violence. In these circumstances, compelled disclosure might well discourage people from giving to the party.

The Court has also considered the constitutional limits on disclosure in other contexts not involving campaign contributions or expenditures. In *McIntyre v. Ohio Elections Commission*, 514 U.S. 334 (1995), the Court struck down a law prohibiting the distribution of anonymous campaign literature under the First Amendment. It rejected the state's asserted interest in informing the electorate as insufficient to justify compelled disclosure. The Court found the prohibition on anonymous campaign literature broader and more intrusive than FECA's disclosure requirements upheld in *Buckley v. Valeo*. And in *Buckley v. American Constitutional Law Foundation*, 525 U.S. 182 (1999) (*ACLF*), the Court struck down a law requiring paid petition circulators to wear a badge with their names and requiring initiative proponents to file reports listing circulators and their income from circulation. It found the interests in anonymity, and thus the potential harm to speech, especially strong in this context.

Although these cases might be understood to suggest rigorous review, the Roberts Court has so far taken a fairly deferential approach to disclosure requirements. One example is *Citizens United*'s upholding of BCRA's disclosure requirements. Another example is *Doe v. Reed*, 130 S. Ct. 2811 (2010) (also discussed in Chapter 8.C). In *Doe v. Reed*, the Court rejected a facial challenge to a state law requiring disclosure of the names and addresses of referendum petition signatories. Applying the test stated in *Buckley* and other campaign finance cases, the majority required only a substantial relation between the disclosure requirement and a sufficiently important governmental interest. While rejecting a facial challenge to the disclosure requirement, the majority left open the possibility of an as-applied challenge, if plaintiffs could produce evidence of threats, harassment, or reprisals against those signing the referendum petition. The exception suggested in *Buckley* and applied in *Socialist Workers* still exists, but there must be evidence—not just speculation—of probable threats, harassment, or reprisals to obtain an exemption to disclosure.

INDEX

References are to pages.

ABSENTEE VOTING
Constitutional issues, 173–75
Reform, 31
State laws, 190–91
Uniformed and Overseas Citizens Absentee Voting Act (UOCAVA), 175, 177

AGE RESTRICTIONS, 28–29

ALIENS
Right to vote, 30

AMERICANS WITH DISABILITIES ACT (ADA), 177

APPORTIONMENT
See Legislative Districting, this index

AS–APPLIED AND FACIAL CHALLENGES, 166, 228–29, 259–61, 286, 323, 324, 326

ASSOCIATIONAL RIGHTS, 252–62, 264–71

AT–LARGE ELECTIONS, 93, 96–98, 113, 116–17, 134, 136, 179

BALLOTS
Butterfly ballot, 200
Florida election controversy, 149, 152–62
Form of, 170, 200
Secret ballot, 20–21
Write-in votes, 98, 165, 237–38, 266–67

BALLOT ACCESS, 165, 262–71, 285

BALLOT MEASURES
Amendments, 215–17
Campaign finance regulation and, 289–91, 304–05, 325–26
Constitutional limits
    Equal Protection 229–35
    First Amendment, 224–29
    Qualifications Clauses, 235–40
    Republican Guarantee Clause, 223–24
Content limitations, 210–19
Disclosure, 213, 227–29, 325–26
Frequency of use, 207–08
Initiatives, 205–40
    Defined, 206
Judicial review of, 221–23
Minority rights and, 229–35
Populism and progressivism, relationship to, 206, 209
Pre-election review, 222–23
Procedural requirements, 219–21
Pros and cons of, 208–09
Qualification of, 209–10, 219–21
    Anonymity concerns, 226, 229
    Paid circulators, use of, 224–26
    Substantial compliance, 221
Recalls, see Recall Elections, this index
Referendum, 205–40
    Defined, 206
Republican form of government and, 205, 223–24
Revisions, 215–17
Separate vote requirement, 211
Single subject rule, 210–15
Substantive limitations, 210–19
Turnout and, 208

BALLOT PROPOSITIONS
See Ballot Measures, this index

BIPARTISAN CAMPAIGN REFORM ACT (BCRA), 297–302, 307–08, 309–11, 320, 323–24, 325

BLANKET PRIMARY, 258–61, 265, 267–68

BURKEAN DEBATE, 5

BUTTERFLY BALLOT, 200

CAMPAIGN FINANCE REGULATION
527 organizations, 311, 313–14
Ballot measure campaigns and, 289–91, 304–05, 325–26
Bipartisan Campaign Reform Act (BCRA), 297–302, 307–08, 309–11, 320, 323–24, 325
Constitutional framework, 280–88
Contribution limits, 275, 281–83, 303–16
    527 organizations, 313–14
    Aggregate limits, 316
    Ballot measures, 304–05
    Competition and competitiveness and, 277–78, 279, 306–08
    Corporations and labor unions, 308–09, 312–13, 315
    Nonprofits, 315
    Political action committees (PACs), 283, 311–13, 316
    Political parties, 309–11
    Residency requirements, 309
    Super PACs, 314–15
Corporations, 289–90, 293–302, 308–09, 311, 312, 315
Disclosure, 275, 278, 279, 285–88, 311–12, 313–14, 315, 322–26
Expenditure limits, 274, 281–84, 288–303
    Ballot measure campaigns, 289–91
    Corporations and labor unions, 293–302
    Judicial elections, 302–03
    Lobbyists, 213
    Nonprofits, 294–95, 297, 299
    Political parties, 291–93
Federal Election Campaign Act (FECA), 281–88, 292–95, 297, 303, 307, 309, 311, 312, 313, 314–15, 317, 323, 324–25
Incumbency and, 277–78, 279, 306–07
Independent expenditures, 280, 282, 284, 288, 289, 291, 292, 293–303, 308, 314, 315, 316
Judicial elections, 302–03

Labor unions, 289, 293–302, 308, 311, 312, 315
Modes of regulation, 274–76
Nonprofit organizations, 294–95, 297, 299, 315
Political action committees (PACs)
    Contribution limits, 283, 311–13, 316
    Corporate and union PACs, 293–94, 297, 299, 302
    Super PACs, 314–15
Political parties, 280, 285–86, 291–93, 307, 309–11
Pros and cons of, 276–80
Public financing, 275, 284–85, 316–22
    Constitutionality, 284–85, 319–22
    Presidential elections, 317–18
    State public financing plans, 318–19
Soft money, 297, 307, 309–11
Spending limits, see Expenditure Limits
Super PACs, 314–15
Third parties and, 285–86, 319, 324–25
Unions, see Labor Unions
Values, 276–80

CIVIC REPUBLICANISM, 6–7

CLOSED PRIMARY, 256, 258

COMMUNITIES OF INTEREST, 71, 73, 74

COMPETITION AND COMPETITIVENESS,
    Generally, 9–11, 55
Campaign finance, 277–78, 279, 306–07
Judicial elections, 262
Legislative districting, 72–73, 78
Major parties, 270–71
Third parties, 270–71

CONSTITUTION OF THE UNITED STATES
Article I, Section 2 of, 14, 29, 33, 36, 52–53, 59, 61, 82
Article I, Section 4 of, 33, 48, 53, 87, 182–83, 239, 246, 249
Article II of, 151–54, 155–56, 160–61,194–95
Article IV, Section 4 of, 47, 223–24
Ballot Measures, Constitutional limits, this index
Due Process Clause, see Fourteenth Amendment
Eighteenth Amendment, 24

Elections Clause, 33, 48, 53, 87, 182–83, 239, 246, 249
Equal Protection Clause, see Fourteenth Amendment
Fifteenth Amendment
     Generally, 34, 93
  At-large elections, 116
  Congressional power under, 96, 108–12
  Enforcement power, 108–12
  Gerrymandering, 37, 48–49, 138
  History, 17–22
  Legislative districting, 138
  Literacy tests, 36
  Restrictions on voting, 43–44
  Voting Rights Act and, 108–12
  White primary, 247–52
  Women's right to vote, 23
First Amendment
  Associational rights, 252–62, 264–71
  Ballot access, 264–71, 285
  Ballot measures, 223, 224–29
  Campaign finance regulation, 273, 278, 281–326
  Gerrymandering, 88
  Term limits, 239
Fourteenth Amendment
     Generally, 4, 17, 34
  Age restrictions, 29
  At-large elections, 116
  Ballot access, 264–71
  Ballot measures, 230–35
  Congressional power under, 108–12
  Due Process Clause, 8, 159, 169, 173, 174, 253, 303
  Election administration, 162–76
  Enforcement power, 108–12
  Equal Protection Clause, 8, 17, 20, 31, 37–39, 49, 51, 52–58, 59, 61, 69, 81–82, 83–92, 93, 114, 128, 137–47, 149, 155–59, 161–62, 169–76, 194, 223, 229–35, 247–48, 264–65, 296
  Felony disenfranchisement, 30–31
  Gerrymandering, 81–92, 136–47
  History, 17–22
  Noncitizens, 30
  One person, one vote, this index

Political question doctrine, 49
Poll tax, 37–39, 157
Privileges or Immunities Clause, 17, 23
Voting Rights Act and, 28–29, 108–12
White primary, 247–51
Women's right to vote, 23–24
Guaranty Clause, see Republican Guarantee Clause
Nineteenth Amendment, 22–25, 34
Political question doctrine, 16, 46–51, 83–92
Privileges or Immunities Clause, see Fourteenth Amendment
Qualifications for Congress, 235–40
Qualifications for voting, 14–16, 29–31, 33, 35–36, 39–44
Republican Guarantee Clause, 47, 49, 51, 223–24
Seventeenth Amendment, 15, 29, 33, 36
Twelfth Amendment, 151
Twenty–First Amendment, 24
Twenty–Fourth Amendment, 20, 34, 38
Twenty–Sixth Amendment, 29, 34

CORRUPTION

Campaign finance regulation and, 276–77, 282–83, 284, 286, 288, 289, 290, 292, 294, 296, 300, 301, 305–06, 308, 310–11, 317, 321, 323

DILUTION

See Vote Dilution, this index

DIRECT DEMOCRACY

Generally, 205–40
See Ballot Measures, this index
See Recall Elections, this index

DISABILITY, 177, 184, 190

DISCLOSURE

Ballot measures, 213, 227–29, 325–26
Campaign finance regulation, 275, 278, 279, 281, 284, 285–88, 311–12, 313–14, 315, 322–26

DISENFRANCHISEMENT

See Right to Vote, this index

DISTRICTING
See Legislative Districting, this index

DUE PROCESS CLAUSE
See Constitution of the United States, Fourteenth Amendment, this index

DURATIONAL RESIDENCY REQUIREMENTS, 29–30, 41

DUVERGER'S LAW, 242–43

EARLY VOTING
Constitutional issues, 169–70, 175–76
Reform, 31–32
State laws, 190–91
Voting Rights Act and, 180

ELECTION ADMINISTRATION
Absentee voting
   Constitutional issues, 173–75
   Reform, 31
   State laws, 190–91
   Uniformed and Overseas Citizens Absentee Voting Act (UOCAVA), 175, 177
Butterfly ballot, 200
Canvasses, 153, 193
Contests, 31, 152–55, 193, 194, 197
Convenience voting, 190–91
Counting of votes, 157, 168, 173–75, 193
Decentralization of, 150
Disabilities, 177, 184, 190
Early voting
   Constitutional issues, 169–70, 175–76
   Reform, 31–32
   State laws, 190–91
   Voting Rights Act and, 180
Election Assistance Commission (EAC), 185
Election litigation, volume, 162
Electronic voting, 171–73
Florida election controversy, 149, 151–62
Help America Vote Act (HAVA), 149, 172, 177, 183–86, 188, 189–90, 191, 192

Institutional arrangements, 186–88
Judicial remedies, 193–203
Language assistance, 181–82
National Voter Registration Act (NVRA, or "Motor Voter"), 177, 182–83, 185, 188
Partisanship in, 150, 158, 187–88
Polling place operations, 191–92
Provisional voting
 Canvassing, 193
 Constitutional issues, 168–69, 174–75
 Help America Vote Act, 184, 185–86
 Reform, 31–32
 Remedies, 195
 State laws, 189–90
Recounts, 31, 149, 153–62, 172, 173, 174, 191, 193, 194, 197
Remedies, 193–203
Turnout, 188
Voter identification
 Constitutionality, 149, 163–68
 Enjoining, 195
 Fraud and, 163–67
 Help America Vote Act, 184
 Poll tax compared, 164
 Reform, 31–32
 State laws, 188–89
 Voting Rights Act, 179–81
Voter registration
 Durational residency and, 30
 False registration forms, 202–03
 Help America Vote Act (HAVA), 184, 186
 Minority voting and, 19, 21, 25, 27, 36, 95–96, 111, 180
 National Voter Registration Act (NVRA, or "Motor Voter"), 177, 182–83, 185, 188
 Polling place operations and, 192
 Provisional voting and, 189–90
 Qualification of ballot measures, 220, 226
 Reform, 31–32
 State laws, 188
 Turnout, 188
 Voting Rights Act (VRA), 95–96, 110, 111, 180, 181

Voting equipment
  Constitutional issues, 162–63,169–73
  Help America Vote Act (HAVA), 183–84
  Polling place operations and, 192
  Reform, 31–32
  Remedies, 196–97
  State laws, 191
  Voting Rights Act (VRA), 179–80
Voting Rights Act, this index

ELECTION ASSISTANCE COMMISSION, 185

ELECTION OFFICIALS, 21, 95, 150, 158, 174, 187–88, 202–03

ELECTIONS CLAUSE
See Constitution, Elections Clause, this index

ELECTORAL COLLEGE, 151–52, 161

ELECTORAL COUNT ACT, 159, 161

ELECTRONIC VOTING, 171–73

EQUAL POPULATION
See One Person, One Vote, this index

EQUAL PROTECTION CLAUSE
See Constitution of the United States, Fourteenth Amendment, this index

FACIAL AND AS–APPLIED CHALLENGES, 166, 228–29, 259–61, 286, 323, 324, 326

FEDERAL ELECTION CAMPAIGN ACT (FECA), 281–88, 292–95, 297, 303, 307, 309, 311, 312, 313, 314–15, 317, 323, 324–25

FEDERAL ELECTION COMMISSION (FEC), 286, 310

FEDERALISM, 50, 108

FELONY DISENFRANCHISEMENT, 13, 30–31, 131, 179

FIFTEENTH AMENDMENT
See Constitution of the United States, this index

FIRST AMENDMENT
See Constitution of the United States, this index

FLORIDA ELECTION CONTROVERSY, 149, 151–62

FOURTEENTH AMENDMENT
See Constitution of the United States, this index

FRANCHISE
See Voting Rights, this index

FRAUD
Absentee ballots, 198
Criminal penalties for, 202–03
Disenfranchisement and, 18, 19
Petition signatures, 225–26
Primaries, 249
Remedies for
    Adjusting vote totals, 197
    Criminal penalties, 202
    Voiding election, 199
Voter identification and, 163–67
Voter registration, 202
Voting fraud, 32, 163–67, 202–03

FREEDOM OF ASSOCIATION
See Constitution of the United States, First Amendment, this
    index

FREEDOM OF SPEECH
See Constitution of the United States, First Amendment, this
    index

FUSION CANDIDACIES, 269–71

GERRYMANDERING
Bipartisan gerrymandering, 78, 81–82
Constitutionality of, 81–92
Partisan gerrymandering, 77–92
Population equality and, 81–83
Racial gerrymandering, 9, 37, 136–47
Sweetheart gerrymandering, 78, 81–82

GRANDFATHER CLAUSES, 20

GUARANTY CLAUSE
See Constitution of the United States, Republican Guarantee Clause, this index

HELP AMERICA VOTE ACT (HAVA), 149, 172, 177, 183–86, 188, 189–90, 191, 192

HISTORY OF VOTING RIGHTS, 13–32

INCUMBENCY
Advantages of, 10
Campaign finance regulation, 277–78, 279, 306–07
Districting, 72–74, 78–81
Judicial review, 8–10
One person, one vote and, 55, 57, 60
Term limits, 235–39

INDEPENDENT CANDIDATES, 68, 97–98, 241–42, 262–66, 285

INDEPENDENT COMMISSIONS, 80, 187–88

INDEPENDENT EXPENDITURES, 280, 282, 284, 288, 289, 291, 292, 293–303, 308, 314, 315, 316, 320

INITIATIVES
See Ballot Propositions, this index

INSTITUTIONAL ARRANGEMENTS, 187–88

INTERPRETATION TESTS
See Literacy and Interpretation Tests, this index

JUDICIAL ELECTIONS, 174, 261–62, 289, 302–03

JUDICIAL REMEDIES
See Remedies, this index

JUDICIAL REVIEW
Generally, 8–12
Ballot measures, 221–23, 230–35
Campaign finance regulation, 280–88
Competition and competitiveness, 8–10

Election administration, 155–76
Incumbency and, 9–10
Legislative districting, 45–69, 81–92
Political question doctrine, this index
Process-based theory, 8–9, 55–56
Remedies, see Remedies, this index
Representation-reinforcement theory, 8–9
Rights-based approach, 11
Structuralist approach, 9
Term limits, 235–40
Voting Rights Act, 99, 107–12

JUSTICIABILITY
See Political Question Doctrine

LANGUAGE ASSISTANCE, 181–82

LEGISLATIVE DISTRICTING
Apportionment, 45–67, 88, 142
Census, 51, 63, 71, 73, 75, 91, 100
Communities of interest, 71, 73, 74
Compactness, 60, 70, 73, 74, 75, 80, 83, 89, 123–24, 127–29, 142, 146
Competition and competitiveness, 72–73, 78
Contiguity, 70, 73, 74, 75, 89, 142
Criteria for, 69–76, 80, 89, 128, 142
Deference to states, 75–76, 100–01
Geographic boundaries, 71
Gerrymandering, this index
Incumbency, 72
Independent commissions, 80
Judicial review, 45–69, 81–92
Malapportionment, 45–67
Minority representation, 73, 78, 93–147, 179, 180
Nesting, 71–72, 73, 74, 75
One person, one vote, this index
Partisanship, 45, 62, 69, 72, 77–92
Political boundaries, 60, 71
Reapportionment, see Apportionment
Voting Rights Act, this index

LEGISLATIVE TERM LIMITS
See Term Limits, this index

LITERACY AND INTERPRETATION TESTS
Constitutionality, 35–36, 38
History, 20, 25, 27, 28, 178
Voting Rights Act, 27, 28, 35–36, 93, 95–96, 178

MAIL VOTING, 190

MAJOR PARTIES
See Parties, this index

MALAPPORTIONMENT, 45–67

MCCAIN–FEINGOLD
See Bipartisan Campaign Reform Act (BCRA), this index

MINOR PARTIES
See Parties, this index

MOTOR VOTER LAW
See National Voter Registration Act (NVRA), this index

NATIONAL VOTER REGISTRATION ACT (NVRA), 177,
182–83, 185, 188

NINETEENTH AMENDMENT
See Constitution of the United States, this index

NONCITIZEN VOTING, 30

ONE PERSON, ONE VOTE
Generally, 9, 46, 51–69, 75
Appointive bodies, 65
Census, 51, 63
Deviations from equality, 59–62
Election administration and, 157–58
Gerrymandering and, 81–83
Incumbency and, 55, 57, 60
Local government, 64–65
Other democratic processes, 67–68
Primary elections, 51–52, 67–68
Remedies, 196

Special purpose districts, 66–67
Voting Rights Act and, 100

OPEN PRIMARY, 255, 257–58

PACS
See Political Action Committees, this index

PARTIES
    Generally, 241–45
Associational rights of, 252–62
Ballot access, 262–71
Campaign finance regulation of, 280, 285–86, 291–93, 307, 309–11
Constitutional obligations of, 245–52
Duverger's Law, 242–43
Governance, 261–62
History, 241
Independent candidates and, 242, 263–65
Legislature, regulation of party in, 244, 251
Major parties,
    Ballot access, 264
    Campaign finance regulation, 285
    Competition and competitiveness, 270–71
    Divided government, 244
    Dominance, 1, 241–42
    Election administration, 150
    Legislative districting, 61, 72–73, 78, 82
    Presidential nominations, 253–55
    Primary elections, 21–22, 25
    Strength of, 242–43
Minor parties, see Third Parties
Obligations under Constitution, 245–52
Partisan Gerrymandering, see Gerrymandering, this index
Party raiding, 256, 267
Party switching, 267
Presidential nominations, 253–55
Primary elections, this index
Sore loser candidacies, 267
Third Parties
    Ballot access, 262–71

Blanket primary, 267–68
Campaign finance regulation, 285–86, 319, 324–25
Duverger's Law, 242–43
Fusion candidacies, 269–71
History, 241–42
Semi–closed primary, 256–57
Two-party system, 241–44, 256, 263, 270

PARTISAN GERRYMANDERING
See Gerrymandering, this index

PLURALISM, 6

POLITICAL ACTION COMMITTEES (PACS)
Contribution limits, 283, 311–13, 316
Corporate and union PACs, 293–94, 297, 299, 302
Super PACs, 314–15

POLITICAL GERRYMANDERING
See Gerrymandering, this index

POLITICAL PARTIES
See Parties, this index

POLITICAL QUESTION DOCTRINE, 16, 46–51, 83–92

POLL TAX
Constitutionality, 34, 37–39, 157
History, 9, 15, 16, 20, 25, 93, 178
Voter identification compared, 164

POLLING PLACE OPERATIONS, 31, 191–92

PRIMARY ELECTIONS
Ballot access, 263
Blanket primary, 258–61, 265, 267–68
Campaign finance regulation, 297, 307, 317
Closed primary, 256, 258
Enjoining, 197
Filing fees, 271
One person, one vote, 51–52, 67–68
Open primary, 255, 257–58
Party raiding in, 267

Political parties, 244, 245–52, 255–61
Racial discrimination in, 21–22, 25, 178, 202, 245–52
Semi-closed primary, 256–57
Turnout in, 268
Voting Rights Act, 115, 178
White Primary, 21–22, 25, 178, 245–52

PRISONERS
Counting, 63–64
Voting rights, 30–31, 179

PROGRESSIVISM, 6, 206, 209

PROPERTY RESTRICTIONS FOR VOTING, 14–16, 39, 40, 47

PROPORTIONAL REPRESENTATION, 73, 85–86, 114, 118–20, 122, 124, 126, 134, 242

PROVISIONAL VOTING
Canvassing, 193
Constitutional issues, 168–70, 173–75
Help America Vote Act, 184, 185–86
Reform, 31–32
Remedies, 195
State laws, 189–90

PUBLIC CHOICE THEORY, 7

PUBLIC FINANCING, 275, 316–22
Constitutionality, 284–85, 288, 319–22
Presidential elections, 317–18
State public financing plans, 318–19

QUALIFICATION OF BALLOT MEASURES, 209–10, 219–21
Anonymity concerns, 226, 229
Paid circulators, use of, 224–26
Substantial compliance, 221

QUALIFICATIONS FOR CONGRESS, 235–40

QUALIFICATIONS FOR VOTING, 14–16, 29, 33, 35–36, 39–44, 96

RACE DISCRIMINATION
See Voting Rights, this index, and Voting Rights Act, this index
Election Administration, 177–82
History, 16–22, 25–28
Representation, 93–147

RACIAL GERRYMANDERING
See Gerrymandering, this index

RACIAL POLARIZATION, 97, 116, 123–26, 131–33

REAPPORTIONMENT
See Legislative Districting, this index

RECALL ELECTIONS
California Governor, 171, 196–97
Congress, 239–40
Constitutional limits, 239–40
Defined, 207
Qualification, 209–10

RECONSTRUCTION, 16–18, 37–38, 93
Second Reconstruction, 25–28

RECOUNTS,
Generally, 31, 193, 194
Florida, 149, 153–62
Judicial remedies, 197
Minnesota, 173–74
Voter-verifiable paper audit trail (VVPAT),172, 173, 191

REDISTRICTING
See Legislative Districting, this index

REFERENDUMS
See Ballot Propositions, this index

REGISTRATION
See Voter Registration, this index

RELIGION
Ballot measures, 212
Communities of interest, 71
Minority protection, 73
Qualification for voting, 14
Religious Freedom Restoration Act, 108

REMEDIES
Generally, 193–95
Adjusting vote totals, 197–99
Civil damages, 201–02
Criminal penalties, 202–03
Enjoining election, 196–97
Enjoining particular practice, 195–96
Florida election litigation, 158–59
Fraud, 197–98, 199, 202
Injunctions, 195–97
Voiding an election, 199–201

REPRESENTATION, THEORIES OF
Burkean debate, 5
Civic republicanism, 6–7
Pluralism, 6
Progressivism, 6
Public choice, 7

REPRESENTATIVE DEMOCRACY
Burkean debate, 5
Direct democracy compared, 6, 205
Madison's view, 6, 205
Republican form of government, 2–4, 47, 205, 223
Role of representatives, 4–5

REPUBLICAN FORM OF GOVERNMENT
See Representative Democracy, this index

REPUBLICAN GUARANTEE CLAUSE
See Constitution of the United States, this index

RESIDENCY
Campaign finance regulation, 309
Qualification for Voting, 29–30, 40–43

RIGHT TO VOTE
See Voting Rights, this index

SECOND RECONSTRUCTION, 25–28

SECRET BALLOT, 20–21

SECTION 2 OF VOTING RIGHTS ACT
See Voting Rights Act, this index

SECTION 4 OF VOTING RIGHTS ACT
See Voting Rights Act, this index

SECTION 5 OF VOTING RIGHTS ACT
See Voting Rights Act, this index

SECTION 203 OF VOTING RIGHTS ACT
See Voting Rights Act, this index

SECTION 1983 ACTIONS, 185–86

SEMI–CLOSED PRIMARY, 256–57

SENATORS, DIRECT ELECTION OF, 15

SEPARATE VOTE REQUIREMENT, 211

SEVENTEENTH AMENDMENT
See Constitution of the United States, this index

SINGLE SUBJECT RULE, 210–15

SOFT MONEY, 297, 307, 309–11

SORE LOSER CANDIDACIES, 267

STATE ACTION
Presidential nominations, 253
White Primary, 247, 250

SUBSTANTIAL COMPLIANCE, 221

SUFFRAGE
See Voting Rights, this index

SUPER PACS, 314–15

TERM LIMITS, 215, 235–40

THIRD PARTIES
See Parties, this index

TURNOUT, 182, 188, 208, 268

TWELFTH AMENDMENT
See Constitution of the United States, this index

TWENTY–FOURTH AMENDMENT
See Constitution of the United States, this index

TWENTY–SIXTH AMENDMENT
See Constitution of the United States, this index

TWO–PARTY SYSTEM, 241–44, 256, 263, 270

**UNIFORMED AND OVERSEAS CITIZENS ABSENTEE
   VOTING ACT (UOCAVA),** 175, 177

VOTE, RIGHT TO
See Voting Rights, this index

VOTE DENIAL, 45, 93, 96, 98, 179

VOTE DILUTION
At-large elections, 96–97
Constitutional standard, 113–17
Defined, 45
Initiative compared, 232
Malapportionment as, 45–46
Qualitative, 45
Quantitative 45
Racial minorities, 113
Second-generation barrier, 93, 112
Section 2 of VRA, 26–27, 28, 113, 118–36
Section 5 of VRA, 98

Vote denial compared, 45, 93, 98, 179

VOTER IDENTIFICATION
Constitutionality, 149, 163–68
Enjoining, 195
Fraud and, 163–67
Help America Vote Act, 184
Poll tax compared, 164
Reform, 31–32
State laws, 188–89
Voting Rights Act, 179–81

VOTER REGISTRATION
Durational residency and, 30
False registration forms, 202
Help America Vote Act (HAVA), 184, 186
Minority voting and, 19, 21, 25, 27, 36, 95–96, 111, 180
National Voter Registration Act (NVRA, or "Motor Voter"), 177,
    182–83, 185, 188
Polling place operations and, 192
Provisional voting and, 189
Qualification of ballot measures, 220, 226
Reforms, 31–32
State laws, 188
Turnout, 188
Voting Rights Act (VRA), 95–96, 110, 111, 180, 181

VOTER TURNOUT
See Turnout, this index

VOTER–VERIFIABLE PAPER AUDIT TRAIL (VVPAT),
    172, 173, 191

VOTING EQUIPMENT
Constitutional issues, 162–63,169–73
Help America Vote Act (HAVA), 183–84
Polling place operations and, 192
Reform, 31–32
Remedies, 196–97
State laws, 191
Voting Rights Act (VRA), 179–80

VOTING FRAUD
See Fraud, this index

VOTING RIGHTS
African Americans, 13, 16–22, 25–28, 31, 35–38, 78, 93, 95, 96,
    102, 103–04, 112, 113–17, 122–26, 130, 132, 135, 137, 138–41,
    143, 144–45, 177–78, 202, 245–52
Age restrictions, 28–29
Aliens, 30
Asian Americans, 28, 181
Constitutional text and structure, 14, 33–35
Durational residency, 29–30, 41
Exclusions based on lack of interest, 39–44
Felons, 13, 30–31, 131, 179
Grandfather clauses, 20
History, 13–32
Latinos, 28, 128–29, 131, 132, 137, 146
Literacy and interpretation tests
    Constitutionality, 35–36, 38
    History, 20, 25, 27, 28, 178
    Voting Rights Act, 27, 28, 35–36, 93, 95–96, 178
Native Americans, 28, 132, 181
Noncitizens, 30
One person, one vote, this index
Poll tax
    Constitutionality, 34, 37–39, 157
    History, 9, 15, 16, 20, 25, 93, 178
    Voter identification compared, 164
Prisoners, 30–31, 179
Property restrictions, 14–16, 39, 40, 47
Qualifications for voting, 14–16, 29, 33, 35–36, 39–44, 96
Racial gerrymandering, this index
Reconstruction, 16–18, 37–38, 93
Religious tests for voting, 14
Residency, 29–30, 41
Second Reconstruction, 25–28
Voter identification, this index
Voter registration, this index
Voting Rights Act, this index
White Primary, 21–22, 25, 178, 202, 245–52

Women, 16, 22–25

VOTING RIGHTS ACT (VRA)
At-large elections, 93, 96–98, 113, 116, 117, 134, 136, 179
Bail out, 110
Effect on number of minority elected officials elected, 137
Election administration and, 163, 177–82
Governance, inapplicability to, 98, 135
History of, 25–28
Language assistance, 181–82
Legislative districting and, 73, 93–94, 96–97, 98, 99–100, 101–06,
    113, 122–36
Literacy tests, 27, 28, 35–36, 93, 95–96, 178
One person, one vote and, 100
Preclearance, see Section 5
Racial gerrymandering, see Gerrymandering, this index
Section 2
    1982 amendments to, 26–27, 112–13, 114, 117, 118–22
    Gingles standard, 122–35
        Bloc voting, 123, 127, 131–33
        Compactness, 123–24, 127–29
        Extension and limitation of, 134–36
        Racial polarization, 123–26, 131–33
    Judicial elections, application to, 135
    Legal standard, 26–27, 118–36
    Proportional representation and, 118–20, 122, 124, 126, 134
    Relationship to Section 5, 94, 112
    Remedies, 134
    Results test, 113, 117, 118–19, 122
    Totality of circumstances, 118–19, 133–34, 135
    Vote dilution, 26–27, 28, 113, 118–36
 Section 4
    Bail out, 110
    Constitutionality, 28, 109, 110–12, 180
    Coverage formula, 27, 28, 95, 109, 110–12, 180, 181
    Language assistance, 181–82
    Literacy tests, 27
 Section 5
    Constitutionality, 28, 94, 107–12, 180
    Legal standard, 27, 101–07

Discriminatory purpose, 106–07
Retrogressive effect, 101–06
Preclearance Process, 94–101
Reauthorizations, 28, 105, 110, 181
Relationship to Section 2, 94, 112
Vote dilution, 96–98, 112
Voting practices subject to, 97–98
Section 203
Language assistance, 181

VOTING TECHNOLOGY
See Voting Equipment

WHITE PRIMARY
Constitutionality, 202, 245–52
History, 21–22, 25, 178

WOMEN'S SUFFRAGE, 16, 22–25

WRITE–IN VOTES, 98, 165, 237–38, 266–67